The Autobiography of Benjamin Franklin

BENJAMIN FRANKLIN

B. Franklin

THE AUTOBIOGRAPHY
OF
BENJAMIN FRANKLIN

NOW FIRST PRINTED IN ENGLAND FROM
THE FULL AND AUTHENTIC TEXT

EDITED
WITH A BIBLIOGRAPHICAL PREFACE
AND AN HISTORICAL ACCOUNT
OF
FRANKLIN'S LATER LIFE

BY
WILLIAM MACDONALD

LONDON
J. M. DENT & CO.
NEW YORK: E. P. DUTTON & CO.
1905

CONTENTS

ILLUSTRATIONS

PREFACE

THOUGH the Autobiography of Benjamin Franklin has been for over a hundred years a familiar and accepted English classic, this is the first occasion on which an edition containing the authentic text of this celebrated work has been given to the world by an English publishing house. This will seem strange news to most readers; and indeed there is a long and interesting story to tell in connection with it. That story fills very pleasantly some eighty prefatory pages in Mr Bigelow's "Life of Franklin"; but here our generosity must be more frugal, our entertainment more hurried.

It was in 1771, in the seventh year of his second mission to England, and while spending a holiday at the country-seat of his friend, Jonathan Shipley, Bishop of St Asaph, that Franklin set about writing some Recollections of his family and his own early life. The composition was addressed to his son William, at that time Governor of New Jersey, and was not intended to come under the eyes of the general world at all. The work, needless to say, gained a great deal by having thus originated as a sort of holiday gaiety, a long retrospective chat, a budget of personal and moral memoranda, written for the gratification and the uses of his own folk at home. It does not appear that he had any thought of carrying the story further than the point which he brought it down to—namely, as far as page 84 of the present volume—in the course of this holiday labour. Apparently, he sent it to his son not long after, and thought no more about it. And, indeed, he soon had plenty to think about; for the difficult and troublous course of the public business with which he was presently connected was matter enough to engage his whole attention. Then came his return to America, and the vivid and laborious days of the commencing Revolution. We next see him, with scarce a breathing space allowed, spirited back into the Old World to take up a new career of labours, difficulties, and anxieties, almost without parallel. But toward the end of this time an extraordinary thing happened; the manuscript which he had written at the Bishop of St Asaph's some twelve years earlier, was returned to him from America by a Pennsylvanian Quaker, Mr Abel James, into whose hands it had fallen. Through what adventures it had passed in the interval we do not know, but assuredly they were not without peril to a small sheaf of papers. At the beginning of the war the Governor of New Jersey had, as became his office, if not his birth, stood for the King against both his father and his country, and had behaved with so much provocation and defiance that his career, until he finally found his way to England, was, to say the least, not a comfortable one. There was a good deal of imprisonment; a good deal of hustling from this place to that; and, of course, confiscation, with the impounding or the scattering and destroying of papers. However, this paper, as the reader will see on turning to page 85, found its way into very good hands.

The desire so seriously expressed by Mr James that this "so pleasing and profitable work" might be "continued up to a later period" was fully shared by the friends, both French and English—Mr Benjamin Vaughan and Dr Price, M. le Veillard, the Duc de la Rochefoucault, and others—to whom Franklin now showed the recovered manuscript. From this moment these were insistent in their demands upon him, their entreaties, that he would recognise the finishing of these Memoirs as the chief duty which he owed to the world. So in 1784, when a greater work to which he had set his hand at a later time had just been happily concluded—when Independence was won, and peace negotiated, and his country accepted by all the world as a nation among the rest—he now yielded to the instance of these friends and set about to complete the Memoirs of his Life. What he was able to add at this time, however, while still residing at Passy, only amounts to eighteen pages (pp. 92-110) of the present volume. In the following year he returned to America; and his enthusiastic friends in Europe were compensated a little for the loss of his company by the hope that now he would be able to complete those Memoirs at last. But again his country forbade. In spite of age and intense physical sufferings, never long intermitted, he was dragged again into the conflict and toil of public life; so that for three years his European friends, ceaselessly importuning him in the same old cause, got little comfort in return except his promises and his hopes. During that time public affairs claimed practically every hour which was rendered effective by the intermissions of his malady. At last, in the late summer of 1788, he was able to take up the long interrupted work and made such headway that he brought the account down to page 199 as it is here printed. But after this, there was never again such an interval. The crushing pressure of pain was harder upon him than heretofore and left him fewer moments in which he could have the confidence to take up again a work requiring such a command of material and so many powers of the mind. Towards the end of the following year, the old man, reluctantly yet uncomplainingly, surrenders the last hope of ever being able to finish the work now. But he tells M. le Veillard that his grandson is making a copy, as far as it goes, which shall be sent to him. Another copy was sent about the same time to Benjamin Vaughan, but what became of it is unknown. Franklin died in the following April, and the bulk of his books, papers, and manuscripts, including the Autobiography, was bequeathed to his grandson, William Temple Franklin.

Already, it will be seen, the Autobiography affords an instance of the adage *habent et sua fata libelli.* As a manuscript, it has had its strange fortunes. As a book, it is to have more. And even of its history as a manuscript, we shall find, there is something further to tell when the last word seems to have been said.

Seldom has an unpublished book been expected with so intense an interest, been waited for with such impatience, as Dr Franklin's Memoirs of his Life: for so the work was generally called. The world wanted it at once, and seemed to count the days till it should be published. It had to count so many, that a great percentage of the enumerators died at their post. It is true that young Temple Franklin showed a lively sense of the value of the bequest which his grandfather had left him, and that within a month after his grandfather's death he wrote to M. le Veillard of his intention to bring out a complete edition of the Works and Correspondence at an early date. Nay more; he came to England a few weeks later, expressly to arrange this publication. But then a wonderful thing occurred. Though still apparently bent on bringing out the edition, and still exceedingly anxious lest M. le Veillard should permit his MS. copy of the Memoirs to come into the hands or under the eyes of any one else, who might purloin or pirate the same, and so impair the value of the bequest for him—he yet suddenly engages himself for three or four months (at a salary, he says) in some mysterious business to which all other interests have to be postponed, and by which he earns, in that time, a clear £7000, for what services no man knows.

Now the fact may not mean much, but it is at least a curious fact that from the moment when he has concluded this most remunerative and mysterious engagement, he begins to display an indifferent zeal in regard to the business which had brought him to England, the publication of his grandfather's works. To M. le Veillard, who is dissatisfied with the reasons for this delay and is privileged to say so, he answers more pertly than is quite becoming in the grandson of his grandfather to such a friend; but tells him (Feb. 28, 1792) that "I am now almost entirely employed in bringing forward the English edition. . . . A few months will, I hope, satisfy your impatience and the public curiosity." But after that there is silence. M. le Veillard, *Gentilhomme ordinaire du Roi*, died on the revolutionary scaffold in 1794. By his demise it was doubtless rendered easier for Temple Franklin to neglect, or to go on deferring, the duties of piety, than would else have been the case. There were those among the living, however, who interested themselves in the matter still. In France it was confidently asserted, as early as 1791, that the Memoirs were to be suppressed because the son and grandson of the great philosopher and statesman were ashamed of his humble beginnings and his homely style. This, of course, was a wildly uninformed venture of the imagination. But as time wore on, and still Franklin's Works did not appear (that is to say, the authoritative and complete, likewise apocalyptic edition thereof — for unauthoritative editions of Franklin's Works, in English and other languages, there were by the dozen presently), another explanation obtained credence, and was openly alleged. For example, in the Preface to a handsome edition published by Longmans in 1806, Temple Franklin was accused of having carried his grandfather's unpublished Works and Correspondence to a better market for such wares than Paternoster Row, and of having made a very good thing of it. He had, in fact, sold his trust to the British Government, and suppressed, if not destroyed, the whole mass of Franklin's unpublished remains for a great price. In July of that year the *Edinburgh Review* quoted this terrible impeachment in full, and supported it. The same charge was repeated in other quarters. Only once did Temple Franklin publicly take notice of these public attacks, and then he chose (in 1807), as the platform on which to defend himself, the pages of an exquisitely obscure English print, published in Paris. If feeling against him was high in this country, it was higher still in France. There the admirers of Franklin were filled with that peculiar horror with which the Latin races regard parricide. That was the word used to describe the conduct of this young man; and even when, at the end of time (*i.e.* in 1817) it was announced that the edition was at last about to appear, the true Franklinians of France would not believe that there was other than a sinister motive for this publication, so tardy as it was. It would be found to be a carefully mutilated collection, contrived at once so as to misrepresent the great man, to conceal the ignominy of his enemies, and to impair the authority and success of the more faithful French edition which the reader had now the privilege of beholding. "The glory of belittling a great man, of *abridging* Franklin," cries M. Charles Malo, "has been reserved for one of his descendants. Ought we to inherit from one we have assassinated?" To a generation thus hostile did Temple Franklin deliver his work, which was published in two forms (a quarto and an octavo form) simultaneously, by

Colburne, of London. It was far from being a complete edition, but the publisher was probably more to blame for that than the editor. And whatever he had suppressed—if he had suppressed anything—here was the Autobiography, given at last, in full, and for the first time in Franklin's own English.

These words need an explanation, for which we must turn back a little. I have already referred to the anxiety of the legatee in regard to the evil uses that might be made of the copy which had been given to M. le Veillard in September 1789. He feared the French translator only less than the English pirate. The first of these fears was prophetic. In 1791 there was published at Paris an anonymous translation of the work, as far as to the *beginning* of the paragraph (p. 84) about the founding of the Philadelphia Library. Shortly afterwards, two separate translations from this book were published in London, and continued to be re-published in succeeding ages. Some of the copies of what professes to be Franklin's Autobiography even now on sale are really reprints of one or other of these English translations of a French translation of an English manuscript. A still more attenuated degree of authenticity was reached when, in 1798, there appeared at Paris an edition of Franklin's works, "traduit de l'anglais, avec des notes, par J. Castera." This gentleman had fallen in with one of the English versions aforesaid; and, supposing it to be the original work, he translated it anew for the purposes of his edition: in which, therefore, we have a French translation of an English translation of a French translation of an English manuscript. Here the brain begins to reel, and a sense of the ultimate baselessness and unsubstantiality of things invades the soul even of the general reader. But, *courage, mon ami!* Surely there is a place of rest in the year

1817—surely we have in W. Temple Franklin's edition every word of the Autobiography that Benjamin Franklin wrote, and no words but his own.

So the world really thought for a space of fifty years; and then there was made that discovery which it is the business of this Preface to make common knowledge henceforth to all the enlightened inhabitants of these islands.

It came about in this manner. One day in the summer of 1866, the Hon. John Bigelow, at that time American Ambassador to the French Court, happened to have to dinner a number of men-of-letters. Amongst them was that accomplished *littérateur* and publicist, M. Édouard Laboulaye, who had lately edited a selection from Franklin's writings. This introducing the general topic, Mr Bigelow took the opportunity of saying a word to those wise men on a matter that had been a good deal in his mind for some time. He wanted to know what had become of the MS. of Franklin's Autobiography, and whether one could not find it if one looked around in that country. He himself believed that, unless it had been destroyed, which seemed unlikely, the incomparable document was at that moment in France, and had been there from the beginning of the century at least. Not to give all his reasons for so thinking, I will mention two historical facts on which he based. First, it had been in France early in the century; for Sir Samuel Romilly had seen it there in 1802, and has left a description of it in his Diary. Second, it was evidently well taken care of; for it had been seen again about fifteen or sixteen years ago by a well-known American book-collector: this was in some French town, though what town Mr Bigelow could not then say. From these premises the only conclusion seemed to be that the manuscript was discoverable upon search being made. M.

Laboulaye said he would make inquiries, and if the thing was in France, he thought he should be able to trace it. Six months passed, nothing had come of this conversation, and it was time for Mr Bigelow to be getting home. Amongst his farewell calls was one to M. Laboulaye; who had still no findings to report, but had engaged some members of the Academy in the quest and was in good hopes. About a month later (on January 19, 1867) Mr Bigelow, being then in London, received from him a letter which began with the joyful phrase "Eureka!" and went on to give the address of the owner of the manuscript and of some other valuable Franklin relics. Mr Bigelow at once wrote to "my cherished friend the late William H. Huntington, in Paris," who seems to have been a man worth living to know. Him he invested with the powers of an Envoy-plenipotentiary, to treat with the present possessors of part of the birthright of all Americans. It turned out that these possessors were the representatives of the Le Veillard family, M. Paul and M. George Senarmont, both of Paris. The negotiations were therefore conducted (as far as the need for despatch allowed) with the degree of consideration due to the feelings of a family so excellent, and the surrender was arranged in such a way as to reduce to its mildest form the sense of bereavement. In a word, the Messieurs de Senarmont had been waiting for a purchaser of the heirlooms at 25,000 francs. "A large price, it is true," says Mr Bigelow, "but a price that did not seem to me beyond their value to an American." To a good American, certainly not; though doubtless there are soulless misers and some criminals in that country as in others. Untrammelled by these baser thoughts, however, and strengthened by the possession of Mr Bigelow's cheque for the amount named, Mr Huntington carried through the whole legal and commercial business connected with the purchasing, packing and despatching of "The le Veillard Collection" in a single day, that day being the 27th of January 1867: nor has any international transaction of equal importance been so gaily chronicled as he has chronicled this one in his letters to Mr Bigelow. May he so smile for ever, though no longer in Paris; and here below let him have honourable mention wherever this story is told.

The collection consisted of three items: (1) a small batch of Letters; (2) a new Portrait of Franklin; (3) an autograph MS. of the Autobiography. Regarding the Letters I need only say that a few were from Franklin and the rest from members of his family. All were addressed to M. le Veillard, and they afford information, which we should not have found elsewhere, regarding Franklin's last attempts to continue the Memoirs, and also regarding the peculiar action, or inaction, of W. Temple Franklin in the matter of bringing out the Works. Of the Portrait it is the less necessary to give an account, because by the great kindness of Mr Bigelow a reproduction of it appears as the frontispiece to this volume. The original is a pastel of undoubted authenticity, done in 1783 by Joseph Siffred Duplessis, an Academician and a portraitist of very high repute in his generation. The picture was a parting gift from Franklin to his friend and neighbour M. le Veillard, who was a gentleman-in-ordinary to the King, and the Mayor of Passy. A portrait of Franklin was named in the lists of Duplessis' works, but it was lost to the world till Mr Bigelow brought it back to light.

Of the Manuscript it is necessary to speak more fully. There are those who have builded wiser than they knew, and others who have found better things than they sought. To the latter category of the fortunate belongs Mr Bigelow. He had wished to recover the MS. of Franklin's Autobiography, merely out of regard to the sentimental interest attaching to a document having such rich associations—biographical, historical, literary—for an American, and not at all because he supposed that the MS. would reveal anything concerning the history of the book or add a page to those "Memoirs of Franklin, written by Himself," which had so long been a familiar English classic. Careful inspection showed, however, that in both these respects the newly found MS. was a *document révélateur*.

For here there was, in the first place, a considerable positive addition. The Autobiography, as published in 1817, breaks off with the arrival of Franklin in London in 1757; whereas here the story was continued to the conclusion, in 1762, of that Pennsylvanian business which had brought him to this country. The *matter* of this continuation was, as a fact, not quite new, though the actual words were now first verified. A French translation published in 1828 had contained this final portion, and the editor explained that it had been communicated to him by the le Veillard family. How the le Veillard family came to be able to communicate anything of the sort was much of a mystery; but the historical certification given to Mr Bigelow along with his purchases by the Messieurs de Senarmont now explained all. The MS. in their possession was not the copy sent to M. le Veillard by Franklin in September 1789, but Franklin's own original copy in his own handwriting, with all his own corrections, erasures, and marginal comments. These additaments—the use of a Lamb word is privileged here, for more reasons than its correctness—these additaments, which increased the interest of the document for the true devotee so greatly, had been in rather an odd way the cause of its preservation. When

Temple Franklin at last took steps to publish his grandfather's Works, he wished to have a fair copy of the Memoirs "for the printers." And being one of these editors—so exceptional, and extraordinary, and fortunate!—who do not fatigue themselves, he coolly asked the le Veillard family to let him have the use of theirs. At this they very naturally exclaimed, and reminded him of the interest and preciousness to them of this souvenir of their illustrious friend, which they were asked to give up. "Oh, as to that," said the very Anglo-Saxon young man, "you can have my copy in exchange; which is not a 'copy' at all, but the original autograph, and so, you see, much more of a souvenir than your own." The conversation has not been officially reported, any more than the great speeches in Thucydides, but no doubt these were the very words. In this way, at any rate, the exchange was made. But Mr Temple Franklin, who did not fatigue himself, had not troubled to compare the two manuscripts, and so had failed to remark that the one which he was giving away contained an important addition (besides the additaments aforesaid) not to be found in the one which he was getting in return. And this difference between the two manuscripts is just what, with our present knowledge from other sources, we should be able to affirm without having seen either of them. For we know that when Franklin caused a copy to be sent to le Veillard in September 1789, he had then brought the story down to June 1757, and considered that he had now done all he would ever be able to do to it. But we also know that in November he had another rally of courage or confidence, and was trying bravely to go on again, and had even some momentary hopes of completing his task yet. Whatever additions resulted from this final effort, they would appear in the autograph copy which he kept beside him, and would be absent from both of those fair copies which were sent to Europe in September. Yet it was from one of these more imperfect copies that Temple Franklin, in forgetfulness rather than indifference, was electing to print. The great lapse of time during which he had kept back the publication would account for this forgetfulness, and thus the pieties neglected invoked a nemesis of a sort; for in the end he was not the possessor of the Complete Autobiography after all, jealously as he had wished to guard that right.

But a detailed comparison of the work as it exists in manuscript and the book as it was given to the world by Temple Franklin, revealed a more important difference between the two. It revealed a pervading lack of identity. In the act of publication, the text had been tampered with throughout. Not only Franklin's spelling and punctuation had been departed from, but a running commentary of silent alterations, corrections, and suppressions of Franklin's own words had been inflicted on every page of the book. Mr Bigelow gives the number of these changes as 1200 in all. They appear to have been in no case dictated by malevolence or by any motive more considerable than the sempiternal impertinence of youth and modernity. The young man was of his own generation, and not of his grandfather's; he was of a generation which abounded in complete letter-writers, and for which the word "elegant" had an unction that has somehow evaporated for us. The manner of speech which was good enough for the grandfather seemed to the grandson, so differently nurtured, to be a trifle untrimmed, homely, sometimes perhaps coarse. Where Franklin can talk of some one "having got a naughty girl with child," the young gentleman of a more modest age can but speak of "having had an intrigue with a young woman of bad character." Where Benjamin talks of "footing it to London," the politer Temple substitutes "walking." A great many are of this character; but a vast number are even more gratuitous. They consist in substituting for the idiomatic, racy, vernacular diction of Franklin—Franklin, who is an Augustan, but has an affinity with stronger writers than the Augustans—something that was in more complete accord with the recognised correctnesses of polite letterpress in the early Nineteenth Century. I have not room for a detailed citation of passages in parallel columns, but what I have said will put the Reader in a way to understand how greatly we are indebted to Mr Bigelow for his kindness in permitting us to use for this edition the True Text of the Autobiography, as published by him in 1868 and subsequently.[1] The composition of the book has been done from a copy of his 3rd Edition, published by Messrs J. B. Lippincott Company, to whom also acknowledgments and thanks are due.

A word, finally, regarding my own contribution to this volume. I have sought to make it in some

[1] Be it added that these improving touches are the only acts of parricide of which the maligned and ill-used Temple Franklin can be convicted. The accusation of having made his grandfather's literary remains the subject of a nefarious deal with the British Government has never been made good. The only piece of positive evidence in favour of the idea is this: that Jefferson speaks of having read a certain passage in the MS. of Franklin's account of the Secret Negotiations carried on during the winter 1774-5; which passage does not appear in the printed version. But I do not think this at all conclusive, in the face of many facts pointing the other way. The delay in bringing out the Edition can be explained on grounds more credible and creditable than those alleged by enemies and enthusiasts. The young man's father was alive, an exiled loyalist, living in England, subsisting on a pension from the King. Here was an influence; here also considerations of prudence, even of seemliness. And as a fact it was immediately after his father's death, and not till then, that Temple Franklin set about, in earnest, the business which had brought him to Europe nearly thirty years earlier. He died soon afterwards.

degree complementary to the Autobiography; but what I mean by complementary needs to be explained. If there are few more charming or veracious books in the world than Franklin's account of his own life, there is perhaps no other book of its kind so insufficient—no other which gives, with all its appearance of unity and coherence, so fragmentary an impression of the whole man as he really was. This is not due merely to the fact that the book was unfinished, but far more to the fact that the man—the whole man—was so wonderful both from the point of view of character and of career. The Autobiography tells us much about a certain busy and notable and well-doing citizen of Philadelphia; and perhaps even of that civic character the dimensions are understated, by an effect of modesty in the chronicler of his doings. But it tells us nothing of a great and famous man of science; it tells us nothing of a revered philosopher, of a man of massive wisdom, vast toleration, endless patience, inexhaustible courage and endurance, and matchless in security and counsel; nor anything of a man of so rare and full social qualities that there was no such companion as he, and the record of his friendships would almost fill a book. And as for a certain Great and Illustrious Franklin—the most famous patriot, the wisest statesman, the most successful diplomatist of his age, a man whose presence in the world filled the mind of his generation—it does not afford us a hint that such an one ever existed. To make up for all these biographical and historical deficiencies of a confessed literary classic would be impossible in less than two volumes. Having to choose and to forego, I have chosen to treat of that aspect and period of Franklin's life which stands in most vivid contrast with the picture presented to us in the pages of the Autobiography. My subject is the historical Franklin, the Franklin with whose name "all Europe rang from side to side." Of necessity, the result is a composition fully more compact of history than of biography, for that was the atmosphere in which he lived. The labour has been to leave out, and yet preserve continuity; also so to write that the uninformed in these matters should be able to read with some comprehension and interest, and that those who know might not find the whole thing superfluous.

As to sympathy, that will depend on whether they agree with the Gods or Cato. For on this occasion I agree with the Gods.

W. M.

LONDON, *October* 25, 1904.

FRANKLIN'S DRAFT SCHEME OF THE AUTOBIOGRAPHY

[*Copie d'un Projêt tres Curieux de Benjamin Franklin—1ere Esquisse de ses Mémoires. Les additions à l'encre rouge sont de la main de Franklin.*] [1]

My writing. Mrs Dogood's letters. Differences arise between my Brother and me (his temper and mine); their cause in general. His Newspaper. The Prosecution he suffered. My Examination. Vote of Assembly. His manner of evading it. Whereby I became free. My attempt to get employ with other Printers. He prevents me. Our frequent pleadings before our Father. The final Breach. My Inducements to quit Boston. Manner of coming to a Resolution. My leaving him and going to New York (return to eating flesh); thence to Pennsylvania. The journey, and its events on the Bay, at Amboy. The road. Meet with Dr Brown. His character. His great work. At Burlington. The Good Woman. On the River. My Arrival at Philadelphia. First Meal and first Sleep. Money left. Employment. Lodging. First acquaintance with my afterward Wife. With J. Ralph. With Keimer. Their characters. Osborne. Watson. The Governor takes notice of me. The Occasion and Manner. His character. Offers to set me up. My return to Boston. Voyage and accidents. Reception. My Father dislikes the proposal. I return to New York and Philadelphia. Governor Burnet. J. Collins. The Money for Vernon. The Governor's Deceit. Collins not finding employment goes to Barbados much in my Debt. Ralph and I go to

[1] This memorandum, probably in the handwriting of M. le Veillard, immediately precedes the Outline in the MS.—B.

England. Disappointment of Governor's Letters. Colonel French his Friend. Cornwallis's Letters. Cabbin. Denham. Hamilton. Arrival in England. Get employment. Ralph not. He is an expense to me. Adventures in England. Write a Pamphlet and print 100. Schemes. Lyons. Dr Pemberton. My diligence, and yet poor through Ralph. My Landlady. Her character. Wygate. Wilkes. Cibber. Plays. Books I borrowed. Preachers I heard. Redmayne. At Watts's. Temperance. Ghost. Conduct and Influence among the Men. Persuaded by Mr Denham to return with him to Philadelphia and be his clerk. Our voyage and arrival. My resolutions in Writing. My Sickness. His Death. Found D. R. married. Go to work again with Keimer. Terms. His ill-usage of me. My Resentment. Saying of Decow. My Friends at Burlington. Agreement with H. Meredith to set up in Partnership. Do so. Success with the Assembly. Hamilton's Friendship. Sewell's History. Gazette. Paper money. Webb. Writing Busy Body. Breintnal. Godfrey. His character. Suit against us. Offer of my Friends, Coleman and Grace. Continue the Business, and M. goes to Carolina. Pamphlet on Paper Money. Gazette from Keimer. Junto credit; its plan. Marry. Library erected. Manner of conducting the project. Its plan and utility. Children. Almanac. The use I made of it. Great industry. Constant study. Father's Remark and Advice upon Diligence. Carolina Partnership. Learn French and German. Journey to Boston after ten years. Affection of my Brother. His Death, and leaving me his Son. Art of Virtue. Occasion. City Watch amended. Post-office. Spotswood. Bradford's Behaviour. Clerk of Assembly. Lose one of my Sons. Project of subordinate Juntos. Write occasionally in the papers. Success in Business. Fire companies. Engines. Go again to Boston in 1743. See Dr Spence. Whitefield. My connection with him. His generosity to me. My returns. Church Differences. My part in them. Propose a College. Not then prosecuted. Propose and establish a Philosophical Society. War. Electricity. My first knowledge of it. Partnership with D. Hall, etc. Dispute in Assembly upon

Defence. Project for it. Plain Truth. Its success. Ten thousand Men raised and disciplined. Lotteries. Battery built. New Castle. My influence in the Council. Colors, Devices, and Mottos. Ladies' Military Watch. Quakers chosen of the Common Council. Put in the commission of the peace. Logan fond of me. His Library. Appointed Postmaster-General. Chosen Assemblyman. Commissioner to treat with Indians at Carlisle and at Easton. Project and establish Academy. Pamphlet on it. Journey to Boston. At Albany. Plan of union of the colonies. Copy of it. Remarks upon it. It fails, and how. Journey to Boston in 1754. Disputes about it in our Assembly. My part in them. New Governor. Disputes with him. His character and sayings to me. Chosen Alderman. Project of Hospital. My share in it. Its success. Boxes. Made a Commissioner of the Treasury. My commission to defend the frontier counties. Raise Men and build Forts. Militia Law of my drawing. Made Colonel. Parade of my Officers. Offence to Proprietor. Assistance to Boston Ambassadors. Journey with Shirley, etc. Meet with Braddock. Assistance to him. To the Officers of his Army. Furnish him with Forage. His concessions to me and character of me. Success of my Electrical Experiments. Medal sent me. Present Royal Society, and Speech of President. Denny's Arrival and Courtship to me. His character. My service to the Army in the affair of Quarters. Disputes about the Proprietor's Taxes continued. Project for paving the City. I am sent to England. Negotiation there. *Canada delenda est.* My Pamphlet. Its reception and effect. Projects drawn from me concerning the Conquest. Acquaintance made and their services to me—Mrs S. M. Small, Sir John P., Mr Wood, Sargent Strahan, and others. Their characters. Doctorate from Edinburgh, St Andrew's. Doctorate from Oxford. Journey to Scotland. Lord Leicester. Mr Prat. De Grey. Jackson. State of Affairs in England. Delays. Eventful Journey into Holland and Flanders. Agency from Maryland. Son's appointment. My Return. Allowance and thanks. Journey to Boston. John Penn, Governor. My conduct toward him. The

Paxton Murders. My Pamphlet. Rioters march to Philadelphia. Governor retires to my House. My conduct. Sent out to the Insurgents. Turn them back. Little thanks. Disputes revived. Resolutions against continuing under Proprietary Government. Another Pamphlet. Cool thoughts. Sent again to England with Petition. Negotiation there. Lord H. His character. Agencies from New Jersey, Georgia, Massachusetts. Journey into Germany, 1766. Civilities received there. Göttingen Observations. Ditto into France in 1767. Ditto in 1769. Entertainment there at the Academy. Introduced to the King and the Mesdames, Mad. Victoria and Mrs Lamagnon. Duc de Chaulnes, M. Beaumont, Le Roy, D'Alibard, Nollet. See Journals. Holland. Reprint my papers and add many. Books presented to me from many authors. My Book translated into French. Lightning Kite. Various Discoveries. My manner of prosecuting that Study. King of Denmark invites me to dinner. Recollect my Father's Proverb. Stamp Act. My opposition to it. Recommendation of J. Hughes. Amendment of it. Examination in Parliament. Reputation it gave me. Caressed by Ministry. Charles Townsend's Act. Opposition to it. Stoves and chimney-plates. Armonica. Acquaintance with Ambassadors. Russian Intimation. Writing in newspapers. Glasses from Germany. Grant of Land in Nova Scotia. Sicknesses. Letters to America returned hither. The consequences. Insurance Office. My character. Costs me nothing to be civil to inferiors; a good deal to be submissive to superiors, etc., etc. Farce of Perpetual Motion. Writing for Jersey Assembly. Hutchinson's Letters. Temple. Suit in Chancery Abuse before the Privy Council. Lord Hillsborough's character and conduct. Lord Dartmouth. Negotiation to prevent the War. Return to America. Bishop of St Asaph. Congress. Assembly. Committee of Safety. Chevaux-de-frise. Sent to Boston, to the Camp. To Canada, to Lord Howe. To France. Treaty, etc.

THE AUTOBIOGRAPHY

Twyford, at the Bishop of St Asaph's,[1] *1771.*

Dear Son: I have ever had pleasure in obtaining any little anecdotes of my ancestors. You may remember the inquiries I made among the remains of my relations when you were with me in England, and the journey I undertook for that purpose. Imagining it may be equally agreeable to[2] you to know the circumstances of my life, many of which you are yet unacquainted with, and expecting the enjoyment of a week's uninterrupted leisure in my present country retirement, I sit down to write them for you. To which I have besides some other inducements. Having emerged from the poverty and obscurity in which I was born and bred, to a state of affluence and some degree of reputation in the world, and having gone so far through life with a considerable share of felicity, the conducing means I made use of, which with the blessing of God so well succeeded, my posterity may like to know, as they may find some of them suitable to their own situations, and therefore fit to be imitated.

That felicity, when I reflected on it, has induced me sometimes to say, that were it offered to my choice, I should have no objection to a repetition of the same life from its beginning, only asking the

[1] The country-seat of Bishop Shipley, the good bishop, as Dr Franklin used to style him.—B.

[2] After the words "agreeable to" the words "some of" were interlined and afterward effaced.—B.

advantages authors have in a second edition to correct some faults of the first. So I might, besides correcting the faults, change some sinister accidents and events of it for others more favourable. But though this were denied, I should still accept the offer. Since such a repetition is not to be expected, the next thing most like living one's life over again seems to be a recollection of that life, and to make that recollection as durable as possible by putting it down in writing.

Hereby, too, I shall indulge the inclination so natural in old men, to be talking of themselves and their own past actions; and I shall indulge it without being tiresome to others, who, through respect to age, might conceive themselves obliged to give me a hearing, since this may be read or not as any one pleases. And, lastly (I may as well confess it, since my denial of it will be believed by nobody), perhaps I shall a good deal gratify my own *vanity*. Indeed, I scarce ever heard or saw the introductory words, "*Without vanity I may say*," etc., but some vain thing immediately followed. Most people dislike vanity in others, whatever share they have of it themselves; but I give it fair quarter wherever I meet with it, being persuaded that it is often productive of good to the possessor, and to others that are within his sphere of action; and therefore, in many cases, it would not be altogether absurd if a man were to thank God for his vanity among the other comforts of life.

And now I speak of thanking God, I desire with all humility to acknowledge that I owe the mentioned happiness of my past life to His kind providence, which lead me to the means I used and gave them success. My belief of this induces me to *hope*, though I must not *presume*, that the same goodness will still be exercised toward me, in continuing that happiness, or enabling me to bear a fatal reverse, which I may experience as others have done; the complexion of my future fortune being known to Him only in whose power it is to bless to us even our afflictions.

The notes one of my uncles (who had the same kind of curiosity in collecting family anecdotes) once put into my hands, furnished me with several particulars relating to our ancestors. From these notes I learned that the family had lived in the same village, Ecton, in Northamptonshire, for three hundred years, and how much longer he knew not (perhaps from the time when the name of Franklin, that before was the name of an order of people, was assumed by them as a surname when others took surnames all over the kingdom), on a freehold of about thirty acres, aided by the smith's business, which had continued in the family till his time, the eldest son being always bred to that business; a custom which he and my father followed as to their eldest sons. When I searched the registers at Ecton, I found an account of their births, marriages and burials from the year 1555 only, there being no registers kept in that parish at any time preceding. By that register I perceived that I was the youngest son of the youngest son for five generations back. My grandfather Thomas, who was born in 1598, lived at Ecton till he grew too old to follow business longer, when he went to live with his son John, a dyer at Banbury, in Oxfordshire, with whom my father served an apprenticeship. There my grandfather died and lies buried. We saw his gravestone in 1758. His eldest son Thomas lived in the house at Ecton, and left it with the land to his only child, a daughter, who, with her husband, one Fisher, of Wellingborough, sold it to Mr Isted, now lord of the manor there. My grandfather had four sons that grew up, viz.: Thomas, John, Benjamin and Josiah. I will give you what account I can of them, at this distance from my papers, and if these are not lost in my absence, you will among them find many more particulars.

Thomas was bred a smith under his father; but, being ingenious, and encouraged in learning (as all my brothers were) by an Esquire Palmer, then the principal gentleman in that parish, he qualified himself for the business of scrivener; became a considerable man in the county; was a chief mover of all public-spirited undertakings for the county or town of Northampton, and his own village, of which many instances were related of him; and much taken notice of and patronized by the then Lord Halifax. He died in 1702, January 6, old style, just four years to a day before I was born. The account we received of his life and character from some old people at Ecton, I remember, struck you as something extraordinary, from its similarity to what you knew of mine. "Had he died on the same day," you said, "one might have supposed a transmigration."

John was bred a dyer, I believe of woolens. Benjamin was bred a silk dyer, serving an apprenticeship at London. He was an ingenious man. I remember him well, for when I was a boy he came over to my father in Boston, and lived in the house with us some years. He lived to a great age. His grandson, Samuel Franklin, now lives in Boston. He left behind him two quarto volumes, MS., of his own poetry, consisting of little occasional pieces addressed to his friends and relations, of which the following, sent to me, is a specimen. He had formed a short-hand of his own, which he taught me, but, never practising it, I have now forgot it. I was named after this uncle, there being a particular affection between him and my father. He was very pious, a great attender of sermons of the best preachers, which he took down in his short-hand,

and had with him many volumes of them. He was also much of a politician; too much, perhaps, for his station. There fell lately into my hands, in London, a collection he had made of all the principal pamphlets relating to public affairs, from 1641 to 1717; many of the volumes are wanting as appears by the numbering, but there still remain eight volumes in folio, and twenty-four in quarto and in octavo. A dealer in old books met with them, and knowing me by my sometimes buying of him, he brought them to me. It seems my uncle must have left them here when he went to America, which was above fifty years since. There are many of his notes in the margins.

This obscure family of ours was early in the Reformation, and continued Protestants through the reign of Queen Mary, when they were sometimes in danger of trouble on account of their zeal against popery. They had got an English Bible, and to conceal and secure it, it was fastened open with tapes under and within the cover of a joint-stool. When my great-great-grandfather read it to his family, he turned up the joint-stool upon his knees, turning over the leaves then under the tapes. One of the children stood at the door to give notice if he saw the apparitor coming, who was an officer of the spiritual court. In that case the stool was turned down again upon its feet, when the Bible remained concealed under it as before. This anecdote I had from my uncle Benjamin. The family continued all of the Church of England till about the end of Charles the Second's reign, when some of the ministers that had been outed for non-conformity holding conventicles in Northamptonshire, Benjamin and Josiah adhered to them, and so continued all their lives: the rest of the family remained with the Episcopal Church.

Josiah, my father, married young, and carried his

wife with three children into New England, about 1682. The conventicles having been forbidden by law, and frequently disturbed, induced some considerable men of his acquaintance to remove to that country, and he was prevailed with to accompany them thither, where they expected to enjoy their mode of religion with freedom. By the same wife he had four children more born there, and by a second wife ten more, in all seventeen; of which I remember thirteen sitting at one time at his table, who all grew up to be men and women, and married; I was the youngest son, and the youngest child but two, and was born in Boston, New England. My mother, the second wife, was Abiah Folger, daughter of Peter Folger, one of the first settlers of New England, of whom honorable mention is made by Cotton Mather, in his church history of that country, entitled Magnalia Christi Americana, as "*a godly, learned Englishman*," if I remember the words rightly. I have heard that he wrote sundry small occasional pieces, but only one of them was printed, which I saw now many years since. It was written in 1675, in the home-spun verse of that time and people, and addressed to those then concerned in the government there. It was in favor of liberty of conscience, and in behalf of the Baptists, Quakers, and other sectaries that had been under persecution, ascribing the Indian wars, and other distresses that had befallen the country, to that persecution, as so many judgments of God to punish so heinous an offense, and exhorting a repeal of those uncharitable laws. The whole appeared to me as written with a good deal of decent plainness and manly freedom. The six concluding lines I remember, though I have forgotten the two first of the stanza; but the purport of them was, that his censures proceeded from good-will, and, therefore, he would be known to be the author.

"Because to be a libeller (says he)
I hate it with my heart;
From Sherburne town, where now I dwell
My name I do put here;
Without offense your real friend,
It is Peter Folgier."

My elder brothers were all put apprentices to different trades. I was put to the grammar-school at eight years of age, my father intending to devote me, as the tithe of his sons, to the service of the Church. My early readiness in learning to read (which must have been very early, as I do not remember when I could not read), and the opinion of all his friends, that I should certainly make a good scholar, encouraged him in this purpose of his. My uncle Benjamin, too, approved of it, and proposed to give me all his short-hand volumes of sermons, I suppose as a stock to set up with, if I would learn his character. I continued, however, at the grammar-school not quite one year, though in that time I had risen gradually from the middle of the class of that year to be the head of it, and farther was removed into the next class above it, in order to go with that into the third at the end of the year. But my father, in the meantime, from a view of the expense of a college education, which having so large a family he could not well afford, and the mean living many so educated weie afterwards able to obtain—reasons that he gave to his friends in my hearing—altered his first intention, took me from the grammar-school, and sent me to a school for writing and arithmetic, kept by a then famous man, Mr George Brownell, very successful in his profession generally, and that by mild, encouraging methods. Under him I acquired fair writing pretty soon, but I failed in the arithmetic, and made no progress in it. At ten years old I was taken home to assist my father in his business, which was that of a tallow-chandler and sope-boiler; a business he was not bred to, but had assumed on his arrival in New England, and on finding his dying trade would not maintain his family, being in little request. Accordingly, I was employed in cutting wick for the candles, filling the dipping mold and the molds for cast candles, attending the shop, going of errands, etc.

I disliked the trade, and had a strong inclination for the sea, but my father declared against it; however, living near the water, I was much in and about it, learnt early to swim well, and to manage boats; and when in a boat or canoe with other boys, I was commonly allowed to govern, especially in any case of difficulty; and upon other occasions I was generally a leader among the boys, and sometimes led them into scrapes, of which I will mention one instance, as it shows an early projecting public spirit, tho' not then justly conducted.

There was a salt-marsh that bounded part of the mill-pond, on the edge of which, at high water, we used to stand to fish for minnows. By much trampling, we had made it a mere quagmire. My proposal was to build a wharff there fit for us to stand upon, and I showed my comrades a large heap of stones, which were intended for a new house near the marsh, and which would very well suit our purpose. Accordingly, in the evening, when the workmen were gone, I assembled a number of my play-fellows, and working with them diligently like so many emmets, sometimes two or three to a stone, we brought them all away and built our little wharff. The next morning the workmen were surprised at missing the stones, which were found in our wharff. Inquiry was made after the removers; we were discovered and complained of; several of us were corrected by our fathers; and, though I pleaded the usefulness of the work, mine convinced me that nothing was useful which was not honest.

I think you may like to know something of his

person and character. He had an excellent constitution of body, was of middle stature, but well set, and very strong; he was ingenious, could draw prettily, was skilled a little in music, and had a clear pleasing voice, so that when he played psalm tunes on his violin and sung withal, as he sometimes did in an evening after the business of the day was over, it was extremely agreeable to hear. He had a mechanical genius too, and, on occasion, was very handy in the use of other tradesmen's tools; but his great excellence lay in a sound understanding and solid judgment in prudential matters, both in private and publick affairs. In the latter, indeed, he was never employed, the numerous family he had to educate and the straitness of his circumstances keeping him close to his trade; but I remember well his being frequently visited by leading people, who consulted him for his opinion in affairs of the town or of the church he belonged to, and showed a good deal of respect for his judgment and advice: he was also much consulted by private persons about their affairs when any difficulty occurred, and frequently chosen an arbitrator between contending parties. At his table he liked to have, as often as he could, some sensible friend or neighbor to converse with, and always took care to start some ingenious or useful topic for discourse, which might tend to improve the minds of his children. By this means he turned our attention to what was good, just, and prudent in the conduct of life; and little or no notice was ever taken of what related to the victuals on the table, whether it was well or ill dressed, in or out of season, of good or bad flavor, preferable or inferior to this or that other thing of the kind, so that I was bro't up in such a perfect inattention to those matters as to be quite indifferent what kind of food was set before me, and so unobservant of it, that to this day if I am asked I can scarce tell a few hours after dinner what I dined upon. This has been a convenience to me in travelling, where my companions have been sometimes very unhappy for want of a suitable gratification of their more delicate, because better instructed, tastes and appetites.

My mother had likewise an excellent constitution: she suckled all her ten children. I never knew either my father or mother to have any sickness but that of which they dy'd, he at 89, and she at 85 years of age. They lie buried together at Boston, where I some years since placed a marble over their grave, with this inscription:

Josiah Franklin,
and
Abiah his wife,
lie here interred.
They lived lovingly together in wedlock
fifty-five years.
Without an estate, or any gainful employment,
By constant labor and industry,
with God's blessing,
They maintained a large family
comfortably,
and brought up thirteen children
and seven grandchildren
reputably.
From this instance, reader,
Be encouraged to diligence in thy calling,
And distrust not Providence.
He was a pious and prudent man;
She, a discreet and virtuous woman.
Their youngest son,
In filial regard to their memory,
Places this stone.
J. F. born 1655, died 1744, Ætat 89.
A. F. born 1667, died 1752, —— 85.

By my rambling digressions I perceive myself to be grown old. I us'd to write more methodically. But one does not dress for private company as for a publick ball. 'Tis perhaps only negligence.

To return: I continued thus employed in my father's business for two years, that is, till I was twelve years old; and my brother John, who was bred to that business, having left my father, married, and set up for himself at Rhode Island, there was all appearance that I was destined to supply his place, and become a tallow-chandler. But my dislike to the trade continuing, my father was under apprehensions that if he did not find one for me more agreeable, I should break away and get to sea, as his son Josiah had done, to his great vexation. He therefore sometimes took me to walk with him, and see joiners, bricklayers, turners, braziers, etc., at their work, that he might observe my inclination, and endeavor to fix it on some trade or other on land. It has ever since been a pleasure to me to see good workmen handle their tools; and it has been useful to me, having learnt so much by it as to be able to do little jobs myself in my house when a workman could not readily be got, and to construct little machines for my experiments, while the intention of making the experiment was fresh and warm in my mind. My father at last fixed upon the cutler's trade, and my uncle Benjamin's son Samuel, who was bred to that business in London, being about that time established in Boston, I was sent to be with him some time on liking. But his expectations of a fee with me displeasing my father, I was taken home again.

From a child I was fond of reading, and all the little money that came into my hands was ever laid out in books. Pleased with the Pilgrim's Progress, my first collection was of John Bunyan's works in separate little volumes. I afterward sold them to enable me to buy R. Burton's Historical Collections; they were small chapmen's books, and cheap, 40 or 50 in all. My father's little library consisted chiefly of books in polemic divinity, most of which I read, and have since often regretted that, at a time when I had such a thirst for knowledge, more proper books had not fallen in my way, since it was now resolved I should not be a clergyman. Plutarch's Lives there was in which I read abundantly, and I still think that time spent to great advantage. There was also a book of De Foe's, called an Essay on Projects, and another of Dr Mather's, called Essays to do Good, which perhaps gave me a turn of thinking that had an influence on some of the principal future events of my life.

This bookish inclination at length determined my father to make me a printer, though he had already one son (James) of that profession. In 1717 my brother James returned from England with a press and letters to set up his business in Boston. I liked it much better than that of my father, but still had a hankering for the sea. To prevent the apprehended effect of such an inclination, my father was impatient to have me bound to my brother. I stood out some time, but at last was persuaded, and signed the indentures when I was yet but twelve years old. I was to serve as an apprentice till I was twenty-one years of age, only I was to be allowed journeyman's wages during the last year. In a little time I made great proficiency in the business, and became a useful hand to my brother. I now had access to better books. An acquaintance with the apprentices of booksellers enabled me sometimes to borrow a small one, which I was careful to return soon and clean. Often I sat up in my room reading the greatest part of the night, when the book was borrowed in the evening and to be returned early in the morning, lest it should be missed or wanted.

And after some time an ingenious tradesman, Mr Matthew Adams, who had a pretty collection of books, and who frequented our printing-house, took notice of me, invited me to his library, and very kindly lent me such books as I chose to read. I now took a fancy to poetry, and made some little pieces; my brother, thinking it might turn to account, encouraged me, and put me on composing occasional ballads. One was called *The Lighthouse Tragedy*, and contained an account of the drowning of Captain Worthilake, with his two daughters: the other was a sailor's song, on the taking of *Teach* (or Blackbeard) the pirate. They were wretched stuff, in the Grub-street-ballad style; and when they were printed he sent me about the town to sell them. The first sold wonderfully, the event being recent, having made a great noise. This flattered my vanity; but my father discouraged me by ridiculing my performances, and telling me verse-makers were generally beggars. So I escaped being a poet, most probably a very bad one; but as prose writing has been of great use to me in the course of my life, and was a principal means of my advancement, I shall tell you how, in such a situation, I acquired what little ability I have in that way.

There was another bookish lad in the town, John Collins by name, with whom I was intimately acquainted. We sometimes disputed, and very fond we were of argument, and very desirous of confuting one another, which disputatious turn, by the way, is apt to become a very bad habit, making people often extremely disagreeable in company by the contradiction that is necessary to bring it into practice; and thence, besides souring and spoiling the conversation, is productive of disgusts and, perhaps enmities where you may have occasion for friendship. I had caught it by reading my father's books of dispute about religion. Persons of good sense, I have since observed, seldom fall into it, except lawyers, university men, and men of all sorts that have been bred at Edinborough.

A question was once, somehow or other, started between Collins and me, of the propriety of educating the female sex in learning, and their abilities for study. He was of opinion that it was improper, and that they were naturally unequal to it. I took the contrary side, perhaps a little for dispute's sake. He was naturally more eloquent, had a ready plenty of words; and sometimes, as I thought, bore me down more by his fluency than by the strength of his reasons. As we parted without settling the point, and were not to see one another again for some time, I sat down to put my arguments in writing, which I copied fair and sent to him. He answered, and I replied. Three or four letters of a side had passed, when my father happened to find my papers and read them. Without entering into the discussion, he took occasion to talk to me about the manner of my writing; observed that, though I had the advantage of my antagonist in correct spelling and pointing (which I ow'd to the printing-house), I fell far short in elegance of expression, in method and in perspicuity, of which he convinced me by several instances. I saw the justice of his remarks, and thence grew more attentive to the manner in writing, and determined to endeavor at improvement.

About this time I met with an odd volume of the *Spectator*. It was the third. I had never before seen any of them. I bought it, read it over and over, and was much delighted with it. I thought the writing excellent, and wished, if possible, to imitate it. With this view I took some of the papers, and, making short hints of the sentiment in each sentence, laid them by a few days, and then, without looking at the book, try'd to compleat the papers again, by expressing each hinted sentiment at length, and as fully as it had been expressed before, in any suitable words that should come to hand. Then I compared my *Spectator* with the original, discovered some of my faults, and corrected them. But I found I wanted a stock of words, or a readiness in recollecting and using them, which I thought I should have acquired before that time if I had gone on making verses; since the continual occasion for words of the same import, but of different length, to suit the measure, or of different sound for the rhyme, would have laid me under a constant necessity of searching for variety, and also have tended to fix that variety in my mind, and make me master of it. Therefore I took some of the tales and turned them into verse; and, after a time, when I had pretty well forgotten the prose, turned them back again. I also sometimes jumbled my collections of hints into confusion, and after some weeks endeavored to reduce them into the best order, before I began to form the full sentences and compleat the paper. This was to teach me method in the arrangement of thoughts. By comparing my work afterwards with the original, I discovered many faults and amended them; but I sometimes had the pleasure of fancying that, in certain particulars of small import, I had been lucky enough to improve the method or the language, and this encouraged me to think I might possibly in time come to be a tolerable English writer, of which I was extreamly ambitious. My time for these exercises and for reading was at night, after work or before it began in the morning, or on Sundays, when I contrived to be in the printing-house alone, evading as much as I could the common attendance on public worship which my father used to exact on me when I was under his care, and which indeed I still thought a duty, though I could not, as it seemed to me, afford time to practise it.

When about 16 years of age I happened to meet with a book, written by one Tryon, recommending a vegetable diet. I determined to go into it. My brother, being yet unmarried, did not keep house, but boarded himself and his apprentices in another family. My refusing to eat flesh occasioned an inconveniency, and I was frequently chid for my singularity. I made myself acquainted with Tryon's manner of preparing some of his dishes, such as boiling potatoes or rice, making hasty pudding, and a few others, and then proposed to my brother, that if he would give me, weekly, half the money he paid for my board, I would board myself. He instantly agreed to it, and I presently found that I could save half what he paid me. This was an additional fund for buying books. But I had another advantage in it. My brother and the rest going from the printing-house to their meals, I remained there alone, and, despatching presently my light repast, which often was no more than a bisket or a slice of bread, a handful of raisins or a tart from the pastry-cook's, and a glass of water, had the rest of the time till their return for study, in which I made the greater progress, from that greater clearness of head and quicker apprehension which usually attend temperance in eating and drinking.

And now it was that, being on some occasion made asham'd of my ignorance in figures, which I had twice failed in learning when at school, I took Cocker's book of Arithmetick, and went through the whole by myself with great ease. I also read Seller's and Shermy's books of Navigation, and became acquainted with the little geometry they contain; but never proceeded far in that science. And I read about this time Locke *on Human Understanding*, and the *Art of Thinking*, by Messrs du Port Royal.

While I was intent on improving my language, I met with an English grammar (I think it was Greenwood's), at the end of which there were two little sketches of the arts of rhetoric and logic, the latter finishing with a specimen of a dispute in the Socratic method; and soon after I procur'd Xenophon's Memorable Things of Socrates, wherein there are many instances of the same method. I was charm'd with it, adopted it, dropt my abrupt contradiction and positive argumentation, and put on the humble inquirer and doubter. And being then, from reading Shaftesbury and Collins, become a real doubter in many points of our religious doctrine, I found this method safest for myself and very embarassing to those against whom I used it; therefore I took a delight in it, practis'd it continually, and grew very artful and expert in drawing people, even of superior knowledge, into concessions, the consequences of which they did not foresee, entangling them in difficulties out of which they could not extricate themselves, and so obtaining victories that neither myself nor my cause always deserved. I continu'd this method some few years, but gradually left it, retaining only the habit of expressing myself in terms of modest diffidence; never using, when I advanced anything that may possibly be disputed, the words *certainly*, *undoubtedly*, or any others that give the air of positiveness to an opinion; but rather say, I conceive or apprehend a thing to be so and so; it appears to me, or *I should think it so or so*, for such and such reasons; or *I imagine it to be so;* or *it is so, if I am not mistaken*. This habit, I believe, has been of great advantage to me when I have had occasion to inculcate my opinions, and persuade men into measures that I have been from time to time engag'd in promoting; and, as the chief ends of conversation are to *inform* or to be *informed*, to *please* or to *persuade*, I wish well-meaning, sensible men would not lessen their power of doing good by a positive, assuming manner, that seldom fails to disgust, tends to create opposition, and to defeat everyone of those purposes for which speech was given to us, to wit, giving or receiving information or pleasure. For, if you would inform, a positive and dogmatical manner in advancing your sentiments may provoke contradiction and prevent a candid attention. If you wish information and improvement from the knowledge of others, and yet at the same time express yourself as firmly fix'd in your present opinions, modest, sensible men, who do not love disputation, will probably leave you undisturbed in the possession of your error. And by such a manner, you can seldom hope to recommend yourself in *pleasing* your hearers, or to persuade those whose concurrence you desire. Pope says, judiciously:

> *"Men should be taught as if you taught them not,*
> *And things unknown propos'd as things forgot;"*

farther recommending to us

> "To speak, tho' sure, with seeming diffidence."

And he might have coupled with this line that which he has coupled with another, I think, less properly,

> "For want of modesty is want of sense."

If you ask, Why less properly? I must repeat the lines,

> "Immodest words admit of no defense,
> For want of modesty is want of sense."

Now, is not *want of sense* (where a man is so unfortunate as to want it) some apology for his *want of modesty*? and would not the lines stand more justly thus?

> "Immodest words admit *but* this defense,
> That want of modesty is want of sense."

This, however, I should submit to better judgments.

My brother had, in 1720 or 1721, begun to print a newspaper. It was the second that appeared in America, and was called the New England Courant. The only one before it was the Boston News-Letter.

I remember his being dissuaded by some of his friends from the undertaking, as not likely to succeed, one newspaper being, in their judgment, enough for America. At this time (1771) there are not less than five-and-twenty. He went on, however, with the undertaking, and after having worked in composing the types and printing off the sheets, I was employed to carry the papers thro' the streets to the customers.

He had some ingenious men among his friends, who amus'd themselves by writing little pieces for this paper, which gain'd it credit and made it more in demand, and these gentlemen often visited us. Hearing their conversations, and their accounts of the approbation their papers were received with, I was excited to try my hand among them; but, being still a boy, and suspecting that my brother would object to printing anything of mine in his paper if he knew it to be mine, I contrived to disguise my hand, and, writing an anonymous paper, I put it in at night under the door of the printing-house. It was found in the morning, and communicated to his writing friends when they call'd in as usual. They read it, commented on it in my hearing, and I had the exquisite pleasure of finding it met with their approbation, and that, in their different guesses at the author, none were named but men of some character among us for learning and ingenuity. I suppose now that I was rather lucky in my judges, and that perhaps they were not really so very good ones as I then esteem'd them.

Encourag'd, however, by this, I wrote and convey'd in the same way to the press several more papers which were equally approv'd; and I kept my secret till my small fund of sense for such performances was pretty well exhausted, and then I discovered it, when I began to be considered a little more by my brother's acquaintance, and in a manner that did not quite please him, as he thought, probably with reason, that it tended to make me too vain. And, perhaps, this might be one occasion of the differences that we began to have about this time. Though a brother, he considered himself as my master, and me as his apprentice, and, accordingly, expected the same services from me as he would from another, while I thought he demean'd me too much in some he requir'd of me, who from a brother expected more indulgence. Our disputes were often brought before our father, and I fancy I was either generally in the right, or else a better pleader, because the judgment was generally in my favor. But my brother was passionate, and had often beaten me, which I took extreamly amiss; and, thinking my apprenticeship very tedious, I was continually wishing for some opportunity of shortening it, which at length offered in a manner unexpected.[1]

One of the pieces in our newspaper on some political point, which I have now forgotten, gave offense to the Assembly. He was taken up, censur'd, and imprison'd for a month, by the speaker's warrant, I suppose, because he would not discover his author. I too was taken up and examin'd before the council; but, tho' I did not give them any satisfaction, they content'd themselves with admonishing me, and dismissed me, considering me, perhaps, as an apprentice, who was bound to keep his master's secrets.

During my brother's confinement, which I resented a good deal, notwithstanding our private differences, I had the management of the paper; and I made bold to give our rulers some rubs in it, which my brother took very kindly, while others

[1] I fancy his harsh and tyrannical treatment of me might be a means of impressing me with that aversion to arbitrary power that has stuck to me through my whole life.

began to consider me in an unfavorable light, as a young genius that had a turn for libelling and satyr. My brother's discharge was accompany'd with an order of the House (a very odd one), that "*James Franklin should no longer print the paper called the New England Courant.*"

There was a consultation held in our printing-house among his friends, what he should do in this case. Some proposed to evade the order by changing the name of the paper; but my brother, seeing inconveniences in that, it was finally concluded on as a better way, to let it be printed for the future under the name of BENJAMIN FRANKLIN; and to avoid the censure of the Assembly, that might fall on him as still printing it by his apprentice, the contrivance was that my old indenture should be return'd to me, with a full discharge on the back of it, to be shown on occasion, but to secure to him the benefit of my service, I was to sign new indentures for the remainder of the term, which were to be kept private. A very flimsy scheme it was; however, it was immediately executed, and the paper went on accordingly, under my name for several months.

At length, a fresh difference arising between my brother and me, I took upon me to assert my freedom, presuming that he would not venture to produce the new indentures. It was not fair in me to take this advantage, and this I therefore reckon one of the first errata of my life; but the unfairness of it weighed little with me, when under the impressions of resentment for the blows his passion too often urged him to bestow upon me, though he was otherwise not an ill-natur'd man: perhaps I was too saucy and provoking.

When he found I would leave him, he took care to prevent my getting employment in any other printing-house of the town, by going round and speaking to every master, who accordingly refus'd to give me work. I then thought of going to New York, as the nearest place where there was a printer; and I was rather inclin'd to leave Boston when I reflected that I had already made myself a little obnoxious to the governing party, and, from the arbitrary proceedings of the Assembly in my brother's case, it was likely I might, if I stay'd, soon bring myself into scrapes; and farther, that my indiscrete disputations about religion began to make me pointed at with horror by good people as an infidel or atheist. I determin'd on the point, but my father now siding with my brother, I was sensible that, if I attempted to go openly, means would be used to prevent me. My friend Collins, therefore, undertook to manage a little for me. He agreed with the captain of a New York sloop for my passage, under the notion of my being a young acquaintance of his, that had got a naughty girl with child, whose friends would compel me to marry her, and therefore I could not appear or come away publicly. So I sold some of my books to raise a little money, was taken on board privately, and as we had a fair wind, in three days I found myself in New York, near 300 miles from home, a boy of but 17, without the least recommendation to, or knowledge of any person in the place, and with very little money in my pocket.

My inclinations for the sea were by this time worne out, or I might now have gratify'd them. But, having a trade, and supposing myself a pretty good workman, I offer'd my service to the printer in the place, old Mr William Bradford, who had been the first printer in Pennsylvania, but removed from thence upon the quarrel of George Keith. He could give me no employment, having little to do, and help enough already; but says he, "My son at Philadelphia has lately lost his principal hand, Aquila Rose, by death; if you go thither, I believe

Old House in Milk Street where Benjamin Franklin was born

From a drawing taken shortly before it was burnt down in 1810

he may employ you." Philadelphia was a hundred miles further; I set out, however, in a boat for Amboy, leaving my chest and things to follow me round by sea.

In crossing the bay, we met with a squall that tore our rotten sails to pieces, prevented our getting into the Kill, and drove us upon Long Island. In our way, a drunken Dutchman, who was a passenger too, fell overboard; when he was sinking, I reached through the water to his shock pate, and drew him up, so that we got him in again. His ducking sobered him a little, and he went to sleep, taking first out of his pocket a book, which he desir'd I would dry for him. It proved to be my old favorite author, Bunyan's Pilgrim's Progress, in Dutch, finely printed on good paper, with copper cuts, a dress better than I had ever seen it wear in its own language. I have since found that it has been translated into most of the languages of Europe, and suppose it has been more generally read than any other book, except perhaps the Bible. Honest John was the first that I know of who mix'd narration and dialogue; a method of writing very engaging to the reader, who in the most interesting parts finds himself, as it were, brought into the company and present at the discourse. De Foe in his Cruso, his Moll Flanders, Religious Courtship, Family Instructor, and other pieces, has imitated it with success; and Richardson has done the same in his Pamela, etc.

When we drew near the island, we found it was at a place where there could be no landing, there being a great surff on the stony beach. So we dropt anchor, and swung round towards the shore. Some people came down to the water edge and hallow'd to us, as we did to them; but the wind was so high, and the surff so loud, that we could not hear so as to understand each other. There were canoes on the shore, and we made signs, and hallow'd that they should fetch us; but they either did not understand us, or thought it impracticable, so they went away, and night coming on, we had no remedy but to wait till the wind should abate; and, in the mean time, the boatman and I concluded to sleep, if we could; and so crowded into the scuttle, with the Dutchman, who was still wet, and the spray beating over the head of our boat, leak'd thro' to us, so that we were soon almost as wet as he. In this manner we lay all night, with very little rest; but, the wind abating the next day, we made a shift to reach Amboy before night, having been thirty hours on the water, without victuals, or any drink but a bottle of filthy rum, and the water we sail'd on being salt.

In the evening I found myself very feverish, and went into bed; but, having read somewhere that cold water drank plentifully was good for a fever, I follow'd the prescription, sweat plentiful most of the night, my fever left me, and in the morning, crossing the ferry, I proceeded on my journey on foot, having fifty miles to Burlington, where I was told I should find boats that would carry me the rest of the way to Philadelphia.

It rained very hard all the day; I was thoroughly soak'd, and by noon a good deal tired; so I stopt at a poor inn, where I staid all night, beginning now to wish that I had never left home. I cut so miserable a figure, too, that I found, by the questions ask'd me, I was suspected to be some runaway servant, and in danger of being taken up on that suspicion. However, I proceeded the next day, and got in the evening to an inn, within eight or ten miles of Burlington, kept by one Dr Brown. He entered into conversation with me while I took some refreshment, and, finding I had read a little, became very sociable and friendly. Our acquaintance continu'd as long as he liv'd. He had been, I imagine, an itinerant doctor, for there was no town in England, or country in Europe, of which he could not give a very particular account. He had some letters, and was ingenious, but much of an unbeliever, and wickedly undertook, some years after, to travestie the Bible in doggrel verse, as Cotton had done Virgil. By this means he set many of the facts in a very ridiculous light, and might have hurt weak minds if his work had been published; but it never was.

At his house I lay that night, and the next morning reach'd Burlington, but had the mortification to find that the regular boats were gone a little before my coming, and no other expected to go before Tuesday, this being Saturday; wherefore I returned to an old woman in the town, of whom I had bought gingerbread to eat on the water, and ask'd her advice. She invited me to lodge at her house till a passage by water should offer; and being tired with my foot travelling, I accepted the invitation. She understanding I was a printer, would have had me stay at that town and follow my business, being ignorant of the stock necessary to begin with. She was very hospitable, gave me a dinner of ox-cheek with great good will, accepting only of a pot of ale in return; and I thought myself fixed till Tuesday should come. However, walking in the evening by the side of the river, a boat came by, which I found was going towards Philadelphia, with several people in her. They took me in, and, as there was no wind, we row'd all the way; and about midnight, not having yet seen the city, some of the company were confident we must have passed it, and would row no farther; the others knew not where we were; so we put toward the shore, got into a creek, landed near an old fence, with the rails of which we made a fire, the night being cold, in October, and there we remained till daylight. Then one of the company knew the place to be Cooper's Creek, a little above Philadelphia, which we saw as soon as we got out of the creek, and arriv'd there about eight or nine o'clock on the Sunday morning, and landed at the Market-street wharf.

I have been the more particular in this description of my journey, and shall be so of my first entry into that city, that you may in your mind compare such unlikely beginnings with the figure I have since made there. I was in my working dress, my best clothes being to come round by sea. I was dirty from my journey; my pockets were stuff'd out with shirts and stockings, and I knew no soul nor where to look for lodging. I was fatigued with travelling, rowing, and want of rest, I was very hungry; and my whole stock of cash consisted of a Dutch dollar, and about a shilling in copper. The latter I gave the people of the boat for my passage, who at first refus'd it, on account of my rowing; but I insisted on their taking it. A man being sometimes more generous when he has but a little money than when he has plenty, perhaps thro' fear of being thought to have but little.

Then I walked up the street, gazing about till near the market-house I met a boy with bread. I had made many a meal on bread, and, inquiring where he got it, I went immediately to the baker's he directed me to, in Second-street, and ask'd for bisket, intending such as we had in Boston; but they, it seems, were not made in Philadelphia. Then I asked for a three-penny loaf, and was told they had none such. So not considering or knowing the difference of money, and the greater cheapness nor the names of his bread, I bad him give me three-penny worth of any sort. He gave me, accordingly, three great puffy rolls. I was surpriz'd at the quantity, but took it, and, having no room in my pockets, walk'd off with a roll under each arm, and eating the other. Thus I went up Market-street as far as Fourth-street, passing by the door of Mr Read, my future wife's father; when she, standing at the door, saw me, and thought I made, as I certainly did, a most awkward, ridiculous appearance. Then I turned and went down Chesnut-street and part of Walnut-street, eating my roll all the way, and, coming round, found myself again at Market-street wharf, near the boat I came in, to which I went for a draught of the river water; and, being filled with one of my rolls, gave the other two to a woman and her child that came down the river in the boat with us, and were waiting to go farther.

Thus refreshed, I walked again up the street, which by this time had many clean-dressed people in it, who were all walking the same way. I joined them, and thereby was led into the great meeting-house of the Quakers near the market. I sat down among them, and, after looking round awhile and hearing nothing said, being very drowsy thro' labor and want of rest the preceding night, I fell fast asleep, and continued so till the meeting broke up, when one was kind enough to rouse me. This was, therefore, the first house I was in, or slept in, in Philadelphia.

Walking down again toward the river, and, looking in the faces of people, I met a young Quaker man, whose countenance I lik'd, and, accosting him, requested he would tell me where a stranger could get lodging. We were then near the sign of the Three Mariners. "Here," says he, "is one place that entertains strangers, but it is not a reputable house; if thee wilt walk with me, I'll show thee a better." He brought me to the Crooked Billet in Water-street. Here I got a dinner; and, while I was eating it, several sly questions were asked me, as it seemed to be suspected from my youth and appearance, that I might be some runaway.

After dinner, my sleepiness return'd, and being shown to a bed, I lay down without undressing, and slept till six in the evening, was call'd to supper, went to bed again very early, and slept soundly till next morning. Then I made myself as tidy as I could, and went to Andrew Bradford the printer's. I found in the shop the old man his father, whom I had seen at New York, and who, travelling on horseback, had got to Philadelphia before me. He introduc'd me to his son, who receiv'd me civilly, gave me a breakfast, but told me he did not at present want a hand, being lately suppli'd with one; but there was another printer in town, lately set up, one Keimer, who, perhaps, might employ me; if not, I should be welcome to lodge at his house, and he would give me a little work to do now and then till fuller business should offer.

The old gentleman said he would go with me to the new printer; and when we found him, "Neighbor," says Bradford, "I have brought to see you a young man of your business; perhaps you may want such a one." He ask'd me a few questions, put a composing stick in my hand to see how I work'd, and then said he would employ me soon, though he had just then nothing for me to do; and, taking old Bradford, whom he had never seen before, to be one of the town's people that had a good will for him, enter'd into a conversation on his present undertaking and prospects; while Bradford, not discovering that he was the other printer's father, on Keimer's saying he expected soon to get the greatest part of the business into his own hands, drew him on by artful questions, and starting little doubts, to explain all his views, what interest he reli'd on, and in what manner he intended to proceed. I, who stood by and heard all, saw immediately that one of them was a crafty old sophister, and the other a mere novice. Bradford left me with Keimer, who was greatly surprised when I told him who the old man was.

Keimer's printing-house, I found, consisted of an old shatter'd press, and one small, worn-out font of English, which he was then using himself, composing an Elegy on Aquila Rose, before mentioned, an ingenious young man, of excellent character, much respected in the town, clerk of the Assembly, and a pretty poet. Keimer made verses too, but very indifferently. He could not be said to write them, for his manner was to compose them in the types directly out of his head. So there being no copy, but one pair of cases, and the Elegy likely to require all the letter, no one could help him. I endeavor'd to put his press (which he had not yet us'd, and of which he understood nothing) into order fit to be work'd with; and, promising to come and print off his Elegy as soon as he should have got it ready, I return'd to Bradford's, who gave me a little job to do for the present, and there I lodged and dieted. A few days after, Keimer sent for me to print off the Elegy. And now he had got another pair of cases, and a pamphlet to reprint, on which he set me to work.

These two printers I found poorly qualified for their business. Bradford had not been bred to it, and was very illiterate; and Keimer, tho' something of a scholar, was a mere compositor, knowing nothing of presswork. He had been one of the French prophets, and could act their enthusiastic agitations. At this time he did not profess any particular religion, but something of all on occasion; was very ignorant of the world, and had, as I afterward found, a good deal of the knave in his composition. He did not like my lodging at Bradford's while I work'd with him. He had a house, indeed, but without furniture, so he could not lodge me; but he got me a lodging at Mr Read's, before mentioned, who was the owner of his house; and, my chest and clothes being come by this time, I made rather a more respectable appearance in the eyes of Miss Read than I had done when she first happen'd to see me eating my roll in the street.

I began now to have some acquaintance among the young people of the town, that were lovers of reading, with whom I spent my evenings very pleasantly; and gaining money by my industry and frugality, I lived very agreeably, forgetting Boston as much as I could, and not desiring that any there should know where I resided, except my friend Collins, who was in my secret, and kept it when I wrote to him. At length, an incident happened that sent me back again much sooner than I had intended. I had a brother-in-law, Robert Holmes, master of a sloop that traded between Boston and Delaware. He being at Newcastle, forty miles below Philadelphia, heard there of me, and wrote me a letter mentioning the concern of my friends in Boston at my abrupt departure, assuring me of their good will to me, and that every thing would be accommodated to my mind if I would return, to which he exhorted me very earnestly. I wrote an answer to his letter, thank'd him for his advice, but stated my reasons for quitting Boston fully and in such a light as to convince him I was not so wrong as he had apprehended.

Sir William Keith, governor of the province, was then at Newcastle, and Captain Holmes, happening to be in company with him when my letter came to hand, spoke to him of me, and show'd him the letter. The governor read it, and seem'd surpris'd when he was told of my age. He said I appear'd a young man of promising parts, and therefore should be encouraged; the printers at Philadelphia were wretched ones; and, if I would set up there, he made no doubt I should succeed; for his part, he would procure me the public business, and do me every other service in his power. This my brother-in-law afterwards told me in Boston, but I knew as yet nothing of it; when, one day, Keimer and I being at work together near the window, we saw the governor and another gentleman (which proved to be Colonel French, of Newcastle), finely dress'd, come directly across the street to our house, and heard them at the door.

Keimer ran down immediately, thinking it a visit to him; but the governor inquir'd for me, came up, and with a condescension and politeness I had been quite unus'd to, made me many compliments, desired to be acquainted with me, blam'd me kindly for not having made myself known to him when I first came to the place, and would have me away with him to the tavern, where he was going with Colonel French to taste, as he said, some excellent Madeira. I was not a little surprised, and Keimer star'd like a pig poison'd. I went, however, with the governor and Colonel French to a tavern, at the corner of Third-street, and over the Madeira he propos'd my setting up my business, laid before me the probabilities of success, and both he and Colonel French assur'd me I should have their interest and influence in procuring the public business of both governments. On my doubting whether my father would assist me in it, Sir William said he would give me a letter to him, in which he would state the advantages, and he did not doubt of prevailing with him. So it was concluded I should return to Boston in the first vessel, with the governor's letter recommending me to my father. In the mean time the intention was to be kept a secret, and I went on working with Keimer as usual, the governor sending for me now and then to dine with him, a very great honor I thought it, and conversing with me in the most affable, familiar, and friendly manner imaginable.

About the end of April, 1724, a little vessel offer'd for Boston. I took leave of Keimer as going to see my friends. The governor gave me an ample letter, saying many flattering things of me to my father, and strongly recommending the project of my setting up at Philadelphia as a thing that must make my fortune. We struck on a shoal in going down the bay, and sprung a leak; we had a blustering time at sea, and were oblig'd to pump almost continually, at which I took my turn. We arriv'd safe, however, at Boston in about a fortnight. I had been absent seven months, and my friends had heard nothing of me; for my br. Holmes was not yet return'd, and had not written about me. My unexpected appearance surpriz'd the family; all were, however, very glad to see me, and made me welcome, except my brother. I went to see him at his printing-house. I was better dress'd than ever while in his service, having a genteel new suit from head to foot, a watch, and my pockets lin'd with near five pounds sterling in silver. He receiv'd me not very frankly, look'd me all over, and turn'd to his work again.

The journeymen were inquisitive where I had been, what sort of a country it was, and how I lik'd it. I prais'd it much, and the happy life I led in it, expressing strongly my intention of returning to it; and, one of them asking what kind of money we had there, I produc'd a handful of silver, and spread it before them, which was a kind of raree-show they had not been us'd to, paper being the money of Boston. Then I took an opportunity of letting them see my watch; and, lastly (my brother still grum and sullen), I gave them a piece of eight to drink, and took my leave. This visit of mine offended him extreamly; for, when my mother some time after spoke to him of a reconciliation, and of her wishes to see us on good terms together, and that we might live for the future as brothers, he said I had insulted him in such a manner before his people that he could never forget or forgive it. In this, however, he was mistaken.

My father received the governor's letter with some apparent surprise, but said little of it to me for some days, when Capt. Holmes returning he showed it to him, ask'd him if he knew Keith, and what kind of man he was; adding his opinion that he must be of small discretion to think of setting a boy up in business who wanted yet three years of being at man's estate. Holmes said what he could in favor of the project, but my father was clear in the impropriety of it, and at last gave a flat denial to it. Then he wrote a civil letter to Sir William, thanking him for the patronage he had so kindly offered me, but declining to assist me as yet in setting up, I being, in his opinion, too young to be trusted with the management of a business so important, and for which the preparation must be so expensive.

My friend and companion Collins, who was a clerk in the post-office, pleas'd with the account I gave him of my new country, determined to go thither also; and, while I waited for my father's determination, he set out before me by land to Rhode Island, leaving his books, which were a pretty collection of mathematicks and natural philosophy, to come with mine and me to New York, where he propos'd to wait for me.

My father, tho' he did not approve Sir William's proposition, was yet pleas'd that I had been able to obtain so advantageous a character from a person of such note where I had resided, and that I had been so industrious and careful as to equip myself so handsomely in so short a time; therefore, seeing no prospect of an accommodation between my brother and me, he gave his consent to my returning again to Philadelphia, advis'd me to behave respectfully to the people there, endeavor to obtain the general esteem, and avoid lampooning and libeling, to which he thought I had too much inclination; telling me, that by steady industry and a prudent parsimony I might save enough by the time I was one-and-twenty to set me up; and that, if I came near the matter, he would help me out with the rest. This was all I could obtain, except some small gifts as tokens of his and my mother's love, when I embark'd again for New York, now with their approbation and their blessing.

The sloop putting in at Newport, Rhode Island, I visited my brother John, who had been married and settled there some years. He received me very affectionately, for he always lov'd me. A friend of his, one Vernon, having some money due to him in Pensilvania, about thirty-five pounds currency, desired I would receive it for him, and keep it till I had his directions what to remit it in. Accordingly, he gave me an order. This afterwards occasion'd me a good deal of uneasiness.

At Newport we took in a number of passengers for New York, among which were two young women, companions, and a grave, sensible, matronlike Quaker woman, with her attendants. I had shown an obliging readiness to do her some little services, which impress'd her I suppose with a degree of good will toward me; therefore, when she saw a daily growing familiarity between me and the two young women, which they appear'd to encourage, she took me aside, and said, "Young man, I am concern'd for thee, as thou has no friend with thee, and seems not to know much of the world, or of the snares youth is expos'd to; depend upon it, those are very bad women; I can see it in all their actions; and if thee art not upon thy guard, they will draw thee into some danger; they are strangers to thee, and I advise thee, in a friendly concern for thy welfare, to have no acquaintance with them." As I seem'd at first not to think so ill of them as she did, she mentioned some things she had observ'd and heard that had escap'd my notice, but now convinc'd me she was right. I thank'd her for her kind advice, and promis'd to follow it. When we arriv'd at New York, they told me where they liv'd, and invited me to come and see them; but I avoided it, and it was well I did; for the next day the captain miss'd a silver spoon and some other things, that had been taken out of his cabbin, and, knowing that these were a couple of strumpets, he got a warrant to search their lodgings, found the stolen goods, and had the thieves punish'd. So, tho' we had escap'd a sunken rock, which we scrap'd upon in the passage, I thought this escape of rather more importance to me.

At New York I found my friend Collins, who had arriv'd there some time before me. We had been intimate from children, and had read the same books together; but he had the advantage of more time for reading and studying, and a wonderful genius for mathematical learning, in which he far outstript me. While I liv'd in Boston, most of my hours of leisure for conversation were spent with him, and he continu'd a sober as well as an industrious lad; was much respected for his learning by several of the clergy and other gentlemen, and seemed to promise making a good figure in life. But, during my absence, he had acquir'd a habit of sotting with brandy; and I found by his own account, and what I heard from others, that he had been drunk every day since his arrival at New York, and behav'd very oddly. He had gam'd, too, and lost his money, so that I was oblig'd to discharge his lodgings, and defray his expenses to and at Philadelphia, which prov'd extremely inconvenient to me.

The then governor of New York, Burnet (son of Bishop Burnet), hearing from the captain that a young man, one of his passengers, had a great many books, desir'd he would bring me to see him. I waited upon him accordingly, and should have taken Collins with me but that he was not sober. The gov'r. treated me with great civility, show'd me his library, which was a very large one, and we had a good deal of conversation about books and authors. This was the second governor who had done me the honor to take notice of me; which, to a poor boy like me, was very pleasing.

We proceeded to Philadelphia. I received on the way Vernon's money, without which we could hardly have finish'd our journey. Collins wished to be employ'd in some counting-house; but, whether they discover'd his dramming by his breath, or by his behaviour, tho' he had some recommendations, he met with no success in any application, and continu'd lodging and boarding at the same house with me, and at my expense. Knowing I had that money of Vernon's, he was continually borrowing of me, still promising repayment as soon as he should be in business. At length he had got so much of it that I was distress'd to think what I should do in case of being call'd on to remit it.

His drinking continu'd, about which we sometimes quarrell'd; for, when a little intoxicated, he was very fractious. Once, in a boat on the Delaware with some other young men, he refused to row in his turn. "I will be row'd home," says he. "We will not row you," says I. "You must, or stay all night on the water," says he, "just as you please." The others said, "Let us row; what signifies it?" But, my mind being soured with his other conduct, I continu'd to refuse. So he swore he would make me row, or throw me overboard; and coming along, stepping on the thwarts, toward me, when he came up and struck at me, I clapped my hand under his crutch, and, rising, pitched him head-foremost into the river. I knew he was a good swimmer, and so was under little concern about him; but before he could get round to lay hold of the boat, we had with a few strokes pull'd her out of his reach; and ever when he drew near the boat, we ask'd if he would row, striking a few strokes to slide her away from him. He was ready to die with vexation, and obstinately would not promise to row. However, seeing him at last beginning to tire, we lifted him in and brought him home dripping wet in the evening. We hardly exchang'd a civil word afterwards, and a West India captain, who had a commission to procure a tutor for the sons of a gentleman at Barbadoes, happening to meet with him, agreed to carry him thither. He left me then, promising to remit me the first money he should receive in order to discharge the debt; but I never heard of him after.

The breaking into this money of Vernon's was one of the first great errata of my life; and this affair show'd that my father was not much out in his judgment when he suppos'd me too young to manage business of importance. But Sir William, on reading his letter, said he was too prudent. There was great difference in persons; and discretion did not always accompany years, nor was youth always without it. "And since he will not set you up," says he, "I will do it myself. Give me an inventory of the things necessary to be had from England, and I will send for them. You shall repay me when you are able; I am resolv'd to have a good printer here, and I am sure you must succeed." This was spoken with such an appearance of cordiality, that I had not the least doubt of his meaning what he said. I had hitherto kept the proposition of my setting up, a secret in Philadelphia, and I still kept it. Had it been known that I depended on the governor, probably some friend, that knew him better, would have advis'd me not to rely on him, as I afterwards heard it as his known character to be liberal of promises which he never meant to keep. Yet, unsolicited as he was by me, how could I think his generous offers insincere? I believ'd him one of the best men in the world.

I presented him an inventory of a little print'g-house, amounting by my computation to about one hundred pounds sterling. He lik'd it, but ask'd me if my being on the spot in England to chuse the types, and see that every thing was good of the kind, might not be of some advantage. "Then," says he, "when there, you may make acquaintances, and establish correspondences in the bookselling and stationery way." I agreed that this might be advantageous. "Then," says he, "get yourself ready to go with Annis;" which was the annual ship, and the only one at that time usually passing between London and Philadelphia. But it would be some months before Annis sail'd, so I continu'd working with Keimer, fretting about the money Collins had got from me, and in daily apprehensions of being call'd upon by Vernon, which, however, did not happen for some years after.

I believe I have omitted mentioning that, in my first voyage from Boston, being becalm'd off Block Island, our people set about catching cod, and hauled up a great many. Hitherto I had stuck to my resolution of not eating animal food, and on this occasion I consider'd, with my master Tryon, the taking every fish as a kind of unprovoked murder, since none of them had, or ever could do us any injury that might justify the slaughter. All this seemed very reasonable. But I had formerly been a great lover of fish, and, when this came hot out of the frying-pan, it smelt admirably well. I balanc'd some time between principle and inclination, till I recollected that, when the fish were opened, I saw smaller fish taken out of their stomachs; then thought I, "If you eat one another, I don't see why we mayn't eat you." So I din'd upon cod very heartily, and continued to eat with other people, returning only now and then occasionally to a vegetable diet. So convenient a thing is it to be a *reasonable creature*, since it enables one to find or make a reason for every thing one has a mind to do.

Keimer and I liv'd on a pretty good familiar footing, and agreed tolerably well, for he suspected nothing of my setting up. He retained a great deal of his old enthusiasms and lov'd argumentation. We therefore had many disputations. I used to work him so with my Socratic method, and had trepann'd him so often by questions apparently so distant from any point we had in hand, and yet by degrees lead to the point, and brought him into difficulties and contradictions, that at last he grew ridiculously cautious, and would hardly answer me the most common question, without asking first, "*What do you intend to infer from that?*" However, it gave him so high an opinion of my abilities in the confuting way, that he seriously proposed my being his colleague in a project he had of setting up a new sect. He was to preach the doctrines, and I was to confound all opponents. When he came to explain with me upon the doctrines, I found several conundrums which I objected to, unless I might have my way a little to, and introduce some of mine.

Keimer wore his beard at full length, because somewhere in the Mosaic law it is said, "*Thou shalt not mar the corners of thy beard.*" He likewise kept the Seventh day, Sabbath; and these two points were essentials with him. I dislik'd both; but agreed to admit them upon condition of his adopting the doctrine of using no animal food. "I doubt," said he, "my constitution will not bear that." I assur'd him it would, and that he would be the better for it. He was usually a great glutton, and I promised myself some diversion in half starving him. He agreed to try the practice, if I would keep him company. I did so, and we held it for three months. We had our victuals dress'd, and brought to us regularly by a woman in the neighborhood, who had from me a list of forty dishes, to be prepar'd for us at different times, in all which there was neither fish, flesh, nor fowl, and the whim suited me the better at this time from the cheapness of it, not costing us above eighteenpence sterling each per week. I have since kept several Lents most strictly, leaving the common diet for that, and that for the common, abruptly, without the least inconvenience, so that I think there is little in the advice of making those changes by easy gradations. I went on pleasantly, but poor Keimer suffered grievously, tired of the project, long'd for the flesh-pots of Egypt, and order'd a roast pig. He invited me and two women friends to dine with him; but, it being brought too soon upon table, he could not resist the temptation, and ate the whole before we came.

I had made some courtship during this time to Miss Read. I had a great respect and affection for her, and had some reason to believe she had the same for me; but, as I was about to take a long voyage, and we were both very young, only a little above eighteen, it was thought most prudent by her mother to prevent our going too far at present, as a marriage, if it was to take place, would be more convenient after my return, when I should be, as I expected, set up in my business. Perhaps, too, she thought my expectations not so well founded as I imagined them to be.

My chief acquaintances at this time were Charles Osborne, Joseph Watson, and James Ralph, all lovers of reading. The two first were clerks to an eminent scrivener or conveyancer in the town, Charles Brogden; the other was clerk to a merchant. Watson was a pious, sensible young man, of great integrity; the others rather more lax in their principles of religion, particularly Ralph, who, as well as Collins, had been unsettled by me, for which they both made me suffer. Osborne was sensible, candid, frank; sincere and affectionate to his friends; but, in literary matters, too fond of criticising. Ralph was ingenious, genteel in his manners, and extremely eloquent; I think I never knew a prettier talker. Both of them great admirers of poetry, and began to try their hands in little pieces. Many pleasant walks we four had together on Sundays into the woods, near Schuylkill, where we read to one another, and conferr'd on what we read.

Ralph was inclin'd to pursue the study of poetry, not doubting but he might become eminent in it, and make his fortune by it, alleging that the best poets must, when they first began to write, make as many faults as he did. Osborne dissuaded him, assur'd him he had no genius for poetry, and advis'd him to think of nothing beyond the business he was bred to; that, in the mercantile way, tho' he had no stock, he might, by his diligence and punctuality, recommend himself to employment as a factor, and in time acquire wherewith to trade on his own account. I approv'd the amusing one's self with poetry now and then, so far as to improve one's language, but no farther.

On this it was propos'd that we should each of us, at our next meeting, produce a piece of our own composing, in order to improve by our mutual observations, criticisms, and corrections. As language and expression were what we had in view, we excluded all considerations of invention by agreeing that the task should be a version of the eighteenth Psalm, which describes the descent of a Deity. When the time of our meeting drew nigh, Ralph called on me first, and let me know his piece was ready. I told him I had been busy, and, having little inclination, had done nothing. He then show'd me his piece for my opinion, and I much approv'd it, as it appear'd to me to have great merit. "Now," says he, "Osborne never will allow the least merit in any thing of mine, but makes 1000 criticisms out of mere envy. He is not so jealous of you; I wish, therefore, you would take this piece, and produce it as yours; I will pretend not to have had time, and so produce nothing. We shall then see what he will say to it." It was agreed, and I immediately transcrib'd it, that it might appear in my own hand.

We met; Watson's performance was read; there were some beauties in it, but many defects. Osborne's was read; it was much better; Ralph did it justice; remarked some faults, but applauded the beauties. He himself had nothing to produce. I was backward; seemed desirous of being excused; had not had sufficient time to correct, etc.; but no excuse could be admitted; produce I must. It was read and repeated; Watson and Osborne gave up the contest, and join'd in applauding it. Ralph only made some criticisms, and propos'd some amendments; but I defended my text. Osborne was against Ralph, and told him he was no better a critic than poet, so he dropt the argument. As they two went home together, Osborne expressed himself still more strongly in favor of what he thought my production; having restrain'd himself before, as he said, lest I should think it flattery. "But who would have imagin'd," said he, "that Franklin had been capable of such a performance; such painting, such force, such fire! He has even improv'd the original. In his common conversation he seems to have no choice of words; he hesitates and blunders; and yet, good God! how he writes!" When we next met, Ralph discovered the trick we had plaid him, and Osborne was a little laught at.

This transaction fixed Ralph in his resolution of becoming a poet. I did all I could to dissuade him from it, but he continued scribbling verses till *Pope* cured him. He became, however, a pretty good prose writer. More of him hereafter. But, as I may not have occasion again to mention the other two, I shall just remark here, that Watson died in my arms a few years after, much lamented, being the best of our set. Osborne went to the West Indies, where he became an eminent lawyer and made money, but died young. He and I had made a serious agreement, that the one who happen'd first to die should, if possible, make a friendly visit to the other, and acquaint him how he found things in that separate state. But he never fulfill'd his promise.

The governor, seeming to like my company, had me frequently to his house, and his setting me up was always mention'd as a fixed thing. I was to take with me letters recommendatory to a number of his friends, besides the letter of credit to furnish me with the necessary money for purchasing the press and types, paper, etc. For these letters I was appointed to call at different times, when they were to be ready; but a future time was still named. Thus he went on till the ship, whose departure too had been several times postponed, was on the point of sailing. Then, when I call'd to take my leave and receive the letters, his secretary, Dr Bard, came out to me and said the governor was extremely busy in writing, but would be down at Newcastle before the ship, and there the letters would be delivered to me.

Ralph, though married, and having one child, had determined to accompany me in this voyage. It was thought he intended to establish a correspondence, and obtain goods to sell on commission; but I found afterwards, that, thro' some discontent with his wife's relations, he purposed to leave her on their hands, and never return again. Having taken leave of my friends, and interchang'd some promises with Miss Read, I left Philadelphia in the ship, which anchor'd at Newcastle. The governor was there; but when I went to his lodging, the secretary came to me from him with the civillest message in the world, that he could not then see me, being engaged in business of the utmost importance, but should send the letters to me on board, wished me heartily a good voyage and a speedy return, etc. I returned on board a little puzzled, but still not doubting.

Mr Andrew Hamilton, a famous lawyer of Philadelphia, had taken passage in the same ship for himself and son, and with Mr Denham, a Quaker merchant, and Messrs Onion and Russel, masters of an iron work in Maryland, had engag'd the great cabin; so that Ralph and I were forced to take up with a berth in the steerage, and none on board knowing us, were considered as ordinary persons. But Mr Hamilton and his son (it was James, since governor) return'd from Newcastle to Philadelphia, the father being recall'd by a great fee to plead for a seized ship; and, just before we sail'd, Colonel French coming on board, and showing me great respect, I was more taken notice of, and, with my friend Ralph, invited by the other gentlemen to come into the cabin, there being now room. Accordingly, we remov'd thither.

Understanding that Colonel French had brought on board the governor's despatches, I ask'd the captain for those letters that were to be under my care. He said all were put into the bag together and he could not then come at them; but, before we landed in England, I should have an opportunity of picking them out; so I was satisfied for the present, and we proceeded on our voyage. We had a sociable company in the cabin, and lived uncommonly well, having the addition of all Mr Hamilton's stores, who had laid in plentifully. In this passage Mr Denham contracted a friendship for me that continued during his life. The voyage was otherwise not a pleasant one, as we had a great deal of bad weather.

When we came into the Channel, the captain kept his word with me, and gave me an opportunity of examining the bag for the governor's letters. I found none upon which my name was put as under my care. I picked out six or seven, that, by the handwriting, I thought might be the promised letters, especially as one of them was directed to Basket, the king's printer, and another to some stationer. We arriv'd in London the 24th of December, 1724. I waited upon the stationer, who came first in my way, delivering the letter as from Governor Keith. "I don't know such a person," says he; but, opening the letter, "O! this is from Riddlesden. I have lately found him to be a compleat rascal, and I will have nothing to do with him, nor receive any letters from him." So, putting the letter into my hand, he turn'd on his heel and left me to serve some customer. I was surprized to find these were not the governor's letters; and, after recollecting and comparing circumstances, I began to doubt his sincerity. I found my friend Denham, and opened the whole affair to him. He let me into Keith's character; told me there was not the least probability that he had written any letters for me; that no one, who knew him, had the smallest dependence on him; and he laught at the notion of the governor's giving me a letter of credit, having, as he said, no credit to give. On my expressing some concern about what I should do, he advised me to endeavor getting some employment in the way of my business. "Among the printers here," said he, "you will improve yourself, and when you return to America, you will set up to greater advantage."

We both of us happen'd to know, as well as the stationer, that Riddlesden, the attorney, was a very knave. He had half ruin'd Miss Read's father by persuading him to be bound for him. By this letter it appear'd there was a secret scheme on foot to the prejudice of Hamilton (suppos'd to be then coming over with us); and that Keith was concerned in it with Riddlesden. Denham, who was a friend of Hamilton's thought he ought to be acquainted with it; so, when he arriv'd in England, which was soon after, partly from resentment and ill-will to Keith and Riddlesden, and partly from good-will to him, I waited on him, and gave him the letter. He thank'd me cordially, the information being of importance to him; and from that time he became my friend, greatly to my advantage afterwards on many occasions.

But what shall we think of a governor's playing such pitiful tricks, and imposing so grossly on a poor ignorant boy! It was a habit he had acquired. He wish'd to please everybody; and, having little to give, he gave expectations. He was otherwise an ingenious, sensible man, a pretty good writer, and a good governor for the people, tho' not for his constituents, the proprietaries, whose instructions he sometimes disregarded. Several of our best laws were of his planning and passed during his administration.

Ralph and I were inseparable companions. We took lodgings together in Little Britain at three shillings and sixpence a week—as much as we could then afford. He found some relations, but they were poor, and unable to assist him. He now let me know his intentions of remaining in London, and that he never meant to return to Philadelphia. He had brought no money with him, the whole he could muster having been expended in paying his passage. I had fifteen pistoles; so he borrowed occasionally of me to subsist, while he was looking out for business. He first endeavored to get into the playhouse, believing himself qualify'd for an actor; but Wilkes, to whom he apply'd, advis'd him candidly not to think of that employment, as it was impossible he should succeed in it. Then he propos'd to Roberts, a publisher in Paternoster Row, to write for him a weekly paper like the Spectator, on certain conditions, which Roberts did not approve. Then he endeavored to get employment as a hackney writer, to copy for the stationers and lawyers about the Temple, but could find no vacancy.

I immediately got into work at Palmer's, then a famous printing-house in Bartholomew Close, and here I continu'd near a year. I was pretty diligent, but spent with Ralph a good deal of my earnings in going to plays and other places of amusement. We had together consumed all my pistoles, and now just rubbed on from hand to mouth. He seem'd quite to forget his wife and child, and I, by degrees, my engagements with Miss Read, to whom I never wrote more than one letter, and that was to let her know I was not likely soon to return. This was another of the great errata of my life, which I should wish to correct if I were to live it over again. In fact, by our expenses, I was constantly kept unable to pay my passage.

At Palmer's I was employed in composing for the second edition of Wollaston's "Religion of Nature." Some of his reasonings not appearing to me well founded, I wrote a little metaphysical piece in which I made remarks on them. It was entitled "A Dissertation on Liberty and Necessity, Pleasure and Pain." I inscribed it to my friend Ralph; I printed a small number. It occasion'd my being more consider'd by Mr Palmer as a young man of some ingenuity, tho' he seriously expostulated with me upon the principles of my pamphlet, which to him appear'd abominable. My printing this pamphlet was another erratum. While I lodg'd in Little Britain, I made an acquaintance with one Wilcox, a bookseller, whose shop was at the next door. He had an immense collection of second-hand books. Circulating libraries were not then in use; but we agreed that, on certain reasonable terms, which I have now forgotten, I might take, read, and return any of his books. This I esteem'd a great advantage, and I made as much use of it as I could.

My pamphlet by some means falling into the hands of one Lyons, a surgeon, author of a book entitled "The Infallibility of Human Judgment," it occasioned an acquaintance between us. He took great notice of me, called on me often to converse on those subjects, carried me to the Horns, a pale alehouse in —— Lane, Cheapside, and introduced me to Dr Mandeville, author of the "Fable of the Bees," who had a club there, of which he was the soul, being a most facetious, entertaining companion. Lyons, too, introduced me to Dr Pemberton, at Batson's Coffee-house, who promis'd to give me an opportunity, some time or other, of seeing Sir Isaac

Newton, of which I was extreamely desirous; but this never happened.

I had brought over a few curiosities, among which the principal was a purse made of the asbestos, which purifies by fire. Sir Hans Sloane heard of it, came to see me, and invited me to his house in Bloomsbury Square, where he show'd me all his curiosities, and persuaded me to let him add that to the number, for which he paid me handsomely.

In our house there lodg'd a young woman, a milliner, who, I think, had a shop in the Cloisters. She had been genteelly bred, was sensible and lively, and of most pleasing conversation. Ralph read plays to her in the evenings, they grew intimate, she took another lodging, and he followed her. They liv'd together some time; but, he being still out of business, and her income not sufficient to maintain them with her child, he took a resolution of going from London, to try for a country school, which he thought himself well qualified to undertake, as he wrote an excellent hand, and was a master of arithmetic and accounts. This, however, he deemed a business below him, and confident of future better fortune, when he should be unwilling to have it known that he once was so meanly employed, he changed his name, and did me the honor to assume mine; for I soon after had a letter from him, acquainting me that he was settled in a small village (in Berkshire, I think it was, where he taught reading and writing to ten or a dozen boys, at sixpence each per week), recommending Mrs T—— to my care, and desiring me to write to him, directing for Mr Franklin, schoolmaster, at such a place.

He continued to write frequently, sending me large specimens of an epic poem which he was then composing, and desiring my remarks and corrections. These I gave him from time to time, but endeavor'd rather to discourage his proceeding. One of Young's Satires was then just published. I copy'd and sent him a great part of it, which set in a strong light the folly of pursuing the Muses with any hope of advancement by them. All was in vain; sheets of the poem continued to come by every post. In the mean time, Mrs T——, having on his account lost her friends and business, was often in distresses, and us'd to send for me, and borrow what I could spare to help her out of them. I grew fond of her company, and, being at that time under no religious restraint, and presuming upon my importance to her, I attempted familiarities (another erratum) which she repuls'd with a proper resentment, and acquainted him with my behaviour. This made a breach between us; and, when he returned again to London, he let me know he thought I had cancell'd all the obligations he had been under to me. So I found I was never to expect his repaying me what I lent to him, or advanc'd for him. This, however, was not then of much consequence, as he was totally unable; and in the loss of his friendship I found myself relieved from a burthen. I now began to think of getting a little money beforehand, and, expecting better work, I left Palmer's to work at Watts's, near Lincoln's Inn Fields, a still greater printing-house. Here I continued all the rest of my stay in London.

At my first admission into this printing-house I took to working at press, imagining I felt a want of the bodily exercise I had been us'd to in America, where presswork is mix'd with composing. I drank only water; the other workmen, near fifty in number, were great guzzlers of beer. On occasion, I carried up and down stairs a large form of types in each hand, when others carried but one in both hands. They wondered to see, from this and several instances, that the *Water-American*, as they called me, was *stronger* than themselves, who drank *strong* beer! We had an alehouse boy who attended always in the house to supply the workmen. My companion at the press drank every day a pint before breakfast, a pint at breakfast with his bread and cheese, a pint between breakfast and dinner, a pint at dinner, a pint in the afternoon about six o'clock, and another when he had done his day's work. I thought it a detestable custom; but it was necessary, he suppos'd, to drink *strong* beer, that he might be *strong* to labor. I endeavored to convince him that the bodily strength afforded by beer could only be in proportion to the grain or flour of the barley dissolved in the water of which it was made; that there was more flour in a pennyworth of bread; and therefore, if he would eat that with a pint of water, it would give him more strength than a quart of beer. He drank on, however, and had four or five shillings to pay out of his wages every Saturday night for that muddling liquor; an expense I was free from. And thus these poor devils keep themselves always under.

Watts, after some weeks, desiring to have me in the composing-room, I left the pressmen; a new bien venu or sum for drink, being five shillings, was demanded of me by the compositors. I thought it an imposition, as I had paid below; the master thought so too, and forbad my paying it. I stood out two or three weeks, was accordingly considered as an excommunicate, and had so many little pieces of private mischief done me, by mixing my sorts, transposing my pages, breaking my matter, etc., etc., if I were ever so little out of the room, and all ascribed to the chappel ghost, which they said ever haunted those not regularly admitted, that, notwithstanding the master's protection, I found myself oblig'd to comply and pay the money, convinc'd of the folly of being on ill terms with those one is to live with continually.

I was now on a fair footing with them, and soon acquir'd considerable influence. I propos'd some reasonable alterations in their chappel[1] laws, and carried them against all opposition, From my example, a great part of them left their muddling breakfast of beer, and bread, and cheese, finding they could with me be suppl'd from a neighboring house with a large porringer of hot water-gruel, sprinkled with pepper, crumb'd with bread, and a bit of butter in it, for the price of a pint of beer, viz., three half-pence. This was a more comfortable as well as cheaper breakfast, and kept their heads clearer. Those who continued sotting with beer all day, were often, by not paying, out of credit at the alehouse, and us'd to make interest with me to get beer; their *light*, as they phrased it, *being out*. I watch'd the pay-table on Saturday night, and collected what I stood engag'd for them, having to pay sometimes near thirty shillings a week on their accounts. This, and my being esteem'd a pretty good *riggite*, that is, a jocular verbal satirist, supported my consequence in the society. My constant attendance (I never making a St. Monday) recommended me to the master; and my uncommon quickness at composing occasioned my being put upon all work of dispatch, which was generally better paid. So I went on now very agreeably.

My lodging in Little Britain being too remote, I

[1] "A printing-house is always called a chapel by the workmen, the origin of which appears to have been, that printing was first carried on in England in an antient chapel converted into a printing-house, and the title has been preserved by tradition The bien venu among the printers answers to the terms entrance and footing among mechanics; thus a journeyman, on entering a printing-house, was accustomed to pay one or more gallons of beer for the good of the chapel: this custom was falling into disuse thirty years ago; it is very properly rejected entirely in the United States."—W. T. F.

found another in Duke-street, opposite to the Romish Chapel. It was two pair of stairs backwards, at an Italian warehouse. A widow lady kept the house; she had a daughter, and a maid servant, and a journeyman who attended the warehouse, but lodg'd abroad. After sending to inquire my character at the house where I last lodg'd she agreed to take me in at the same rate, 3s. 6d. per week; cheaper, as she said, from the protection she expected in having a man lodge in the house. She was a widow, an elderly woman; had been bred a Protestant, being a clergyman's daughter, but was converted to the Catholic religion by her husband, whose memory she much revered; had lived much among people of distinction, and knew a thousand anecdotes of them as far back as the times of Charles the Second. She was lame in her knees with the gout, and, therefore, seldom stirred out of her room, so sometimes wanted company; and hers was so highly amusing to me, that I was sure to spend an evening with her whenever she desired it. Our supper was only half an anchovy each, on a very little strip of bread and butter, and half a pint of ale between us; but the entertainment was in her conversation. My always keeping good hours, and giving little trouble in the family, made her unwilling to part with me; so that, when I talk'd of a lodging I had heard of, nearer my business, for two shillings a week, which, intent as I now was on saving money, made some difference, she bid me not think of it, for she would abate me two shillings a week for the future; so I remained with her at one shilling and sixpence as long as I staid in London.

In a garret of her house there lived a maiden lady of seventy, in the most retired manner, of whom my landlady gave me this account: that she was a Roman Catholic, had been sent abroad when young, and lodg'd in a nunnery with an intent of becoming a nun; but, the country not agreeing with her, she returned to England, where, there being no nunnery, she had vow'd to lead the life of a nun, as near as might be done in those circumstances. Accordingly, she had given all her estate to charitable uses, reserving only twelve pounds a year to live on, and out of this sum she still gave a great deal in charity, living herself on water-gruel only, and using no fire but to boil it. She had lived many years in that garret, being permitted to remain there gratis by successive Catholic tentants of the house below, as they deemed it a blessing to have her there. A priest visited her to confess her every day. "I have ask'd her," says my landlady, "how she, as she liv'd, could possibly find so much employment for a confessor?" "Oh," said she, "it is impossible to avoid *vain thoughts.*" I was permitted once to visit her. She was chearful and polite, and convers'd pleasantly. The room was clean, but had no other furniture than a matras, a table with a crucifix and book, a stool which she gave me to sit on, and a picture over the chimney of Saint Veronica displaying her handkerchief, with the miraculous figure of Christ's bleeding face on it, which she explained to me with great seriousness. She look'd pale, but was never sick; and I give it as another instance on how small an income, life and health may be supported.

At Watts's printing-house I contracted an acquaintance with an ingenious young man, one Wygate, who, having wealthy relations, had been better educated than most printers; was a tolerable Latinist, spoke French, and lov'd reading. I taught him and a friend of his to swim at twice going into the river, and they soon became good swimmers. They introduc'd me to some gentlemen from the country, who went to Chelsea by water to see the College and Don Saltero's curiosities. In our return, at the request of the company, whose curiosity Wygate had excited, I stripped and leaped into the river, and swam from near Chelsea to Blackfryar's, performing on the way many feats of activity, both upon and under water, that surpris'd and pleas'd those to whom they were novelties.

I had from a child been ever delighted with this exercise, had studied and practis'd all Thevenot's motions and positions, added some of my own, aiming at the graceful and easy as well as the useful. All these I took this occasion of exhibiting to the company, and was much flatter'd by their admiration; and Wygate, who was desirous of becoming a master, grew more and more attach'd to me on that account, as well as from the similarity of our studies. He at length proposed to me travelling all over Europe together, supporting ourselves everywhere by working at our business. I was once inclined to it; but, mentioning it to my good friend Mr Denham, with whom I often spent an hour when I had leisure, he dissuaded me from it, advising me to think only of returning to Pennsilvania, which he was now about to do.

I must record one trait of this good man's character. He had formerly been in business at Bristol, but failed in debt to a number of people, compounded and went to America. There, by a close application to business as a merchant, he acquir'd a plentiful fortune in a few years. Returning to England in the ship with me, he invited his old creditors to an entertainment, at which he thank'd them for the easy composition they had favored him with, and, when they expected nothing but the treat, every man at the first remove found under his plate an order on a banker for the full amount of the unpaid remainder with interest.

He now told me he was about to return to Philadelphia, and should carry over a great quantity of goods in order to open a store there. He propos'd to take me over as his clerk, to keep his books, in which he would instruct me, copy his letters, and attend the store. He added, that, as soon as I should be acquainted with mercantile business, he would promote me by sending me with a cargo of flour and bread, etc., to the West Indies, and procure me commissions from others which would be profitable; and, if I manag'd well, would establish me handsomely. The thing pleas'd me; for I was grown tired of London, remembered with pleasure the happy months I had spent in Pennsylvania, and wish'd again to see it; therefore I immediately agreed on the terms of fifty pounds a year, Pennsylvania money; less, indeed, than my present gettings as a compositor, but affording a better prospect.

I now took leave of printing, as I thought, for ever, and was daily employed in my new business, going about with Mr Denham among the tradesmen to purchase various articles, and seeing them pack'd up, doing errands, calling upon workmen to dispatch, etc.; and, when all was on board, I had a few days' leisure. On one of these days, I was, to my surprise, sent for by a great man I knew only by name, a Sir William Wyndham, and I waited upon him. He had heard by some means or other of my swimming from Chelsea to Blackfriar's, and of my teaching Wygate and another young man to swim in a few hours. He had two sons, about to set out on their travels; he wish'd to have them first taught swimming, and proposed to gratify me handsomely if I would teach them. They were not yet come to town, and my stay was uncertain, so I could not undertake it; but, from this incident, I thought it likely that, if I were to remain in England and open a swimming-school, I might get a good deal of money; and it struck me so strongly, that, had the overture been sooner made me, probably I should not so soon have returned to America. After many years, you and I had something of more importance to do with one of these sons of Sir William Wyndham, become Earl of Egremont, which I shall mention in its place.

Thus I spent about eighteen months in London; most part of the time I work'd hard at my business, and spent but little upon myself except in seeing plays and in books. My friend Ralph had kept me poor; he owed me about twenty-seven pounds, which I was now never likely to receive; a great sum out of my small earnings! I lov'd him, notwithstanding, for he had many amiable qualities. I had by no means improv'd my fortune; but I had picked up some very ingenious acquaintance, whose conversation was of great advantage to me; and I had read considerably.

We sail'd from Gravesend on the 23rd of July, 1726. For the incidents of the voyage, I refer you to my Journal, where you will find them all minutely related. Perhaps the most important part of that journal is the *plan*[1] to be found in it, which I formed at sea, for regulating my future conduct in life. It is the more remarkable, as being formed when I was so young, and yet being pretty faithfully adhered to quite thro' to old age,

We landed in Philadelphia on the 11th of Octber, where I found sundry alterations. Keith was no longer governor, being superseded by Major Gordon. I met him walking the streets as a common citizen. He seem'd a little asham'd at seeing me, but pass'd without saying any thing. I should have been as much asham'd at seeing Miss Read, had not her friends, despairing with reason of my return after

[1] The "Journal" was printed by Sparks, from a copy made at Reading in 1787. But it does not contain the *Plan*.—Ed.

the receipt of my letter, persuaded her to marry another, one Rogers, a potter, which was done in my absence. With him, however, she was never happy, and soon parted from him, refusing to cohabit with him or bear his name, it being now said that he had another wife. He was a worthless fellow, tho' an excellent workman, which was the temptation to her friends. He got into debt, ran away in 1727 or 1728, went to the West Indies, and died there. Keimer had got a better house, a shop well supply'd with stationery, plenty of new types, a number of hands, tho' none good, and seem'd to have a great deal of business.

Mr Denham took a store in Water-street, where we open'd our goods; I attended the business diligently, studied accounts, and grew, in a little time, expert at selling. We lodg'd and boarded together; he counsell'd me as a father, having a sincere regard for me. I respected and loved him, and we might have gone on together very happy; but, in the beginning of February, $172\frac{6}{7}$, when I had just pass'd my twenty-first year, we both were taken ill. My distemper was a pleurisy, which very nearly carried me off. I suffered a good deal, gave up the point in my mind, and was rather disappointed when I found myself recovering, regretting, in some degree, that I must now, some time or other, have all that disagreeable work to do over again. I forget what his distemper was; it held him a long time, and at length carried him off. He left me a small legacy in a nuncupative will, as a token of his kindness for me, and he left me once more to the wide world; for the store was taken into the care of his executors, and my employment under him ended.

My brother-in-law, Holmes, being now at Philadelphia, advised my return to my business; and Keimer tempted me, with an offer of large wages by the year, to come and take the management of his printing-house, that he might better attend his stationer's shop. I had heard a bad character of him in London from his wife and her friends, and was not fond of having any more to do with him. I tri'd for farther employment as a merchant's clerk; but, not readily meeting with any, I clos'd again with Keimer. I found in his house these hands: Hugh Meredith, a Welsh Pensilvanian, thirty years of age, bred to country work; honest, sensible, had a great deal of solid observation, was something of a reader, but given to drink. Stephen Potts, a young countryman of full age, bred to the same, of uncommon natural parts, and great wit and humour, but a little idle. These he had agreed with at extream low wages per week, to be rais'd a shilling every three months, as they would deserve by improving in their business; and the expectation of these high wages, to come on hereafter, was what he had drawn them in with. Meredith was to work at press, Potts at book-binding, which he, by agreement, was to teach them, though he knew neither one nor t'other. John ——, a wild Irishman, brought up to no business, whose service, for four years, Keimer had purchased from the captain of a ship; he, too, was to be made a pressman. George Webb, an Oxford scholar, whose time for four years he had likewise bought, intending him for a compositor, of whom more presently; and David Harry, a country boy, whom he had taken apprentice.

I soon perceiv'd that the intention of engaging me at wages so much higher than he had been us'd to give, was, to have these raw, cheap hands form'd thro' me; and, as soon as I had instructed them, then they being all articled to him, he should be able to do without me. I went on, however, very cheerfully, put his printing-house in order, which had been in great confusion, and brought his hands by degrees to mind their business and to do it better.

It was an odd thing to find an Oxford scholar in the situation of a bought servant. He was not more than eighteen years of age, and gave me this account of himself; that he was born in Gloucester, educated at a grammar-school there, had been distinguish'd among the scholars for some apparent superiority in performing his part, when they exhibited plays; belong'd to the Witty Club there, and had written some pieces in prose and verse, which were printed in the Gloucester newspapers; thence he was sent to Oxford; where he continued about a year, but not well satisfi'd, wishing of all things to see London, and become a player. At length, receiving his quarterly allowance of fifteen guineas, instead of discharging his debts he walk'd out of town, hid his gown in a furze bush, and footed it to London, where, having no friends to advise him, he fell into bad company, soon spent his guineas, found no means of being introduc'd among the players, grew necessitous, pawn'd his cloaths, and wanted bread. Walking the street very hungry, and not knowing what to do with himself, a crimp's bill was put into his hand, offering immediate entertainment and encouragement to such as would bind themselves to serve in America. He went directly, sign'd the indentures, was put into the ship, and came over, never writing a line to acquaint his friends what was become of him. He was lively, witty, good-natur'd, and a pleasant companion, but idle, thoughtless, and imprudent to the last degree.

John, the Irishman, soon ran away; with the rest I began to live very agreeably, for they all respected me the more, as they found Keimer incapable of instructing them, and that from me they learned something daily. We never worked on Saturday, that being Keimer's Sabbath, so I had two days for reading. My acquaintance with ingenious people in the town increased. Keimer himself treated me with great civility and apparent regard, and nothing now made me uneasy but my debt to Vernon, which I was yet unable to pay, being hitherto but a poor œconomist. He, however, kindly made no demand of it.

Our printing-house often wanted sorts, and there was no letter-founder in America; I had seen types cast at James's in London, but without much attention to the manner; however, I now contrived a mould, made use of the letters we had as puncheons, struck the matrices in lead, and thus supply'd in a pretty tolerable way all deficiencies. I also engrav'd several things on occasion; I made the ink; I was warehouseman, and everything, and, in short, quite a fac-totum.

But, however serviceable I might be, I found that my services became every day of less importance, as the other hands improv'd in the business; and, when Keimer paid my second quarter's wages, he let me know that he felt them too heavy, and thought I should make an abatement. He grew by degrees less civil, put on more of the master, frequently found fault, was captious, and seem'd ready for an outbreaking. I went on, nevertheless, with a good deal of patience, thinking that his encumber'd circumstances were partly the cause. At length a trifle snapt our connections; for, a great noise happening near the court-house, I put my head out of the window to see what was the matter. Keimer, being in the street, look'd up and saw me, call'd out to me in a loud voice and angry tone to mind my business, adding some reproachful words, that nettled me the more for their publicity, all the neighbors who were looking out on the same occasion being witnesses how I was treated. He came up immediately into the printing-house, continu'd the quarrel, high words pass'd on both sides, he gave me the quarter's warning we had stipulated, expressing a wish that he had not been oblig'd to so long a warning. I told him his wish was unnecessary, for I would leave him that instant; and so, taking my hat, walk'd out of doors, desiring Meredith, whom I saw below, to take care of some things I left, and bring them to my lodgings.

Meredith came accordingly in the evening, when we talked my affair over. He had conceiv'd a great regard for me, and was very unwilling that I should leave the house while he remain'd in it. He dissuaded me from returning to my native country, which I began to think of; he reminded me that Keimer was in debt for all he possess'd; that his creditors began to be uneasy; that he kept his shop miserably, sold often without profit for ready money, and often trusted without keeping accounts; that he must therefore fail, which would make a vacancy I might profit of. I objected my want of money. He then let me know that his father had a high opinion of me, and, from some discourse that had pass'd between them, he was sure would advance money to set us up, if I would enter into partnership with him. "My time," says he, "will be out with Keimer in the spring; by that time we may have our press and types in from London. I am sensible I am no workman; if you like it, your skill in the business shall be set against the stock I furnish, and we will share the profits equally."

The proposal was agreeable, and I consented; his father was in town and approv'd of it; the more as he saw I had great influence with his son, had prevail'd on him to abstain long from dram-drinking, and he hop'd might break him off that wretched habit entirely, when we came to be so closely connected. I gave an inventory to the father, who carry'd it to a merchant; the things were sent for, the secret was to be kept till they should arrive, and in the mean time I was to get work, if I could, at the other printing-house. But I found no vacancy there, and so remain'd idle a few days, when Keimer, on a prospect of being employ'd to print some paper money in New Jersey, which would require cuts and various types that I only could supply, and apprehending Bradford might engage me and get the job from him, sent me a very civil message, that old friends should not part for a few words, the effect of sudden passion, and wishing me to return. Meredith persuaded me to comply, as it would give more opportunity for his improvement under my daily instructions; so I return'd, and we went on more smoothly than for some time before. The New Jersey jobb was obtain'd, I contriv'd a copperplate press for it, the first that had been seen in the country; I cut several ornaments and checks for the bills. We went together to Burlington, where I executed the whole to satisfaction; and he received so large a sum for the work as to be enabled thereby to keep his head much longer above water.

At Burlington I made an acquaintance with many principal people of the province. Several of them had been appointed by the Assembly a committee to attend the press, and take care that no more bills were printed than the law directed. They were therefore, by turns, constantly with us, and generally he who attended, brought with him a friend or two for company. My mind having been much more improv'd by reading than Keimer's, I suppose it was for that reason my conversation seem'd to be more valu'd. They had me to their houses, introduced me to their friends, and show'd me much civility; while he, tho' the master, was a little neglected. In truth, he was an odd fish; ignorant of common life, fond of rudely opposing receiv'd opinions, slovenly to extream dirtiness, enthusiastic in some points of religion, and a little knavish withal.

We continu'd there near three months; and by that time I could reckon among my acquired friends, Judge Allen, Samuel Bustill, the secretary of the Province, Isaac Pearson, Joseph Cooper, and several of the Smiths, members of Assembly, and Isaac Decow, the surveyor-general. The latter was a shrewd, sagacious old man, who told me that he began for himself, when young, by wheeling clay for the brickmakers, learned to write after he was of age, carri'd the chain for surveyors, who taught him surveying, and he had now by his industry, acquir'd a good estate; and says he, "I foresee that you will soon work this man out of his business, and make a fortune in it at Philadelphia." He had not then the least intimation of my intention to set up there or anywhere. These friends were afterwards of great use to me, as I occasionally was to some of them. They all continued their regard for me as long as they lived.

Before I enter upon my public appearance in business, it may be well to let you know the then state of my mind with regard to my principles and morals, that you may see how far those influenc'd the future events of my life. My parents had early given me religious impressions, and brought me through my childhood piously in the Dissenting way. But I was scarce fifteen, when, after doubting by turns of several points, as I found them disputed in the different books I read, I began to doubt of Revelation itself. Some books against Deism fell into my hands; they were said to be the substance of sermons preached at Boyle's Lectures. It happened that they wrought an effect on me quite contrary to what was intended by them; for the arguments of the Deists, which were quoted to be refuted, appeared to me much stronger than the refutations; in short, I soon became a thorough Deist. My arguments perverted some others, particularly Collins and Ralph; but, each of them having afterwards wrong'd me greatly without the least compunction, and recollecting Keith's conduct towards me (who was another freethinker), and my own towards Vernon and Miss Read, which at times gave me great trouble, I began to suspect that this doctrine, tho' it might be true, was not very useful. My London pamphlet, which had for its motto these lines of Dryden:

> "Whatever is, is right. Though purblind man
> Sees but a part o' the chain, the nearest link:
> His eyes not carrying to the equal beam,
> That poises all above;"

and from the attributes of God, his infinite wisdom, goodness and power, concluded that nothing could possibly be wrong in the world, and that vice and virtue were empty distinctions, no such things existing, appear'd now not so clever a performance as I once thought it; and I doubted whether some error had not insinuated itself unperceiv'd into my argument, so as to infect all that follow'd, as is common in metaphysical reasonings.

I grew convinc'd that *truth, sincerity* and *integrity* in dealings between man and man were of the utmost importance to the felicity of life; and I form'd written resolutions, which still remain in my journal book, to practice them ever while I lived. Revelation had indeed no weight with me, as such; but I entertain'd an opinion that, though certain actions might not be bad *because* they were forbidden by it, or good *because* it commanded them, yet probably these actions might be forbidden *because* they were bad for us, or commanded *because* they were beneficial to us, in their own natures, all the circumstances of things considered. And this persuasion, with the kind hand of Providence, or some guardian angel, or accidental favorable circumstances and situations, or all together, preserved me, thro' this dangerous time of youth, and the hazardous situations I was sometimes in among strangers, remote from the eye and advice of my father, without any willful gross immorality or injustice, that might have been expected from my want of religion. I say willful, because the instances I have mentioned had something of *necessity* in them, from my youth, inexperience, and the knavery of others. I had therefore a tolerable character to begin the world with; I valued it properly, and determin'd to preserve it.

We had not been long return'd to Philadelphia before the new types arriv'd from London. We settled with Keimer, and left him by his consent before he heard of it. We found a house to hire near the market, and took it. To lessen the rent, which was then but twenty-four pounds a year, tho' I have since known it to let for seventy, we took in Thomas Godfrey, a glazier, and his family, who were to pay a considerable part of it to us, and we to board with them. We had scarce opened our letters and put our press in order, before George House, an acquaintance of mine, brought a countryman to us, whom he had met in the street inquiring for a printer. All our cash was now expended in the variety of particulars we had been obliged to procure, and this countryman's five shillings, being our first-fruits, and coming so seasonably, gave me more pleasure than any crown I have since earned; and the gratitude I felt toward House has made me often more ready than perhaps I should otherwise have been to assist young beginners.

There are croakers in every country, always boding its ruin. Such a one then lived in Philadelphia; a person of note, an elderly man, with a wise look and a very grave manner of speaking; his name was Samuel Mickle. This gentleman, a stranger to me, stopt one day at my door, and asked me if I was the young man who had lately opened a new printing-house. Being answered in the affirmative, he said he was sorry for me, because it was an expensive undertaking, and the expense would be lost; for Philadelphia was a sinking place, the people already half-bankrupts, or near being so; all appearances to the contrary, such as new buildings and the rise of rents, being to his certain knowledge fallacious; for they were, in fact, among the things that would soon ruin us. And he gave me such a detail of misfortunes now existing, or that were soon to exist, that he left me half melancholy. Had I known him before I engaged in this business, probably I never should have done it. This man continued to live in this decaying place, and to declaim in the same strain, refusing for many years to buy a house there, because all was going to destruction; and at last I had the pleasure of seeing him give five times as much for one as he might have bought it for when he first began his croaking.

I should have mentioned before, that, in the autumn of the preceding year, I had form'd most of my ingenious acquaintance into a club of mutual improvement, which we called the JUNTO; we met on Friday evenings. The rules that I drew up required that every member, in his turn, should produce one or more queries on any point of Morals, Politics, or Natural Philosophy, to be discuss'd by the company; and once in three months produce and read an essay of his own writing, on any subject he pleased. Our debates were to be under the direction of a president, and to be conducted in the sincere spirit of inquiry after truth, without fondness for dispute, or desire of victory; and, to prevent warmth, all expressions of positiveness in opinions, or direct contradiction, were after some time made contraband, and prohibited under small pecuniary penalties.

The first members were Joseph Breintnal, a copyer of deeds for the scriveners, a good-natur'd, friendly, middle-ag'd man, a great lover of poetry, reading all he could meet with, and writing some that was tolerable; very ingenious in many little Nicknackeries, and of sensible conversation.

Thomas Godfrey, a self-taught mathematician, great in his way, and afterwards inventor of what is now called Hadley's Quadrant. But he knew little out of his way, and was not a pleasing companion; as, like most great mathematicians I have met with, he expected universal precision in everything said, or was for ever denying or distinguishing upon trifles, to the disturbance of all conversation. He soon left us.

Nicholas Scull, a surveyor, afterwards surveyor-general, who lov'd books, and sometimes made a few verses.

William Parsons, bred a shoemaker, but, loving reading, had acquir'd a considerable share of mathematics, which he first studied with a view to astrology, that he afterwards laught at it. He also became surveyor-general.

William Maugridge, a joiner, a most exquisite mechanic, and a solid, sensible man.

Hugh Meredith, Stephen Potts, and George Webb I have characteriz'd before.

Robert Grace, a young gentleman of some fortune, generous, lively, and witty; a lover of punning and of his friends.

And William Coleman, then a merchant's clerk, about my age, who had the coolest, clearest head, the best heart, and the exactest morals of almost any man I ever met with. He became afterwards a merchant of great note, and one of our provincial judges. Our friendship continued without interruption to his death, upwards of forty years; and the club continued almost as long, and was the best school of philosophy, morality, and politics that then existed in the province; for our queries, which were read the week preceding their discussion, put us upon reading with attention upon the several subjects, that we might speak more to the purpose; and here, too, we acquired better habits of conversation, every thing being studied in our rules which might prevent our disgusting each other. From hence the long continuance of the club, which I shall have frequent occasion to speak further of hereafter.

But my giving this account of it here is to show something of the interest I had, every one of these exerting themselves in recommending business to us. Breintnal particularly procur'd us from the Quakers the printing forty sheets of their history, the rest being to be done by Keimer; and upon this we work'd exceedingly hard, for the price was low. It was a folio, pro patria size, in pica, with long primer notes. I compos'd of it a sheet a day, and Meredith worked it off at press; it was often eleven at night, and sometimes later, before I had finished my distribution for the next day's work, for the little jobbs sent in by our other friends now and then put us back. But so determin'd I was to continue doing a sheet a day of the folio, that one night, when, having impos'd my forms, I thought my day's work over, one of them by accident was broken, and two pages reduced to pi, I immediately distributed and compos'd it over again before I went to bed; and this industry, visible to our neighbors, began to give us character and credit; particularly, I was told, that mention being made of the new printing-office at the merchants' Every-night club, the general opinion was that it must fail, there being already two printers in the place, Keimer and Bradford;

but Dr Baird (whom you and I saw many years after at his native place, St. Andrew's in Scotland) gave a contrary opinion: "For the industry of that Franklin," says he, "is superior to any thing I ever saw of the kind; I see him still at work when I go home from club, and he is at work again before his neighbors are out of bed." This struck the rest, and we soon after had offers from one of them to supply us with stationery; but as yet we did not chuse to engage in shop business.

I mention this industry the more particularly and the more freely, tho' it seems to be talking in my own praise, that those of my posterity, who shall read it, may know the use of that virtue, when they see its effects in my favour throughout this relation.

George Webb, who had found a female friend that lent him wherewith to purchase his time of Keimer, now came to offer himself as a journeyman to us. We could not then employ him; but I foolishly let him know as a secret that I soon intended to begin a newspaper, and might then have work for him. My hopes of success, as I told him, were founded on this, that the then only newspaper, printed by Bradford, was a paltry thing, wretchedly manag'd, no way entertaining, and yet was profitable to him; I therefore thought a good paper would scarcely fail of good encouragement. I requested Webb not to mention it; but he told it to Keimer, who immediately, to be beforehand with me, published proposals for printing one himself, on which Webb was to be employ'd. I resented this; and, to counteract them, as I could not yet begin our paper, I wrote several pieces of entertainment for Bradford's paper, under the title of the Busy Body, which Breintnal continu'd some months. By this means the attention of the publick was fixed on that paper, and Keimer's proposals, which we burlesqu'd and ridicul'd, were disregarded. He began his paper, however, and, after carrying it on three quarters of a year, with at most only ninety subscribers, he offered it to me for a trifle; and I, having been ready some time to go on with it, took it in hand directly; and it prov'd in a few years extremely profitable to me.

I perceive that I am apt to speak in the singular number, though our partnership still continu'd; the reason may be that, in fact, the whole management of the business lay upon me. Meredith was no compositor, a poor pressman, and seldom sober. My friends lamented my connection with him, but I was to make the best of it.

Our first papers made a quite different appearance from any before in the province; a better type, and better printed; but some spirited remarks of my writing, on the dispute then going on between Governor Burnet and the Massachussets Assembly, struck the principal people, occasioned the paper and the manager of it to be much talk'd of, and in a few weeks brought them all to be our subscribers.

Their example was follow'd by many, and our number went on growing continually. This was one of the first good effects of my having learnt a little to scribble; another was, that the leading men, seeing a newspaper now in the hands of one who could also handle a pen, thought it convenient to oblige and encourage me. Bradford still printed the votes, and laws, and other publick business. He had printed an address of the House to the governor, in a coarse, blundering manner, we reprinted it elegantly and correctly, and sent one to every member. They were sensible of the difference: it strengthened the hands of our friends in the House, and they voted us their printers for the year ensuing.

Among my friends in the House I must not forget Mr Hamilton, before mentioned, who was then returned from England, and had a seat in it. He interested himself for me strongly in that instance, as he did in many others afterward, continuing his patronage till his death.[1]

Mr Vernon, about this time, put me in mind of the debt I ow'd him, but did not press me. I wrote him an ingenuous letter of acknowledgment, crav'd his forbearance a little longer, which he allow'd me, and as soon as I was able, I paid the principal with interest, and many thanks; so that erratum was in some degree corrected.

But now another difficulty came upon me which I had never the least reason to expect. Mr Meredith's father, who was to have paid for our printing-house, according to the expectations given me, was able to advance only one hundred pounds currency, which had been paid; and a hundred more was due to the merchant, who grew impatient, and su'd us all. We gave bail, but saw that, if the money could not be rais'd in time, the suit must soon come to a judgment and execution, and our hopeful prospects must, with us, be ruined, as the press and letters must be sold for payment, perhaps at half price.

In this distress two true friends, whose kindness I have never forgotten, nor ever shall forget while I can remember any thing, came to me separately, unknown to each other, and, without any application from me, offering each of them to advance me all the money that should be necessary to enable me to take the whole business upon myself, if that should be practicable; but they did not like my continuing the partnership with Meredith, who, as they said, was often seen drunk in the streets, and playing at low games in alehouses, much to our discredit. These two friends were William Coleman and Robert Grace. I told them I could not propose a separation while any prospect remain'd of the Meredith's fulfilling their part of our agreement, because

[1] I got his son once £500 [marg. note].

I thought myself under great obligations to them for what they had done, and would do if they could; but, if they finally fail'd in their performance, and our partnership must be dissolv'd, I should then think myself at liberty to accept the assistance of my friends.

Thus the matter rested for some time, when I said to my partner, "Perhaps your father is dissatisfied at the part you have undertaken in this affair of ours, and is unwilling to advance for you and me what he would for you alone. If that is the case, tell me, and I will resign the whole to you, and go about my business." "No," said he, "my father has really been disappointed, and is really unable; and I am unwilling to distress him farther. I see this is a business I am not fit for. I was bred a farmer, and it was a folly in me to come to town, and put myself, at thirty years of age, an apprentice to learn a new trade. Many of our Welsh people are going to settle in North Carolina, where land is cheap. I am inclin'd to go with them, and follow my old employment. You may find friends to assist you. If you will take the debts of the company upon you; return to my father the hundred pound he has advanced; pay my little personal debts, and give me thirty pounds and a new saddle, I will relinquish the partnership, and leave the whole in your hands." I agreed to this proposal: it was drawn up in writing, sign'd, and seal'd immediately. I gave him what he demanded, and he went soon after to Carolina, from whence he sent me next year two long letters, containing the best account that had been given of that country, the climate, the soil, husbandry, etc., for in those matters he was very judicious. I printed them in the papers, and they gave great satisfaction to the publick.

As soon as he was gone, I recurr'd to my two friends; and because I would not give an unkind preference to either, I took half of what each had offered and I wanted of one, and half of the other; paid off the company's debts, and went on with the business in my own name, advertising that the partnership was dissolved. I think this was in or about the year 1729.

About this time there was a cry among the people for more paper money, only fifteen thousand pounds being extant in the province, and that soon to be sunk. The wealthy inhabitants oppos'd any addition, being against all paper currency, from an apprehension that it would depreciate, as it had done in New England, to the prejudice of all creditors. We had discuss'd this point in our Junto, where I was on the side of an addition, being persuaded that the first small sum struck in 1723 had done much good by increasing the trade, employment, and number of inhabitants in the province, since I now saw all the old houses inhabited, and many new ones building: whereas I remembered well, that when I first walk'd about the streets of Philadelphia, eating my roll, I saw most of the houses in Walnut Street, between Second and Front streets, with bills on their doors, "To be let"; and many likewise in Chestnut-street and other streets, which made me then think the inhabitants of the city were deserting it one after another.

Our debates possess'd me so fully of the subject, that I wrote and printed an anonymous pamphlet on it, entitled "*The Nature and Necessity of a Paper Currency.*" It was well receiv'd by the common people in general; but the rich men dislik'd it, for it increas'd and strengthen'd the clamor for more money, and they happening to have no writers among them that were able to answer it, their opposition slacken'd, and the point was carried by a majority in the House. My friends there, who conceiv'd I had been of some service, thought fit to reward me by employing me in printing the money; a very profitable jobb and a great help to me. This was another advantage gain'd by my being able to write.

The utility of this currency became by time and experience so evident as never afterwards to be much disputed; so that it grew soon to fifty-five thousand pounds, and in 1739 to eighty thousand pounds, since which it arose during war to upwards of three hundred and fifty thousand pounds, trade, building, and inhabitants all the while increasing, tho' I now think there are limits beyond which the quantity may be hurtful.

I soon after obtain'd, thro' my friend Hamilton, the printing of the Newcastle paper money, another profitable jobb as I then thought it; small things appearing great to those in small circumstances; and these, to me, were really great advantages, as they were great encouragements. He procured for me, also, the printing of the laws and votes of that government, which continu'd in my hands as long as I follow'd the business.

I now open'd a little stationer's shop. I had in it blanks of all sorts, the correctest that ever appear'd among us, being assisted in that by my friend Breintnal. I had also paper, parchment, chapmen's books, etc. One Whitemash, a compositor I had known in London, an excellent workman, now came to me, and work'd with me constantly and diligently; and I took an apprentice, the son of Aquila Rose.

I began now gradually to pay off the debt I was under for the printing-house. In order to secure my credit and character as a tradesman, I took care not only to be in *reality* industrious and frugal, but to avoid all appearances to the contrary. I drest plainly; I was seen at no places of idle diversion. I never went out a fishing or shooting; a book, indeed, sometimes debauch'd me from my work, but that was seldom, snug, and gave no scandal; and, to show that I was not above my business, I sometimes brought home the paper I purchas'd at the stores thro' the streets on a wheelbarrow. Thus being esteem'd an industrious, thriving young man, and paying duly for what I bought, the merchants who imported stationery solicited my custom; others proposed supplying me with books, and I went on swimmingly. In the mean time, Keimer's credit and business declining daily, he was at last forc'd to sell his printing-house to satisfy his creditors. He went to Barbadoes, and there lived some years in very poor circumstances.

His apprentice, David Harry, whom I had instructed while I work'd with him, set up in his place at Philadelphia, having bought his materials. I was at first apprehensive of a powerful rival in Harry, as his friends were very able, and had a good deal of interest. I therefore propos'd a partnership to him, which he, fortunately for me, rejected with scorn. He was very proud, dress'd like a gentleman, liv'd expensively, took much diversion and pleasure abroad, ran in debt, and neglected his business; upon which, all business left him; and, finding nothing to do, he followed Keimer to Barbadoes, taking the printing-house with him. There this apprentice employ'd his former master as a journeyman; they quarrel'd often; Harry went continually behindhand, and at length was forc'd to sell his types and return to his country work in Pensilvania. The person that bought them employ'd Keimer to use them, but in a few years he died.

There remained now no competitor with me at Philadelphia but the old one, Bradford; who was rich and easy, did a little printing now and then by straggling hands, but was not very anxious about the business. However, as he kept the post-office, it was imagined he had better opportunities of obtaining news; his paper was thought a better distributer of advertisements than mine, and therefore had many more, which was a profitable thing to him, and a disadvantage to me; for, tho' I did indeed receive and send papers by the post, yet the publick opinion was otherwise, for what I did send was by bribing the riders, who took them privately, Bradford being unkind enough to forbid it, which occasion'd some resentment on my part; and I thought so meanly of him for it, that, when I afterward came into his situation, I took care never to imitate it.

I had hitherto continu'd to board with Godfrey, who lived in part of my house with his wife and children, and had one side of the shop for his glazier's business, tho' he worked little, being always absorbed in his mathematics. Mrs Godfrey projected a match for me with a relation's daughter, took opportunities of bringing us often together, till a serious courtship on my part ensu'd, the girl being in herself very deserving. The old folks encourag'd me by continual invitations to supper, and by leaving us together, till at length it was time to explain. Mrs Godfrey manag'd our little treaty. I let her know that I expected as much money with their daughter as would pay off my remaining debt for the printing-house, which I believe was not then above a hundred pounds. She brought me word they had no such sum to spare; I said they might mortgage their house in the loan-office. The answer to this, after some days, was, that they did not approve the match; that, on inquiry of Bradford, they had been informed the printing business was not a profitable one; the types would soon be worn out, and more wanted; that S. Keimer and D. Harry had failed one after the other, and I should probably soon follow them; and, therefore, I was forbidden the house, and the daughter shut up.

Whether this was a real change of sentiment or only artifice, on a supposition of our being too far engaged in affection to retract, and therefore that we should steal a marriage, which would leave them at liberty to give or withhold what they pleas'd, I know not; but I suspected the latter, resented it, and went no more. Mrs Godfrey brought me afterward some more favorable accounts of their disposition, and would have drawn me on again; but I declared absolutelv my resolution to have nothing more to do with that family. This was resented by the Godfreys; we differ'd, and they removed, leaving me the whole house, and I re-resolved to take no more inmates.

But this affair having turned my thoughts to marriage, I look'd round me and made overtures of acquaintance in other places; but soon found that, the business of a printer being generally thought a poor one, I was not to expect money with a wife, unless with such a one as I should not otherwise think agreeable. In the mean time, that hard-to-be-governed passion of youth hurried me frequently into intrigues with low women that fell in my way, which were attended with some expense and great inconvenience, besides a continual risque to my health by a distemper which of all things I dreaded, though by great good luck I escaped it. A friendly correspondence as neighbors and old acquaintances had continued between me and Mrs Read's family, who all had a regard for me from the time of my first lodging in their house. I was often invited there and consulted in their affairs, wherein I sometimes was of service. I piti'd poor Miss Read's unfortunate situation, who was generally dejected, seldom cheerful, and avoided company. I considered my giddiness and inconstancy when in London as in a great degree the cause of her unhappiness, tho' the mother was good enough to think the fault more her own than mine, as she had prevented our marrying before I went thither, and persuaded the other match in my absence. Our mutual affection was revived, but there were now great objections to our union. The match was indeed looked upon as invalid, a preceding wife being said to be living in England; but this could not easily be prov'd, because of the distance; and, tho' there was a report of his death, it was not certain. Then, tho' it should be true, he had left many debts, which his successor might be call'd upon to pay. We ventured, however, over all these difficulties, and I took her to wife, September 1st, 1730. None of the inconveniences happened that we had apprehended; she proved a good and faithful helpmate, assisted me much by attending the shop; we throve together, and have ever mutually endeavor'd to make each other happy. Thus I corrected that great *erratum* as well as I could.

About this time, our club meeting, not at a tavern, but in a little room of Mr Grace's, set apart for that purpose, a proposition was made by me, that, since our books were often referr'd to in our disquisitions upon the queries, it might be convenient to us to have them altogether where we met, that upon occasion they might be consulted; and by thus clubbing our books to a common library, we should, while we lik'd to keep them together, have each of us the advantage of using the books of all the other members, which would be nearly as beneficial as if each owned the whole. It was lik'd and agreed to, and we fill'd one end of the room with such books as we could best spare. The number was not so great as we expected; and tho' they had been of great use, yet some inconveniences occurring for want of due care of them, the collection, after about a year, was separated, and each took his books home again.

And now I set on foot my first project of a public nature, that for a subscription library. I drew up the proposals, got them put into form by our great scrivener, Brockden, and, by the help of my friends in the Junto, procured fifty subscribers of forty shillings each to begin with, and ten shillings a year for fifty years, the term our company was to continue. We afterwards obtain'd a charter, the company being increased to one hundred: this was the mother of all the North American subscription libraries, now so numerous. It is become a great thing itself, and continually increasing. These libraries have improved the general conversation of the Americans, made the common tradesmen and farmers as intelligent as most gentlemen from other countries, and perhaps have contributed in some degree to the stand so generally made throughout the colonies in defence of their privileges.

Memo. Thus far was written with the intention express d in the beginning and therefore contains several little family anecdotes of no importance to others. What follows was written many years after in compliance with the advice contain'd in these letters, and accordingly intended for the public. The affairs of the Revolution occasion'd the interruption.

Letter from Mr Abel James, with Notes of my Life (received in Paris).

"MY DEAR AND HONORED FRIEND: I have often been desirous of writing to thee, but could not be reconciled to the thought, that the letter might fall into the hands of the British, lest some printer or busy-body should publish some part of the contents, and give our friend pain, and myself censure.

"Some time since there fell into my hands, to my great joy, about twenty-three sheets in thy own handwriting, containing an account of the parentage and life of thyself, directed to thy son, ending in the year 1730, with which there were notes, likewise in thy writing; a copy of which I inclose, in hopes it may be a means, if thou continued it up to a later period, that the first and latter part may be put together; and if it is not yet continued, I hope thee will not delay it. Life is uncertain, as the preacher tells us; and what will the world say if kind, humane, and benevolent Ben. Franklin should leave his friends and the world deprived of so pleasing and profitable a work; a work which would be useful and entertaining not only to a few, but to millions? The influence writings under that class have on the minds of youth is very great, and has nowhere appeared to me so plain, as in our public friend's journals. It almost insensibly leads the youth into the resolution of endeavoring to become as good and eminent as the journalist. Should thine, for instance, when published (and I think it could not fail of it), lead the youth to equal the industry and temperance of thy early youth, what a blessing with that class would such a work be! I know of no character living, nor many of them put together, who has so much in his power as thyself to promote a greater spirit of industry and early attention to business, frugality, and temperance with the American youth. Not that I think the work would have no other merit and use in the world, far from it; but the first is of such vast importance that I know nothing that can equal it."

The foregoing letter and the minutes accompanying it being shown to a friend, I received from him the following:

Letter from Mr Benjamin Vaughan.

"PARIS, *January* 31, 1783.

"MY DEAREST SIR: When I had read over your sheets of minutes of the principal incidents of your life, recovered for you by your Quaker acquaintance, I told you I would send you a letter expressing my reasons why I thought it would be useful to complete and publish it as he desired. Various concerns have for some time past prevented this letter being written, and I do not know whether it was worth any expectation; happening to be at leisure, however, at present, I shall by writing, at least interest and instruct myself; but as the terms I am inclined to use may tend to offend a person of your manners, I shall only tell you how I would address any other person, who was as good and as great as yourself, but less diffident. I would say to him, Sir, I solicit the history of your life from the following motives: Your history is so remarkable, that if you do not give it, somebody else will certainly give it; and perhaps so as nearly to do as much harm, as your own management of the thing might do good. It will moreover present a table of the internal circumstances of your country, which will very much tend to invite to it settlers of virtuous and manly minds. And considering the eagerness with which such information is sought by them, and the extent of your reputation, I do not know of a more efficacious advertisement than your biography would give. All that has happened to you is also connected with the detail of the manners and situation of a rising people; and in this respect I do not think that the writings of Cæsar and Tacitus can be more interesting to a true judge of human nature and society. But these, sir, are small reasons, in my opinion, compared with the chance which your life will give for the forming of future great men; and in conjunction with your Art of Virtue (which you design to publish) of improving the features of private character, and consequently of aiding all happiness, both public and domestic. The two works I allude to, sir, will in particular give a noble rule and example of self-education. School and other education constantly proceed upon false principles, and show a clumsy apparatus pointed at a false mark; but your apparatus is simple, and the mark a true one; and while parents and young persons are left destitute of other just means of estimating and becoming prepared for a reasonable course in life, your discovery that the thing is in many a man's private power, will be invaluable! Influence upon the private character, late in life, is not only an influence late in life, but a weak influence. It is in youth that we plant our chief habits and prejudices; it is in youth that we take our party as to profession, pursuits and matrimony. In youth, therefore, the turn is given; in youth the education even of the next generation is given; in youth the private and public character is determined; and the term of life extending but from youth to age, life ought to begin well from youth, and more especially before we take our party as to our principal objects. But your biography will not merely teach self-education, but the education of a wise man; and the wisest man will receive lights and improve his progress, by seeing detailed the conduct of another wise man. And why are weaker men to be deprived of such helps, when we see our race has been blundering on in the dark, almost without a guide in this particular, from the farthest trace of time? Show then, sir, how much is to be done, both to sons and fathers; and invite all wise men to become like yourself, and other men to become wise. When we see how cruel statesmen and warriors can be to the human race, and how absurd distinguished men can be to their acquaintance, it will be instructive to observe the instances multiply of pacific, acquiescing manners; and to find how compatible it is to be great and domestic, enviable and yet good-humored.

"The little private incidents which you will also have to relate, will have considerable use, as we want, above all things, rules of prudence in ordinary affairs; and it will be curious to see how you have acted in these. It will be so far a sort of key to life, and explain many things that all men ought to have once explained to them, to give them a chance of becoming wise by foresight. The nearest thing to having experience of one's own, is to have other people's affairs brought before us in a shape that is interesting; this is sure to happen from your pen; our affairs and management will have an air of simplicity or importance that will not fail to strike; and I am convinced you have conducted them with as much originality as if you had been conducting discussions in politics or philosophy; and what more worthy of experiments and system (its importance and its errors considered) than human life?

"Some men have been virtuous blindly, others have speculated fantastically, and others have been shrewd to bad purposes; but you, sir, I am sure, will give under your hand, nothing but what is at the same moment, wise, practical and good. Your account of yourself (for I suppose the parallel I am drawing for Dr Franklin, will hold not only in point of character, but of private history) will show that you are ashamed of no origin; a thing the more important, as you prove how little necessary all origin is to happiness, virtue, or greatness. As no end likewise happens without a means, so we shall find, sir, that even you yourself framed a plan by which you became considerable; but at the same time we may see that though the event is flattering, the means are as simple as wisdom could make them; that is, depending upon nature, virtue, thought and habit. Another thing demonstrated will be the propriety of every man's waiting for his time for appearing upon the stage of the world. Our sensations being very much fixed to the moment, we are apt to forget that more moments are to follow the first, and consequently that man should arrange his conduct so as to suit the whole of a life. Your attribution appears to have been applied to your life, and the passing moments of it have been enlivened with content and enjoyment, instead of being tormented with foolish impatience or regrets. Such a conduct is easy for those who make virtue and themselves in countenance by examples of other truly great men, of whom patience is so often the characteristic. Your Quaker correspondent, sir (for here again I will suppose the subject of my letter resembling Dr Franklin), praised your frugality, diligence and temperance, which he considered as a pattern for all youth; but it is singular that he should have forgotten your modesty and your disinterestedness, without which you never could have waited for your advancement, or found your situation in the mean time comfortable; which is a strong lesson to show the poverty of glory and the importance of regulating our minds. If this correspondent had known the nature of your reputation as well as I do, he would have said, Your former writings and measures would secure attention to your Biography, and Art of Virtue; and your Biography and Art of Virtue, in return, would secure attention to them. This is an advantage attendant upon a various character, and which brings all that belongs to it into greater play; and it is the more useful, as perhaps more persons are at a loss for the means of improving their minds and characters, than they are for the time or the inclination to do it. But there is one concluding reflection, sir, that will shew the use of your life as a mere piece of biography. This style of writing seems a little gone out of vogue, and yet it is a very useful one; and your specimen of it may be particularly serviceable, as it will make a subject of comparison with the lives of various public cutthroats and intriguers, and with absurd monastic self-tormentors or vain literary triflers. If it encourages more writings of the same kind with your own, and induces more men to spend lives fit to be written, it will be worth all Plutarch's Lives put together. But being tired of figuring to myself a character of which every feature suits only one man in the world, without giving him the praise of it, I shall end my letter, my dear Dr Franklin, with a personal application to your proper self. I am earnestly desirous, then, my dear sir, that you should let the world into the traits of your genuine character, as civil broils may otherwise tend to disguise or traduce it. Considering your great age, the caution of your character, and your peculiar style of thinking, it is not likely that any one besides yourself can be sufficiently master of the facts of your life, or the intentions of your mind. Besides all this, the immense revolution of the present period, will necessarily turn our attention towards the author of it, and when virtuous principles have been pretended in it, it will be highly important to shew that such have really influenced; and, as your own character will be the principal one to receive a scrutiny, it is proper (even for its effects upon your vast and rising country, as well as upon England and upon Europe) that it should stand respectable and eternal. For the furtherance of human happiness, I have always maintained that it is necessary to prove that man is not even at present a vicious and detestable animal; and still more to prove that good management may greatly amend him; and it is for much the same reason, that I am anxious to see the opinion established, that there are fair characters existing among the individuals of the race; for the moment that all men, without exception, shall be conceived abandoned, good people will cease efforts deemed to be hopeless, and perhaps think of taking their share in the scramble of life, or at least of making it comfortable principally for themselves. Take then, my dear sir, this work most speedily into hand: shew yourself good as you are good; temperate as you are temperate; and above all things, prove yourself as one, who from your infancy have loved justice, liberty and concord, in a way that has made it natural and consistent for you to have acted, as we have seen you act in the last seventeen years of your life. Let Englishmen be made not only to respect, but even to love you. When they think well of individuals in your native country, they will go nearer to thinking well of your country; and when your countrymen see themselves well thought of by Englishmen, they will go nearer to thinking well of England. Extend your views even further; do not stop at those who speak the English tongue, but after having settled so many points in nature and politics, think of bettering the whole race of men. As I have not read any part of the life in question, but know only the character that lived it, I write somewhat at hazard. I am sure, however, that the life and the treatise I allude to (on the Art of Virtue) will necessarily fulfil the chief of my expectations; and still more so if you take up the measure of suiting these performances to the several views above stated. Should they even prove unsuccessful in all that a sanguine admirer of yours hopes from them, you will at least have framed pieces to interest the human mind; and whoever gives a feeling of pleasure that is innocent to man, has added so much to the fair side of a life otherwise too much darkened by anxiety and too much injured by pain. In the hope, therefore, that you will listen to the prayer addressed to you in this letter, I beg to subscribe myself, my dearest sir, etc., etc.,

"Signed, BENJ. VAUGHAN."

Continuation of the Account of my Life, begun at Passy, near Paris, 1784.

It is some time since I receiv'd the above letters, but I have been too busy till now to think of complying with the request they contain. It might, too, be much better done if I were at home among my papers, which would aid my memory, and help to ascertain dates; but my return being uncertain, and having just now a little leisure, I will endeavor to recollect and write what I can; if I live to get home, it may there be corrected and improv'd.

Not having any copy here of what is already written, I know not whether an account is given of the means I used to establish the Philadelphia public library, which, from a small beginning, is now become so considerable, though I remember to have come down to near the time of that transaction (1730). I will therefore begin here with an account of it, which may be struck out if found to have been already given.

At the time I establish'd myself in Pennsylvania, there was not a good bookseller's shop in any of the colonies to the southward of Boston. In New York and Philad'a the printers were indeed stationers; they sold only paper, etc., almanacs, ballads, and a few common school-books. Those who lov'd reading were oblig'd to send for their books from England; the members of the Junto had each a few. We had left the alehouse, where we first met, and hired a room to hold our club in. I propos'd that we should all of us bring our books to that room, where they would not only be ready to consult in our conferences, but become a common benefit, each of us being at liberty to borrow such as he wish'd to read at home. This was accordingly done, and for some time contented us.

Finding the advantage of this little collection, I propos'd to render the benefit from books more common, by commencing a public subscription library. I drew a sketch of the plan and rules that would be necessary, and got a skilful conveyancer, Mr Charles Brockden, to put the whole in form of articles of agreement to be subscribed, by which each subscriber engag'd to pay a certain sum down for the first purchase of books, and an annual contribution for increasing them. So few were the readers at that time in Philadelphia, and the majority of us so poor, that I was not able, with great industry, to find more than fifty persons, mostly young tradesmen, willing to pay down for this purpose forty shillings each, and ten shillings per annum. On this little fund we began. The books were imported; the library was opened one day in the week for lending to the subscribers, on their promissory notes to pay double the value if not duly returned. The institution soon manifested its utility, was imitated by other towns, and in other provinces. The libraries were augmented by donations; reading became fashionable; and our people, having no publick amusements to divert their attention from study, became better acquainted with books, and in a few years were observ'd by strangers to be better instructed and more intelligent than people of the same rank generally are in other countries.

When we were about to sign the above-mentioned articles, which were to be binding on us, our heirs, etc., for fifty years, Mr Brockden, the scrivener, said to us, "You are young men, but it is scarcely probable that any of you will live to see the expiration of the term fix'd in the instrument." A number of us, however, are yet living; but the instrument was after a few years rendered null by a charter that incorporated and gave perpetuity to the company.

The objections and reluctances I met with in soliciting the subscriptions, made me soon feel the impropriety of presenting one's self as the proposer of any useful project, that might be suppos'd to raise one's reputation in the smallest degree above that of one's neighbors, when one has need of their assistance to accomplish that project. I therefore put myself as much as I could out of sight, and stated it as a scheme of a *number of friends*, who had requested me to go about and propose it to such as they thought lovers of reading. In this way my affair went on more smoothly, and I ever after practis'd it on such occasions; and, from my frequent successes, can heartily recommend it. The present little sacrifice of your vanity will afterwards be amply repaid. If it remains a while uncertain to whom the merit belongs, some one more vain than yourself will be encouraged to claim it, and then even envy will be disposed to do you justice by plucking those assumed feathers, and restoring them to their right owner.

This library afforded me the means of improvement by constant study, for which I set apart an hour or two each day, and thus repair'd in some degree the loss of the learned education my father once intended for me. Reading was the only amusement I allow'd myself. I spent no time in taverns, games, or frolicks of any kind; and my industry in my business continu'd as indefatigable as it was necessary. I was indebted for my printing-house; I had a young family coming on to be educated, and I had to contend with for business two printers, who were established in the place before me. My circumstances, however, grew daily easier. My original habits of frugality continuing, and my father having, among his instructions to me when a boy, frequently repeated a proverb of Solomon, "Seest thou a man diligent in his calling, he shall stand before kings, he shall not stand before mean men," I from thence considered industry as a means of obtaining wealth and distinction, which encourag'd me, tho' I did not think that I should ever literally *stand before kings*, which, however, has since happened; for I have stood before *five*, and even had the honour of sitting down with one, the King of Denmark, to dinner.

We have an English proverb that says, "*He that would thrive, must ask his wife.*" It was lucky for me that I had one as much dispos'd to industry and frugality as myself. She assisted me cheerfully in my business, folding and stitching pamphlets, tending shop, purchasing old linen rags for the paper-makers, etc., etc. We kept no idle servants, our table was plain and simple, our furniture of the cheapest. For instance, my breakfast was a long time bread and milk (no tea), and I ate it out of a twopenny earthen porringer, with a pewter spoon. But mark how luxury will enter families, and make a progress, in spite of principle: being call'd one morning to breakfast, I found it in a China bowl, with a spoon of silver! They had been bought for me without my knowledge by my wife, and had cost her the enormous sum of three-and-twenty shillings, for which she had no other excuse or apology to make, but that she thought *her* husband deserv'd a silver spoon and China bowl as well as any of his neighbors. This was the first appearance of plate and China in our house, which afterward, in a course of years, as our wealth increas'd, augmented gradually to several hundred pounds in value.

I had been religiously educated as a Presbyterian; and tho' some of the dogmas of that persuasion, such as *the eternal decrees of God*, *election*, *reprobation*, *etc.*, appeared to me unintelligible, others doubtful, and I early absented myself from the public assemblies of the sect, Sunday being my studying day, I never was without some religious principles. I never doubted, for instance, the existence of the Deity; that he made the world, and govern'd it by his Providence; that the most acceptable service of God was the doing good to man; that our souls are immortal; and that all crime will be punished, and virtue rewarded, either here or hereafter. These I esteem'd the essentials of every religion; and, being to be found in all the religions we had in our country, I respected them all, tho' with different degrees of respect, as I found them more or less mix'd with other articles, which, without any tendency to inspire, promote, or confirm morality, serv'd principally to divide us, and make us unfriendly to one another. This respect to all, with an opinion that the worst had some good effects, induc'd me to avoid all discourse that might tend to lessen the good opinion another might have of his own religion; and as our province increas'd in people, and new places of worship were continually wanted, and generally erected by voluntary contribution, my mite for such purpose, whatever might be the sect, was never refused.

Tho' I seldom attended any public worship, I had still an opinion of its propriety, and of its utility when rightly conducted, and I regularly paid my annual subscription for the support of the only Presbyterian minister or meeting we had in Philadelphia. He us'd to visit me sometimes as a friend, and admonish me to attend his administrations, and I was now and then prevail'd on to do so, once for five Sundays successively. Had he been in my opinion a good preacher, perhaps I might have continued, notwithstanding the occasion I had for the Sunday's leisure in my course of study; but his discourses were chiefly either polemic arguments, or explications of the peculiar doctrines of our sect, and were all to me very dry, uninteresting, and unedifying, since not a single moral principle was inculcated or enforc'd, their aim seeming to be rather to make us Presbyterians than good citizens.

At length he took for his text that verse of the fourth chapter of Philippians, "*Finally, brethren, whatsoever things are true, honest, just, pure, lovely, or of good report, if there be any virtue, or any praise, think on these things.*" And I imagin'd, in a sermon on such a text, we could not miss of having some morality. But he confin'd himself to five points only, as meant by the apostle, viz.: 1. Keeping holy the Sabbath day. 2. Being diligent in reading the holy Scriptures. 3. Attending duly the publick worship. 4. Partaking of the Sacrament. 5. Paying a due respect to God's ministers. These might be all good things; but, as they were not the kind of good things that I expected from that text, I despaired of ever meeting with them from any other, was disgusted, and attended his preaching no more. I had some years before compos'd a little Liturgy, or form of prayer, for my own private use (viz., in 1728), entitled, *Articles of Belief and Acts of Religion.* I return'd to the use of this, and went no more to the public assemblies. My conduct might be blameable, but I leave it, without attempting further to excuse it; my present purpose being to relate facts, and not to make apologies for them.

It was about this time I conceiv'd the bold and arduous project of arriving at moral perfection. I wish'd to live without committing any fault at any time; I would conquer all that either natural inclination, custom, or company might lead me into. As I knew, or thought I knew, what was right and wrong, I did not see why I might not always do the one and avoid the other. But I soon found I had undertaken a task of more difficulty than I had imagined. While my care was employ'd in guarding against one fault, I was often surprised by another; habit took the advantage of inattention; inclination was sometimes too strong for reason. I concluded, at length, that the mere speculative conviction that it was our interest to be completely virtuous, was not sufficient to prevent our slipping; and that the contrary habits must be broken, and good ones acquired and established, before we can have any dependence on a steady, uniform rectitude of conduct. For this purpose I therefore contrived the following method.

In the various enumerations of the moral virtues I had met with in my reading, I found the catalogue more or less numerous, as different writers included more or fewer ideas under the same name. Temperance, for example, was by some confined to eating and drinking, while by others it was extended to mean the moderating every other pleasure, appetite, inclination, or passion, bodily or mental, even to our avarice and ambition. I propos'd to myself, for the sake of clearness, to use rather more names, with fewer ideas annex'd to each, than a few names with more ideas; and I included under thirteen names of virtues all that at that time occurr'd to me as necessary or desirable, and annexed to each a short precept, which fully express'd the extent I gave to its meaning.

These names of virtues, with their precepts, were:

1. Temperance.

Eat not to dullness; drink not to elevation.

2. Silence.

Speak not but what may benefit others or yourself; avoid trifling conversation.

3. Order.

Let all your things have their places; let each part of your business have its time.

4. Resolution.

Resolve to perform what you ought; perform without fail what you resolve.

5. Frugality.

Make no expense but to do good to others or yourself; *i.e.*, waste nothing.

6. Industry.

Lose no time; be always employ'd in something useful; cut off all unnecessary actions.

7. Sincerity.

Use no hurtful deceit; think innocently and justly, and, if you speak, speak accordingly.

8. Justice.

Wrong none by doing injuries, or omitting the benefits that are your duty.

9. Moderation.

Avoid extreams; forbear resenting injuries so much as you think they deserve.

10. Cleanliness.

Tolerate no uncleanliness in body, cloaths, or habitation.

11. Tranquillity.

Be not disturbed at trifles, or at accidents common or unavoidable.

12. Chastity.

Rarely use venery but for health or offspring, never to dulness, weakness, or the injury of your own or another's peace or reputation.

13. Humility.

Imitate Jesus and Socrates.

My intention being to acquire the *habitude* of all these virtues, I judg'd it would be well not to distract my attention by attempting the whole at once, but to fix it on one of them at a time; and, when I should be master of that, then to proceed to another, and so on, till I should have gone thro' the thirteen;

and, as the previous acquisition of some might facilitate the acquisition of certain others, I arrang'd them with that view, as they stand above. Temperance first, as it tends to procure that coolness and clearness of head, which is so necessary where constant vigilance was to be kept up, and guard maintained against the unremitting attraction of ancient habits, and the force of perpetual temptations. This being acquir'd and establish'd, Silence would be more easy; and my desire being to gain knowledge at the same time that I improv'd in virtue, and considering that in conversation it was obtain'd rather by the use of the ears than of the tongue, and therefore wishing to break a habit I was getting into of prattling, punning, and joking, which only made me acceptable to trifling company, I gave *Silence* the second place. This and the next, *Order*, I expected would allow me more time for attending to my project and my studies. *Resolution*, once become habitual, would keep me firm in my endeavors to obtain all the subsequent virtues; *Frugality* and Industry freeing me from my remaining debt, and producing affluence and independence, would make more easy the practice of Sincerity and Justice, etc., etc. Conceiving then, that, agreeably to the advice of Pythagoras in his Golden Verses, daily examination would be necessary, I contrived the following method for conducting that examination.

I made a little book, in which I allotted a page for each of the virtues. I rul'd each page with red ink, so as to have seven columns, one for each day of the week, marking each column with a letter for the day. I cross'd these columns with thirteen red lines, marking the beginning of each line with the first letter of one of the virtues, on which line, and in its proper column, I might mark, by a little black spot, every fault I found upon examination to have been committed respecting that virtue upon that day.

Form of the pages.

TEMPERANCE.							
EAT NOT TO DULNESS; DRINK NOT TO ELEVATION.							
	S.	M.	T.	W.	T.	F.	S.
T.							
S.	*	*		*		*	
O.	**	*	*		*	*	*
R.			*			*	
F.		*			*		
I			*				
S.							
J.							
M.							
C.							
T.							
C.							
H.							

I determined to give a week's strict attention to each of the virtues successively. Thus, in the first week, my great guard was to avoid every the least offence against *Temperance*, leaving the other virtues to their ordinary chance, only marking every evening the faults of the day. Thus, if in the first week I could keep my first line, marked T, clear of spots, I suppos'd the habit of that virtue so much strengthen'd, and its opposite weaken'd, that I might venture extending my attention to include the next, and for the following week keep both lines clear of spots. Proceeding thus to the last, I could go thro' a course compleat in thirteen weeks, and four courses in a year. And like him who, having a garden to weed, does not attempt to eradicate all the bad herbs at once, which would exceed his reach and his strength, but works on one of the beds at a time, and, having accomplish'd the first, proceeds to a second, so I should have, I hoped, the encouraging pleasure of seeing on my pages the progress I made in virtue, by clearing successively my lines of their spots, till in the end, by a number of courses, I should be happy in viewing a clean book, after a thirteen weeks' daily examination.

This my little book had for its motto these lines from Addison's *Cato:*

> "Here will I hold. If there's a power above us
> (And that there is, all nature cries aloud
> Thro' all her works), He must delight in virtue;
> And that which he delights in must be happy."

Another from Cicero,

> "O vitæ Philosophia dux! O virtutum indagatrix expultrixque vitiorum! Unus dies, bene et ex præceptis tuis actus, peccanti immortalitati est anteponendus."

Another from the Proverbs of Solomon, speaking of wisdom or virtue:

> "Length of days is in her right hand, and in her left hand riches and honour. Her ways are ways of pleasantness, and all her paths are peace." iii. 16, 17.

And conceiving God to be the fountain of wisdom, I thought it right and necessary to solicit his assistance for obtaining it; to this end I formed the following little prayer, which was prefix'd to my tables of examination, for daily use.

> "*O powerful Goodness! bountiful Father! merciful Guide! Increase in me that wisdom which discovers my truest interest. Strengthen my*

resolutions to perform what that wisdom dictates. Accept my kind offices to thy other children as the only return in my power for thy continual favours to me."

I used also sometimes a little prayer which I took from Thomson's Poems, viz.:

"Father of light and life, thou Good Supreme!
O teach me what is good; teach me Thyself!
Save me from folly, vanity, and vice,
From every low pursuit; and fill my soul
With knowledge, conscious peace, and virtue pure;
Sacred, substantial, never-fading bliss!"

The precept of *Order* requiring that *every part of my business should have its allotted time*, one page in my little book contain'd the following scheme of employment for the twenty-four hours of a natural day.

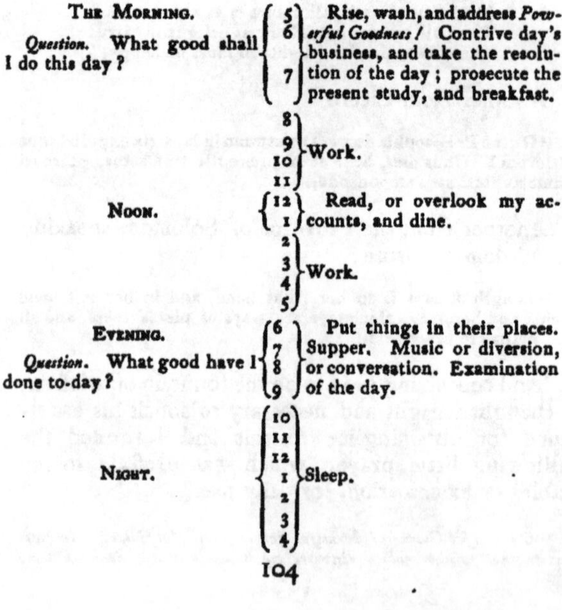

THE MORNING. *Question.* What good shall I do this day?	5 6 7	Rise, wash, and address *Powerful Goodness!* Contrive day's business, and take the resolution of the day; prosecute the present study, and breakfast.
	8 9 10 11	Work.
NOON.	12 1	Read, or overlook my accounts, and dine.
	2 3 4 5	Work.
EVENING. *Question.* What good have I done to-day?	6 7 8 9	Put things in their places. Supper. Music or diversion, or conversation. Examination of the day.
NIGHT.	10 11 12 1 2 3 4	Sleep.

I enter'd upon the execution of this plan for self-examination, and continu'd it with occasional intermissions for some time. I was surpris'd to find myself so much fuller of faults than I had imagined; but I had the satisfaction of seeing them diminish. To avoid the trouble of renewing now and then my little book, which, by scraping out the marks on the paper of old faults to make room for new ones in a new course, became full of holes, I transferr'd my tables and precepts to the ivory leaves of a memorandum book, on which the lines were drawn with red ink, that made a durable stain, and on those lines I mark'd my faults with a black-lead pencil, which marks I could easily wipe out with a wet sponge. After a while I went thro' one course only in a year, and afterward only one in several years, till at length I omitted them entirely, being employ'd in voyages and business abroad, with a multiplicity of affairs that interfered; but I always carried my little book with me.

My scheme of ORDER gave me the most trouble; and I found that, tho' it might be practicable where a man's business was such as to leave him the disposition of his time, that of a journeyman printer, for instance, it was not possible to be exactly observed by a master, who must mix with the world, and often receive people of business at their own hours. *Order*, too, with regard to places for things, papers, etc., I found extreamly difficult to acquire. I had not been early accustomed to it, and, having an exceeding good memory, I was not so sensible of the inconvenience attending want of method. This article, therefore, cost me so much painful attention, and my faults in it vexed me so much, and I made so little progress in amendment, and had such frequent relapses, that I was almost ready to give up the attempt, and content myself with a faulty character in that respect, like the man who, in buying an ax of a smith, my neighbour, desired to have the whole of its surface as bright as the edge. The smith consented to grind it bright for him if he would turn the wheel; he turn'd, while the smith press'd the broad face of the ax hard and heavily on the stone, which made the turning of it very fatiguing. The man came every now and then from the wheel to see how the work went on, and at length would take his ax as it was, without farther grinding. "No," said the smith, "turn on, turn on; we shall have it bright by-and-by; as yet, it is only speckled." "Yes," says the man, "*but I think I like a speckled ax best.*" And I believe this may have been the case with many, who, having, for want of some such means as I employ'd, found the difficulty of obtaining good and breaking bad habits in other points of vice and virtue, have given up the struggle, and concluded that "*a speckled ax was best*"; for something, that pretended to be reason, was every now and then suggesting to me that such extream nicety as I exacted of myself might be a kind of foppery in morals, which, if it were known, would make me ridiculous; that a perfect character might be attended with the inconvenience of being envied and hated; and that a benevolent man should allow a few faults in himself, to keep his friends in countenance.

In truth, I found myself incorrigible with respect to Order; and now I am grown old, and my memory bad, I feel very sensibly the want of it. But, on the whole, tho' I never arrived at the perfection I had been so ambitious of obtaining, but fell far short of it, yet I was, by the endeavour, a better and a happier man than I otherwise should have been if I had not attempted it; as those who aim at perfect writing by imitating the engraved copies, tho' they never reach the wish'd-for excellence of those copies, their hand is mended by the endeavor, and is tolerable while it continues fair and legible.

It may be well my posterity should be informed that to this little artifice, with the blessing of God, their ancestor ow'd the constant felicity of his life, down to his 79th year, in which this is written. What reverses may attend the remainder is in the hand of Providence; but, if they arrive, the reflection on past happiness enjoy'd ought to help his bearing them with more resignation. To Temperance he ascribes his long-continued health, and what is still left to him of a good constitution; to Industry and Frugality, the early easiness of his circumstances and acquisition of his fortune, with all that knowledge that enabled him to be a useful citizen, and obtained for him some degree of reputation among the learned; to Sincerity and Justice, the confidence of his country, and the honorable employs it conferred upon him; and to the joint influence of the whole mass of the virtues, even in the imperfect state he was able to acquire them, all that evenness of temper, and that cheerfulness in conversation, which makes his company still sought for, and agreeable even to his younger acquaintance. I hope, therefore, that some of my descendants may follow the example and reap the benefit.

It will be remark'd that, tho' my scheme was not wholly without religion, there was in it no mark of any of the distinguishing tenets of any particular sect. I had purposely avoided them; for, being fully persuaded of the utility and excellency of my method, and that it might be serviceable to people in all religions, and intending some time or other to publish it, I would not have any thing in it that should prejudice any one, of any sect, against it. I purposed writing a little comment on each virtue, in which I would have shown the advantages of possessing it, and the mischiefs attending its opposite vice; and I should have called my book THE ART OF VIRTUE,[1] because it would have shown the means and manner of obtaining virtue, which would have distinguished it from the mere exhortation to be good, that does not instruct and indicate the means, but is like the apostle's man of verbal charity, who only without showing to the naked and hungry how or where they might get clothes or victuals, exhorted them to be fed and clothed.—James ii. 15, 16.

But it so happened that my intention of writing and publishing this comment was never fulfilled. I did, indeed, from time to time, put down short hints of the sentiments, reasonings, etc., to be made use of in it, some of which I have still by me; but the necessary close attention to private business in the earlier part of my life, and public business since, have occasioned my postponing it; for, it being connected in my mind with *a great and extensive project*, that required the whole man to execute, and which an unforeseen succession of employs prevented my attending to, it has hitherto remain'd unfinish'd.

In this piece it was my design to explain and enforce this doctrine, that vicious actions are not hurtful because they are forbidden, but forbidden because they are hurtful, the nature of man alone considered; that it was, therefore, every one's interest to be virtuous who wish'd to be happy even in this world; and I should, from this circumstance (there being always in the world a number of rich merchants, nobility, states, and princes, who have need of honest instruments for the management of their affairs, and such being so rare), have endeavored to convince young persons that no qualities were so likely to make a poor man's fortune as those of probity and integrity.

[1] Nothing so likely to make a man's fortune as virtue.—*Marg. note.*

My list of virtues contain'd at first but twelve; but a Quaker friend having kindly informed me that I was generally thought proud; that my pride show'd itself frequently in conversation; that I was not content with being in the right when discussing any point, but was overbearing, and rather insolent, of which he convinc'd me by mentioning several instances; I determined endeavouring to cure myself, if I could, of this vice or folly among the rest, and I added *Humility* to my list, giving an extensive meaning to the word.

I cannot boast of much success in acquiring the *reality* of this virtue, but I had a good deal with regard to the *appearance* of it. I made it a rule to forbear all direct contradiction to the sentiments of others, and all positive assertion of my own. I even forbid myself, agreeably to the old laws of our Junto, the use of every word or expression in the language that imported a fix'd opinion, such as *certainly*, *undoubtedly*, etc., and I adopted, instead of them, *I conceive*, *I apprehend*, or *I imagine* a thing to be so or so; or it *so appears to me at present.* When another asserted something that I thought an error, I deny'd myself the pleasure of contradicting him abruptly, and of showing immediately some absurdity in his proposition; and in answering I began by observing that in certain cases or circumstances his opinion would be right, but in the present case there *appear'd* or *seem'd* to me some difference, etc. I soon found the advantage of this change in my manner; the conversations I engag'd in went on more pleasantly. The modest way in which I propos'd my opinions procur'd them a readier reception and less contradiction; I had less mortification when I was found to be in the wrong, and I more easily prevail'd with others to give up their mistakes and join with me when I happened to be in the right.

And this mode, which I at first put on with some violence to natural inclination, became at length so easy, and so habitual to me, that perhaps for these fifty years past no one has ever heard a dogmatical expression escape me. And to this habit (after my character of integrity) I think it principally owing that I had early so much weight with my fellow-citizens when I proposed new institutions, or alterations in the old, and so much influence in public councils when I became a member; for I was but a bad speaker, never eloquent, subject to much hesitation in my choice of words, hardly correct in language, and yet I generally carried my points.

In reality, there is, perhaps, no one of our natural passions so hard to subdue as *pride*. Disguise it, struggle with it, beat it down, stifle it, mortify it as much as one pleases, it is still alive, and will every now and then peep out and show itself; you will see it, perhaps, often in this history; for, even if I could conceive that I had compleatly overcome it, I should probably be proud of my humility.

[Thus far written at Passy, 1784.]

[*"I am now about to write at home, August,* 1788, *but can not have the help expected from my papers, many of them being lost in the war. I have, however, found the following."*] [1]

HAVING mentioned *a great and extensive project* which I had conceiv'd, it seems proper that some account should be here given of that project and its object. Its first rise in my mind appears in the following little paper, accidentally preserv'd, viz.:

Observations on my reading history, in Library, May 19th, 1731.

"That the great affairs of the world, the wars, revolutions, etc., are carried on and affected by parties.

"That the view of these parties is their present general interest, or what they take to be such.

"That the different views of these different parties occasion all confusion.

"That while a party is carrying on a general design, each man has his particular private interest in view.

"That as soon as a party has gain'd its general point, each member becomes intent upon his particular interest; which, thwarting others, breaks that party into divisions, and occasions more confusion.

"That few in public affairs act from a meer view of the good of their country, whatever they may pretend; and, tho' their actings bring real good to their country, yet men primarily considered that

[1] This is a marginal memorandum.—B.

their own and their country's interest was united, and did not act from a principle of benevolence.

"That fewer still, in public affairs, act with a view to the good of mankind.

"There seems to me at present to be great occasion for raising a United Party for Virtue, by forming the virtuous and good men of all nations into a regular body, to be govern'd by suitable good and wise rules, which good and wise men may probably be more unanimous in their obedience to, than common people are to common laws.

"I at present think that whoever attempts this aright, and is well qualified, can not fail of pleasing God, and of meeting with success. B. F."

Revolving this project in my mind, as to be undertaken hereafter, when my circumstances should afford me the necessary leisure, I put down from time to time, on pieces of paper, such thoughts as occurr'd to me respecting it. Most of these are lost; but I find one purporting to be the substance of an intended creed, containing, as I thought, the essentials of every known religion, and being free of every thing that might shock the professors of any religion. It is express'd in these words, viz.:

"That there is one God, who made all things.

"That he governs the world by his providence.

"That he ought to be worshiped by adoration, prayer, and thanksgiving.

"But that the most acceptable service of God is doing good to man.

"That the soul is immortal.

"And that God will certainly reward virtue and punish vice, either here or hereafter."[1]

My ideas at that time were, that the sect should be begun and spread at first among young and single

[1] In the Middle Ages, Franklin, if such a phenomenon as Franklin were possible in the Middle Ages, would probably have been the founder of a monastic order.—B.

men only; that each person to be initiated should not only declare his assent to such creed, but should have exercised himself with the thirteen weeks' examination and practice of the virtues, as in the before-mention'd model; that the existence of such a society should be kept a secret, till it was become considerable, to prevent solicitations for the admission of improper persons, but that the members should each of them search among his acquaintance for ingenuous, well-disposed youths, to whom, with prudent caution, the scheme should be gradually communicated; that the members should engage to afford their advice, assistance, and support to each other in promoting one another's interests, business, and advancement in life; that, for distinction, we should be call'd *The Society of the Free and Easy:* free, as being, by the general practice and habit of the virtues, free from the dominion of vice; and particularly by the practice of industry and frugality, free from debt, which exposes a man to confinement, and a species of slavery to his creditors.

This is as much as I can now recollect of the project, except that I communicated it in part to two young men, who adopted it with some enthusiasm; but my then narrow circumstances, and the necessity I was under of sticking close to my business, occasion'd my postponing the further prosecution of it at that time; and my multifarious occupations, public and private, induc'd me to continue postponing, so that it has been omitted till I have no longer strength or activity left sufficient for such an enterprise; tho' I am still of opinion that it was a practicable scheme, and might have been very useful, by forming a great number of good citizens; and I was not discourag'd by the seeming magnitude of the undertaking, as I have always thought that one man of tolerable abilities may work great changes, and accomplish great affairs among mankind, if he first forms a good plan, and, cutting off all amusements or other employments that would divert his attention, makes the execution of that same plan his sole study and business.

In 1732 I first publish'd my Almanack, under the name of *Richard Saunders*; it was continu'd by me about twenty-five years, commonly call'd *Poor Richard's Almanack.* I endeavor'd to make it both entertaining and useful, and it accordingly came to be in such demand, that I reap'd considerable profit from it, vending annually near ten thousand. And observing that it was generally read, scarce any neighborhood in the province being without it, I consider'd it as a proper vehicle for conveying instruction among the common people, who bought scarcely any other books; I therefore filled all the little spaces that occurr'd between the remarkable days in the calendar with proverbial sentences, chiefly such as inculcated industry and frugality, as the means of procuring wealth, and thereby securing virtue; it being more difficult for a man in want, to act always honestly, as, to use here one of those proverbs, *it is hard for an empty sack to stand upright.*

These proverbs, which contained the wisdom of many ages and nations, I assembled and form'd into a connected discourse prefix'd to the Almanack of 1757, as the harangue of a wise old man to the people attending an auction. The bringing all these scatter'd counsels thus into a focus enabled them to make greater impression. The piece, being universally approved, was copied in all the newspapers of the Continent; reprinted in Britain on a broad side, to be stuck up in houses; two translations were made of it in French, and great numbers bought by the clergy and gentry, to distribute gratis among their poor parishioners and tenants. In Pennsylvania, as it discouraged useless expense in foreign superfluities, some thought it had its share of influence in producing that growing plenty of money which was observable for several years after its publication.

I considered my newspaper, also, as another means of communicating instruction, and in that view frequently reprinted in it extracts from the Spectator, and other moral writers; and sometimes publish'd little pieces of my own, which had been first compos'd for reading in our Junto. Of these are a Socratic dialogue, tending to prove that, whatever might be his parts and abilities, a vicious man could not properly be called a man of sense; and a discourse on self-denial, showing that virtue was not secure till its practice became a habitude, and was free from the opposition of contrary inclinations. These may be found in the papers about the beginning of 1735.

In the conduct of my newspaper, I carefully excluded all libelling and personal abuse, which is of late years become so disgraceful to our country. Whenever I was solicited to insert any thing of that kind, and the writers pleaded, as they generally did, the liberty of the press, and that a newspaper was like a stage-coach, in which any one who would pay had a right to a place, my answer was, that I would print the piece separately if desired, and the author might have as many copies as he pleased to distribute himself, but that I would not take upon me to spread his detraction; and that, having contracted with my subscribers to furnish them with what might be either useful or entertaining, I could not fill their papers with private altercation, in which they had no concern, without doing them manifest injustice. Now, many of our printers make no scruple of gratifying the malice of individuals by false accusations of the fairest characters among ourselves, augmenting animosity even to the producing of duels; and are, moreover, so indiscreet as to print scurrilous reflections on the government of neighboring states, and even on the conduct of our best national allies, which may be attended with the most pernicious consequences. These things I mention as a caution to young printers, and that they may be encouraged not to pollute their presses and disgrace their profession by such infamous practices, but refuse steadily, as they may see by my example that such a course of conduct will not, on the whole, be injurious to their interests.

In 1733 I sent one of my journeymen to Charleston, South Carolina, where a printer was wanting. I furnish'd him with a press and letters, on an agreement of partnership, by which I was to receive one-third of the profits of the business, paying one-third of the expense. He was a man of learning, and honest but ignorant in matters of account; and, tho' he sometimes made me remittances, I could get no account from him, nor any satisfactory state of our partnership while he lived. On his decease, the business was continued by his widow, who, being born and bred in Holland, where, as I have been inform'd, the knowledge of accounts makes a part of female education, she not only sent me as clear a state as she could find of the transactions past, but continued to account with the greatest regularity and exactness every quarter afterwards, and managed the business with such success, that she not only brought up reputably a family of children, but, at the expiration of the term, was able to purchase of me the printing-house, and establish her son in it.

I mention this affair chiefly for the sake of recommending that branch of education for our young females, as likely to be of more use to them and their children, in case of widowhood, than either music or dancing, by preserving them from losses by imposition of crafty men, and enabling them to continue, perhaps, a profitable mercantile house, with establish'd correspondence, till a son is grown up fit to undertake and go on with it, to the lasting advantage and enriching of the family.

About the year 1734 there arrived among us from Ireland a young Presbyterian preacher, named Hemphill, who delivered with a good voice, and apparently extempore, most excellent discourses, which drew together considerable numbers of different persuasions, who join'd in admiring them. Among the rest, I became one of his constant hearers, his sermons pleasing me, as they had little of the dogmatical kind, but inculcated strongly the practice of virtue, or what in the religious stile are called good works. Those, however, of our congregation, who considered themselves as orthodox Presbyterians, disapprov'd his doctrine, and were join'd by most of the old clergy, who arraign'd him of heterodoxy before the synod, in order to have him silenc'd. I became his zealous partisan, and contributed all I could to raise a party in his favour, and we combated for him a while with some hopes of success. There was much scribbling pro and con upon the occasion; and finding that, tho' an elegant preacher, he was but a poor writer, I lent him my pen and wrote for him two or three pamphlets, and one piece in the Gazette of April, 1735. Those pamphlets, as is generally the case with controversial writings, tho' eagerly read at the time, were soon out of vogue, and I question whether a single copy of them now exists.

During the contest an unlucky occurrence hurt his cause exceedingly. One of our adversaries having heard him preach a sermon that was much admired, thought he had somewhere read the sermon before, or at least a part of it. On search, he found that part quoted at length, in one of the British Reviews, from a discourse of Dr Foster's. This detection gave many of our party disgust, who accordingly abandoned his cause, and occasion'd our more speedy discomfiture in the synod. I stuck by him, however, as I rather approv'd his giving us good sermons compos'd by others, than bad ones of his own manufacture, tho' the latter was the practice of our common teachers. He afterward acknowledg'd to me that none of those he preach'd were his own; adding, that his memory was such as enabled him to retain and repeat any sermon after one reading only. On our defeat, he left us in search elsewhere of better fortune, and I quitted the congregation, never joining it after, tho' I continu'd many years my subscription for the support of its ministers.

I had begun in 1733 to study languages; I soon made myself so much a master of the French as to be able to read the books with ease. I then undertook the Italian. An acquaintance, who was also learning it, us'd often to tempt me to play chess with him. Finding this took up too much of the time I had to spare for study, I at length refus'd to play any more, unless on this condition, that the victor in every game should have a right to impose a task, either in parts of the grammar to be got by heart, or in translations, etc., which tasks the vanquish'd was to perform upon honour, before our next meeting. As we play'd pretty equally, we thus beat one another into that language. I afterwards with a little painstaking, acquir'd as much of the Spanish as to read their books also.

I have already mention'd that I had only one year's instruction in a Latin school, and that when very young, after which I neglected that language entirely. But, when I had attained an acquaintance with the French, Italian, and Spanish, I was surpriz'd to find, on looking over a Latin Testament, that I understood so much more of that language than I had imagined, which encouraged me to apply myself again to the study of it, and I met with more success, as those preceding languages had greatly smooth'd my way.

From these circumstances, I have thought that there is some inconsistency in our common mode of teaching languages. We are told that it is proper to begin first with the Latin, and, having acquir'd that, it will be more easy to attain those modern languages which are deriv'd from it; and yet we do not begin with the Greek, in order more easily to acquire the Latin. It is true that, if you can clamber and get to the top of a staircase without using the steps, you will more easily gain them in descending; but certainly, if you begin with the lowest you will with more ease ascend to the top; and I would therefore offer it to the consideration of those who superintend the education of our youth, whether, since many of those who begin with the Latin quit the same after spending some years without having made any great proficiency, and what they have learnt becomes almost useless, so that their time has been lost, it would not have been better to have begun with the French, proceeding to the Italian, etc.; for, tho', after spending the same time, they should quit the study of languages and never arrive at the Latin, they would, however, have acquired another tongue or two, that, being in modern use, might be serviceable to them in common life.

After ten years' absence from Boston, and having become easy in my circumstances, I made a journey thither to visit my relations, which I could not sooner well afford. In returning, I call'd at Newport to see my brother, then settled there with his printing-house. Our former differences were forgotten, and our meeting was very cordial and affectionate. He was fast declining in his health, and requested of me that, in case of his death, which he apprehended not far distant, I would take home his son, then but ten years of age, and bring him up to the printing business. This I accordingly perform'd, sending him a few years to school before I took him into the office. His mother carried on the business till he was grown up, when I assisted him with an assortment of new types, those of his father being in a manner worn out. Thus it was that I made my brother ample amends for the service I had depriv'd him of by leaving him so early.

In 1736 I lost one of my sons, a fine boy of four years old, by the small-pox, taken in the common way. I long regretted bitterly, and still regret that I had not given it to him by inoculation. This I mention for the sake of parents who omit that operation, on the supposition that they should never forgive themselves if a child died under it; my example showing that the regret may be the same either way, and that, therefore, the safer should be chosen.

Our club, the Junto, was found so useful, and afforded such satisfaction to the members, that several were desirous of introducing their friends, which could not well be done without exceeding what we had settled as a convenient number, viz., twelve. We had from the beginning made it a rule to keep our institution a secret, which was pretty well observ'd; the intention was to avoid applications of improper persons for admittance, some of whom, perhaps, we might find it difficult to refuse. I was one of those who were against any addition to our number, but, instead of it, made in writing a proposal, that every member separately should endeavor to form a subordinate club, with the same rules respecting queries, etc., and without informing them of the connection with the Junto. The advantages proposed were, the improvement of so many more young citizens by the use of our institutions; our better acquaintance with the general sentiments of the inhabitants on any occasion, as the Junto member might propose what queries we should desire, and was to report to the Junto what pass'd in his separate club; the promotion of our particular interests in business by more extensive recommendation, and the increase of our influence in public affairs, and our power of doing good by spreading thro' the several clubs the sentiments of the Junto.

The project was approv'd, and every member undertook to form his club, but they did not all succeed. Five or six only were compleated, which were called by different names, as the Vine, the Union, the Band, etc. They were useful to themselves, and afforded us a good deal of amusement, information, and instruction, besides answering, in some considerable degree, our views of influencing the public opinion on particular occasions, of which I shall give some instances in course of time as they happened.

My first promotion was my being chosen, in 1736, clerk of the General Assembly. The choice was made that year without opposition; but the year following, when I was again propos'd (the choice, like that of the members, being annual), a new member made a long speech against me, in order to favour some other candidate. I was, however, chosen, which was the more agreeable to me, as, besides the pay for the immediate service as clerk, the place gave me a better opportunity of keeping up an interest among the members, which secur'd to me the business of printing the votes, laws, paper money, and other occasional jobbs for the public, that, on the whole, were very profitable.

I therefore did not like the opposition of this new member, who was a gentleman of fortune and education, with talents that were likely to give him, in time, great influence in the House, which, indeed, afterwards happened. I did not, however, aim at gaining his favour by paying any servile respect to him, but, after some time, took this other method. Having heard that he had in his library a certain very scarce and curious book, I wrote a note to him, expressing my desire of perusing that book, and requesting he would do me the favour of lending it to me for a few days. He sent it immediately, and I return'd it in about a week with another note, expressing strongly my sense of the favour. When we next met in the House, he spoke to me (which he had never done before), and with great civility; and he ever after manifested a readiness to serve me on all occasions, so that we became great friends, and our friendship continued to his death. This is another instance of the truth of an old maxim I had learned, which says, "*He that has once done you a kindness will be more ready to do you another, than he whom you yourself have obliged.*" And it shows how much more profitable it is prudently to remove, than to resent, return, and continue inimical proceedings.

In 1737, Colonel Spotswood, late governor of Virginia, and then postmaster-general, being dissatisfied with the conduct of his deputy at Philadelphia, respecting some negligence in rendering, and inexactitude of his accounts, took from him the commission and offered it to me. I accepted it readily, and found it of great advantage; for, tho' the salary was small, it facilitated the correspondence that improv'd my newspaper, increas'd the number demanded, as well as the advertisements to be inserted, so that it came to afford me a considerable income. My old competitor's newspaper declin'd proportionably, and I was satisfy'd without retaliating his refusal, while postmaster, to permit my papers being carried by the riders. Thus he suffer'd greatly from his neglect in due accounting; and I mention it as a lesson to those young men who may be employ'd in managing affairs for others, that they should always render accounts, and make remittances, with great clearness and punctuality. The character of observing such a conduct is the most powerful of all recommendations to new employments and increase of business.

I began now to turn my thoughts a little to public affairs, beginning, however, with small matters. The city watch was one of the first things that I conceiv'd to want regulation. It was managed by the constables of the respective wards in turn; the constable warned a number of housekeepers to attend him for the night. Those who chose never to attend, paid him six shillings a year to be excus'd, which was suppos'd to be for hiring substitutes, but was, in reality, much more than was necessary for that purpose, and made the constableship a place of profit; and the constable, for a little drink, often got such ragamuffins about him as a watch, that respectable housekeepers did not choose to mix with. Walking the rounds, too, was often neglected, and most of the nights spent in tippling. I thereupon wrote a paper to be read in Junto, representing these irregularities, but insisting more particularly on the inequality of this six-shilling tax of the constables, respecting the circumstances of those who paid it, since a poor widow housekeeper, all whose property to be guarded by the watch did not perhaps exceed the value of fifty pounds, paid as much as the wealthiest merchant, who had thousands of pounds' worth of goods in his stores.

On the whole, I proposed as a more effectual watch, the hiring of proper men to serve constantly in that business; and as a more equitable way of supporting the charge, the levying a tax that should be proportion'd to the property. This idea, being approv'd by the Junto, was communicated to the other clubs, but as arising in each of them; and though the plan was not immediately carried into execution, yet, by preparing the minds of people for the change, it paved the way for the law obtained a few years after, when the members of our clubs were grown into more influence.

About this time I wrote a paper (first to be read in Junto, but it was afterward publish'd) on the different accidents and carelessnesses by which houses were set on fire, with cautions against them, and means proposed of avoiding them. This was much spoken of as a useful piece, and gave rise to a project, which soon followed it, of forming a company for the more ready extinguishing of fires, and mutual assistance in removing and securing of goods when in danger. Associates in this scheme were presently found, amounting to thirty. Our articles of agreement oblig'd every member to keep always in good order, and fit for use, a certain number of leather buckets, with strong bags and baskets (for packing and transporting of goods), which were to be brought to every fire; and we agreed to meet once a month and spend a social evening together, in discoursing and communicating such ideas as occurred to us upon the subject of fires, as might be useful in our conduct on such occasions.

The utility of this institution soon appeared, and many more desiring to be admitted than we thought convenient for one company, they were advised to form another, which was accordingly done; and this went on, one new company being formed after another, till they became so numerous as to include most of the inhabitants who were men of property; and now, at the time of my writing this, tho' upward of fifty years since its establishment, that which I first formed, called the Union Fire Company, still subsists and flourishes, tho' the first members are all deceas'd but myself and one, who is older by a year than I am. The small fines that have been paid by members for absence at the monthly meetings have been apply'd to the purchase of fire-engines, ladders, fire-hooks, and other useful implements for each company, so that I question whether there is a city in the world better provided with the means of putting a stop to beginning conflagrations; and, in fact, since these institutions, the city has never lost by fire more than one or two houses at a time, and the flames have often been extinguished before the house in which they began has been half consumed.

In 1739 arrived among us from Ireland the Reverend Mr Whitefield, who had made himself remarkable there as an itinerant preacher. He was at first permitted to preach in some of our churches; but the clergy, taking a dislike to him, soon refus'd him their pulpits, and he was oblig'd to preach in the fields. The multitudes of all sects and denominations that attended his sermons were enormous, and it was matter of speculation to me, who was one of the number, to observe the extraordinary influence of his oratory on his hearers, and how much they admir'd and respected him, notwithstanding his common abuse of them, by assuring them they were naturally *half beasts and half devils*. It was wonderful to see the change soon made in the manners of our inhabitants. From being thoughtless or indifferent about religion, it seem'd as if all the world were growing religious, so that one could not walk thro' the town in an evening without hearing psalms sung in different families of every street.

And it being found inconvenient to assemble in the open air, subject to its inclemencies, the building of a house to meet in was no sooner propos'd, and persons appointed to receive contributions, but sufficient sums were soon receiv'd to procure the ground and erect the building, which was one hundred feet long and seventy broad, about the size of Westminster Hall; and the work was carried on with such spirit as to be finished in a much shorter time than could have been expected. Both house and ground were vested in trustees, expressly for the use of any preacher of any religious persuasion who might desire to say something to the people at Philadelphia; the design in building not being to accommodate any particular sect, but the inhabitants in general; so that even if the Mufti of Constantinople were to send a missionary to preach Mohammedanism to us, he would find a pulpit at his service.

Mr Whitefield, in leaving us, went preaching all the way thro' the colonies to Georgia. The settlement of that province had lately been begun, but, instead of being made with hardy, industrious husbandmen, accustomed to labor, the only people fit for such an enterprise, it was with families of broken shop-keepers and other insolvent debtors, many of indolent and idle habits, taken out of the jails, who, being set down in the woods, unqualified for clearing land, and unable to endure the hardships of a new settlement, perished in numbers, leaving many helpless children unprovided for. The sight of their miserable situation inspir'd the benevolent heart of Mr Whitefield with the idea of building an Orphan House there, in which they might be supported and educated. Returning northward, he preach'd up this charity, and made large collections, for his eloquence had a wonderful power over the hearts and purses of his hearers, of which I myself was an instance.

I did not disapprove of the design, but, as Georgia was then destitute of materials and workmen, and it was proposed to send them from Philadelphia at a great expense, I thought it would have been better to have built the house here, and brought the children to it. This I advis'd; but he was resolute in his first project, rejected my counsel, and I therefor refus'd to contribute. I happened soon after to attend one of his sermons, in the course of which I perceived he intended to finish with a collection, and I silently resolved he should get nothing from me. I had in my pocket a handful of copper money, three or four silver dollars, and five pistoles in gold. As he proceeded I began to soften, and concluded to give the coppers. Another stroke of his oratory made me asham'd of that, and determin'd me to give the silver; and he finish'd so admirably, that I empty'd my pocket wholly into the collector's dish, gold and all. At this sermon there was also one of our club, who, being of my sentiments respecting the building in Georgia, and suspecting a collection might be intended, had, by precaution, emptied his pockets before he came from home. Towards the conclusion of the discourse, however, he felt a strong desire to give, and apply'd to a neighbour, who stood near him, to borrow some money for the purpose. The application was unfortunately [made] to perhaps the only man in the company who had the firmness not to be affected by the preacher. His answer was, "*At any other time, Friend Hopkinson, I would lend to thee freely; but not now, for thee seems to be out of thy right senses.*"

Some of Mr Whitefield's enemies affected to suppose that he would apply these collections to his own private emolument; but I, who was intimately acquainted with him (being employed in printing his Sermons and Journals, etc.), never had the least suspicion of his integrity, but am to this day decidedly of opinion that he was in all his conduct a perfectly *honest man*; and methinks my testimony in his favour ought to have the more weight, as we had no religious connection. He us'd, indeed, sometimes to pray for my conversion, but never had the satisfaction of believing that his prayers were heard. Ours was a mere civil friendship, sincere on both sides, and lasted to his death.

The following instance will show something of the terms on which we stood. Upon one of his arrivals from England at Boston, he wrote to me that he should come soon to Philadelphia, but knew not where he could lodge when there, as he understood his old friend and host, Mr Benezet, was removed to Germantown. My answer was, "You know my house; if you can make shift with its scanty accommodations, you will be most heartily welcome." He reply'd, that if I made that kind offer for Christ's sake, I should not miss of a reward. And I returned, "*Don't let me be mistaken; it was not for Christ's sake, but for your sake.*" One of our common acquaintance jocosely remark'd, that, knowing it to be the custom of the saints, when they received any favour, to shift the burden of the obligation from off their own shoulders, and place it in heaven, I had contriv'd to fix it on earth.

The last time I saw Mr Whitefield was in London, when he consulted me about his Orphan House concern, and his purpose of appropriating it to the establishment of a college.

He had a loud and clear voice, and articulated his words and sentences so perfectly, that he might be heard and understood at a great distance, especially as his auditories, however numerous, observ'd the most exact silence. He preach'd one evening from the top of the Court-house steps, which are in the middle of Market-street, and on the west side of Second-street, which crosses it at right angles. Both streets were fill'd with his hearers to a considerable distance. Being among the hindmost in Market-street, I had the curiosity to learn how far he could be heard, by retiring backwards down the street towards the river; and I found his voice distinct till I came near Front-street, when some noise in that street obscur'd it. Imagining then a semicircle, of which my distance should be the radius, and that it were fill'd with auditors, to each of whom I allow'd two square feet, I computed that he might well be heard by more than thirty thousand. This reconcil'd me to the newspaper accounts of his having preach'd to twenty-five thousand people in the fields, and to the antient histories of generals haranguing whole armies, of which I had sometimes doubted.

By hearing him often, I came to distinguish easily between sermons newly compos'd, and those which he had often preach'd in the course of his travels. His delivery of the latter was so improv'd by frequent repetitions that every accent, every emphasis, every modulation of voice, was so perfectly well turn'd and well plac'd, that, without being interested in the subject, one could not help being pleas'd with the discourse; a pleasure of much the same kind with that receiv'd from an excellent piece of musick. This is an advantage itinerant preachers have over those who are stationary, as the latter can not well improve their delivery of a sermon by so many rehearsals.

His writing and printing from time to time gave great advantage to his enemies; unguarded expressions, and even erroneous opinions, delivered in preaching, might have been afterwards explain'd or qualifi'd by supposing others that might have accompani'd them, or they might have been deny'd; but *litera scripta manet*. Critics attack'd his writings violently, and with so much appearance of reason as to diminish the number of his votaries and prevent their encrease; so that I am of opinion if he had never written any thing, he would have left behind him a much more numerous and important sect, and his reputation might in that case have been still growing, even after his death, as there being nothing of his writing on which to found a censure and give him a lower character, his proselytes would be left at liberty to feign for him as great a variety of excellences as their enthusiastic admiration might wish him to have possessed.

My business was now continually augmenting, and my circumstances growing daily easier, my newspaper having become very profitable, as being for a time almost the only one in this and the neighbouring provinces. I experienced, too, the truth of the observation, "*that after getting the first hundred pound, it is more easy to get the second,*" money itself being of a prolific nature.

The partnership at Carolina having succeeded, I was encourag'd to engage in others, and to promote several of my workmen, who had behaved well, by establishing them with printing-houses in different colonies, on the same terms with that in Carolina. Most of them did well, being enabled at the end of our term, six years, to purchase the types of me and go on working for themselves, by which means several families were raised. Partnerships often finish in quarrels; but I was happy in this, that mine were all carried on and ended amicably, owing, I think, a good deal to the precaution of having very explicitly settled, in our articles, every thing to be done by or expected from each partner, so that there was nothing to dispute, which precaution I would therefore recommend to all who enter into partnerships; for, whatever esteem partners may have for, and confidence in each other at the time of the contract, little jealousies and disgusts may arise, with ideas of inequality in the care and burden of the business, etc., which are attended often with breach of friendship and of the connection, perhaps with lawsuits and other disagreeable consequences.

I had, on the whole, abundant reason to be satisfied with my being established in Pennsylvania. There were, however, two things that I regretted, there being no provision for defense, nor for a compleat education of youth; no militia, nor any college. I therefore, in 1743, drew up a proposal for establishing an academy; and at that time, thinking the Reverend Mr Peters, who was out of employ, a fit person to superintend such an institution, I communicated the project to him; but he, having more profitable views in the service of the proprietaries, which succeeded, declin'd the undertaking; and, not knowing another at that time suitable for such a trust, I let the scheme lie a while dormant. I succeeded better the next year, 1744, in proposing and establishing a Philosophical Society. The paper I wrote for that purpose will be found among my writings, when collected.

With respect to defense, Spain having been several years at war against Great Britain, and being at length join'd by France, which brought us into great danger; and the laboured and long-continued endeavour of our governor, Thomas, to prevail with our Quaker Assembly to pass a militia law, and make other provisions for the security of the province, having proved abortive, I determined to try what might be done by a voluntary association of the people. To promote this, I first wrote and published a pamphlet, entitled PLAIN TRUTH, in which I stated our defenceless situation in strong lights, with the necessity of union and discipline for our defense, and promis'd to propose in a few days an association, to be generally signed for that purpose. The pamphlet had a sudden and surprising effect. I was call'd upon for the instrument of association, and having settled the draft of it with a few friends, I appointed a meeting of the citizens in the large building before mentioned. The house was pretty full; I had prepared a number of printed copies, and provided pens and ink dispers'd all over the room. I harangued them a little on the subject, read the paper, and explained it, and then distributed the copies, which were eagerly signed, not the least objection being made.

When the company separated, and the papers were collected, we found above twelve hundred hands; and, other copies being dispersed in the country, the subscribers amounted at length to upward of ten thousand. These all furnished themselves as soon as they could with arms, formed themselves into companies and regiments, chose their own officers, and met every week to be instructed in the manual exercise, and other parts of military discipline. The women, by subscriptions among themselves, provided silk colors, which they presented to the companies, painted with different devices and mottos, which I supplied.

The officers of the companies composing the Philadelphia regiment, being met, chose me for their colonel; but, conceiving myself unfit, I declin'd that station, and recommended Mr Lawrence, a fine person, and man of influence, who was accordingly appointed. I then propos'd a lottery to defray the expense of building a battery below the town, and furnishing it with cannon. It filled expeditiously, and the battery was soon erected, the merlons being fram'd of logs and fill'd with earth. We bought some old cannon from Boston, but, these not being sufficient, we wrote to England for more, soliciting, at the same time, our proprietaries for some assistance, tho' without much expectation of obtaining it.

Meanwhile, Colonel Lawrence, William Allen, Abram Taylor, Esqr., and myself were sent to New York by the associators, commission'd to borrow some cannon of Governor Clinton. He at first refus'd us peremptorily; but at dinner with his council, where there was great drinking of Madeira wine, as the custom of that place then was, he softened by degrees, and said he would lend us six. After a few more bumpers he advanc'd to ten; and at length he very good-naturedly conceded eighteen. They were fine cannon, eighteen-pounders, with their carriages, which we soon transported and mounted on our battery, where the associators kept a nightly guard while the war lasted, and among the rest I regularly took my turn of duty there as a common soldier.

My activity in these operations was agreeable to the governor and council; they took me into confidence, and I was consulted by them in every measure wherein their concurrence was thought useful to the association. Calling in the aid of religion, I propos'd to them the proclaiming a fast, to promote reformation, and implore the blessing of Heaven on our undertaking. They embrac'd the motion; but, as it was the first fast ever thought of in the province, the secretary had no precedent from which to draw the proclamation. My education in New England, where a fast is proclaimed every year, was here of some advantage: I drew it in the accustomed stile, it was translated into German, printed in both languages, and divulg'd thro' the province. This gave the clergy of the different sects an opportunity of influencing their congregations to join in the association, and it would probably have been general among all but Quakers if the peace had not soon interven'd.

It was thought by some of my friends that, by my activity in these affairs, I should offend that sect, and thereby lose my interest in the Assembly of the province, where they formed a great majority. A young gentleman who had likewise some friends in the House, and wished to succeed me as their clerk, acquainted me that it was decided to displace me at the next election; and he, therefore, in good will, advis'd me to resign, as more consistent with my honour than being turn'd out. My answer to him was, that I had read or heard of some public man who made it a rule never to ask for an office, and never to refuse one when offer'd to him. "I approve," says I, "of his rule, and will practice it with a small addition; I shall never *ask*, never *refuse*, nor ever *resign* an office. If they will have my office of clerk to dispose of to another, they shall take it from me. I will not, by giving it up, lose my right of some time or other making reprisals on my adversaries." I heard, however, no more of this; I was chosen again unanimously as usual at the next election. Possibly, as they dislik'd my late intimacy with the members of council, who had join'd the governors in all the disputes about military preparations, with which the House had long been harass'd, they might have been pleas'd if I would voluntarily have left them; but they did not care to displace me on account merely of my zeal for the association, and they could not well give another reason.

Indeed I had some cause to believe that the defense of the country was not disagreeable to any of them, provided they were not requir'd to assist in it. And I found that a much greater number of them than I could have imagined, tho' against offensive war, were clearly for the defensive. Many pamphlets *pro and con* were publish'd on the subject, and some by good Quakers, in favour of defense, which I believe convinc'd most of their younger people.

A transaction in our fire company gave me some insight into their prevailing sentiments. It had been propos'd that we should encourage the scheme for building a battery by laying out the present stock, then about sixty pounds, in tickets of the lottery. By our rules, no money could be dispos'd of till the next meeting after the proposal. The company consisted of thirty members, of which twenty-two were Quakers, and eight only of other persuasions. We eight punctually attended the meeting; but, tho' we thought that some of the Quakers would join us, we were by no means sure of a majority. Only one Quaker, Mr James Morris, appear'd to oppose the measure. He expressed much sorrow that it had ever been propos'd, as he said *Friends* were all against it, and it would create such discord as might break up the company. We told him that we saw no reason for that; we were the minority, and if *Friends* were against the measure, and outvoted us, we must and should, agreeably to the usage of all societies, submit. When the hour for business arriv'd it was mov'd to put the vote; he allow'd we might then do it by the rules, but, as he could assure us that a number of members intended to be present for the purpose of opposing it, it would be but candid to allow a little time for their appearing.

While we were disputing this, a waiter came to tell me two gentlemen below desir'd to speak with me. I went down, and found they were two of our Quaker members. They told me there were eight of them assembled at a tavern just by; that they were determin'd to come and vote with us if there should be occasion, which they hop'd would not be the case, and desir'd we would not call for their assistance if we could do without it, as their voting for such a measure might embroil them with their elders and friends. Being thus secure of a majority, I went up, and after a little seeming hesitation, agreed to a delay of another hour. This Mr Morris allow'd to be extreamly fair. Not one of his opposing friends appear'd, at which he express'd great surprize; and, at the expiration of the hour, we carry'd the resolution eight to one; and as, of the twenty-two Quakers, eight were ready to vote with us, and thirteen, by their absence, manifested that they were not inclin'd to oppose the measure, I afterward estimated the proportion of Quakers sincerely against defense as one to twenty-one only; for these were all regular members of that society, and in good reputation among them, and had due notice of what was propos'd at that meeting.

The honorable and learned Mr Logan, who had always been of that sect, was one who wrote an address to them, declaring his approbation of defensive war, and supporting his opinion by many strong arguments. He put into my hands sixty pounds to be laid out in lottery tickets for the battery, with directions to apply what prizes might be drawn wholly to that service. He told me the following anecdote of his old master, William Penn, respecting defense. He came over from England, when a young man, with that proprietary, and as his secretary. It was war-time, and their ship was chas'd by an armed vessel, suppos'd to be an enemy. Their captain prepar'd for defense; but told William Penn, and his company of Quakers, that he did not expect their assistance, and they might retire into the cabin, which they did, except James Logan, who chose to stay upon deck, and was quarter'd to a gun. The suppos'd enemy prov'd a friend, so there was no fighting; but when the secretary went down to communicate the intelligence, William Penn rebuk'd him severely for staying upon deck, and undertaking to assist in defending the vessel, contrary to the principles of *Friends*, especially as it had not been required by the captain. This reproof, being before all the company, piqu'd the secretary, who answer'd, "*I being thy servant, why did thee not order me to come down? But thee was willing enough that I should stay and help to fight the ship when thee thought there was danger.*"

My being many years in the Assembly, the majority of which were constantly Quakers, gave me frequent opportunities of seeing the embarrassment given them by their principle against war, whenever application was made to them, by order of the crown, to grant aids for military purposes. They were unwilling to offend government, on the one hand, by a direct refusal; and their friends, the body of the Quakers, on the other, by a compliance contrary to their principles; hence a variety of evasions to avoid complying, and modes of disguising the compliance when it became unavoidable. The common mode at last was, to grant money under the phrase of its being "*for the king's use,*" and never to inquire how it was applied.

But, if the demand was not directly from the crown, that phrase was found not so proper, and some other was to be invented. As, when powder was wanting (I think it was for the garrison at Louisburg), and the government of New England solicited a grant of some from Pennsilvania, which was much urg'd on the House by Governor Thomas, they could not grant money to buy powder, because that was an ingredient of war; but they voted an aid to New England of three thousand pounds, to be put into the hands of the governor, and appropriated it for the purchasing of bread, flour, wheat, or *other grain.* Some of the council, desirous of giving the House still further embarrassment, advis'd the governor not to accept provision, as not being the thing he had demanded; but he reply'd, "I shall take the money, for I understand very well their meaning; other grain is gunpowder," which he accordingly bought, and they never objected to it.[1]

[1] See the votes.—[*Marg. note.*]

It was in allusion to this fact that, when in our fire company we feared the success of our proposal in favour of the lottery, and I had said to my friend Mr Syng, one of our members, "If we fail, let us move the purchase of a fire-engine with the money; the Quakers can have no objection to that; and then, if you nominate me and I you as a committee for that purpose, we will buy a great gun, which is certainly a *fire-engine*." "I see," says he, "you have improv'd by being so long in the Assembly; your equivocal project would be just a match for their wheat or *other grain*."

These embarrassments that the Quakers suffer'd from having establish'd and published it as one of their principles that no kind of war was lawful, and which, being once published, they could not afterwards, however they might change their minds, easily get rid of, reminds me of what I think a more prudent conduct in another sect among us, that of the Dunkers. I was acquainted with one of its founders, Michael Welfare, soon after it appear'd. He complain'd to me that they were grievously calumniated by the zealots of other persuasions, and charg'd with abominable principles and practices, to which they were utter strangers. I told him this had always been the case with new sects, and that, to put a stop to such abuse, I imagin'd it might be well to publish the articles of their belief, and the rules of their discipline. He said that it had been propos'd among them, but not agreed to, for this reason: "When we were first drawn together as a society," says he, "it had pleased God to enlighten our minds so far as to see that some doctrines, which we once esteemed truths, were errors; and that others, which we had esteemed errors, were real truths. From time to time He has been pleased to afford us farther light, and our principles have been improving, and our errors diminishing. Now we are not sure that we are arrived at the end of this progression, and at the perfection of spiritual or theological knowledge; and we fear that, if we should once print our confession of faith, we should feel ourselves as if bound and confin'd by it, and perhaps be unwilling to receive further improvement, and our successors still more so, as conceiving what we their elders and founders had done, to be something sacred, never to be departed from."

This modesty in a sect is perhaps a singular instance in the history of mankind, every other sect supposing itself in possession of all truth, and that those who differ are so far in the wrong; like a man traveling in foggy weather, those at some distance before him on the road he sees wrapped up in the fog, as well as those behind him, and also the people in the fields on each side, but near him all appears clear, tho' in truth he is as much in the fog as any of them. To avoid this kind of embarrassment, the Quakers have of late years been gradually declining the public service in the Assembly and in the magistracy, choosing rather to quit their power than their principle.

In order of time, I should have mentioned before, that having, in 1742, invented an open stove for the better warming of rooms, and at the same time saving fuel, as the fresh air admitted was warmed in entering, I made a present of the model to Mr Robert Grace, one of my early friends, who, having an iron-furnace, found the casting of the plates for these stoves a profitable thing, as they were growing in demand. To promote that demand, I wrote and published a pamphlet, entitled "*An Account of the new-invented Pennsylvania Fireplaces; wherein their Construction and Manner of Operation is particularly explained; their Advantages above every other Method of warming Rooms demonstrated; and all Objections that have been raised against the Use of them answered and obviated,"* etc. This pamphlet had a good effect. Gov'r. Thomas was so pleas'd with the construction of this stove, as described in it, that he offered to give me a patent for the sole vending of them for a term of years; but I declin'd it from a principle which has ever weighed with me on such occasions, viz., *That, as we enjoy great advantages from the inventions of others, we should be glad of an opportunity to serve others by any invention of ours; and this we should do freely and generously.*

An ironmonger in London however, assuming a good deal of my pamphlet, and working it up into his own, and making some small changes in the machine, which rather hurt its operation, got a patent for it there, and made, as I was told, a little fortune by it. And this is not the only instance of patents taken out for my inventions by others, tho' not always with the same success, which I never contested, as having no desire of profiting by patents myself, and hating disputes. The use of these fireplaces in very many houses, both of this and the neighbouring colonies, has been, and is, a great saving of wood to the inhabitants.

Peace being concluded, and the association business therefore at an end, I turn'd my thoughts again to the affair of establishing an academy. The first step I took was to associate in the design a number of active friends, of whom the Junto furnished a good part; the next was to write and publish a pamphlet, entitled *Proposals Relating to the Education of Youth in Pennsylvania.* This I distributed among the principal inhabitants gratis; and as soon as I could suppose their minds a little prepared by the perusal of it, I set on foot a subscription for opening and supporting an academy; it was to be paid in quotas yearly for five years; by so dividing it, I judg'd the subscription might be larger, and I believed it was so, amounting to no less, if I remember right, than five thousand pounds.

In the introduction to these proposals, I stated their publication, not as an act of mine, but of some *publick-spirited gentlemen*, avoiding as much as I could, according to my usual rule, the presenting myself to the publick as the author of any scheme for their benefit.

The subscribers, to carry the project into immediate execution, chose out of their number twenty-four trustees, and appointed Mr Francis, then attorney-general, and myself to draw up constitutions for the government of the academy; which being done and signed, a house was hired, masters engag'd, and the schools opened, I think, in the same year, 1749.

The scholars increasing fast, the house was soon found too small, and we were looking out for a piece of ground, properly situated, with intention to build, when Providence threw into our way a large house ready built, which, with a few alterations, might well serve our purpose. This was the building before mentioned, erected by the hearers of Mr Whitefield, and was obtained for us in the following manner.

It is to be noted that the contributions to this building being made by people of different sects, care was taken in the nomination of trustees, in whom the building and ground was to be vested, that a predominancy should not be given to any sect, lest in time that predominancy might be a means of appropriating the whole to the use of such sect, contrary to the original intention. It was therefore that one of each sect was appointed, viz., one Church-of-England man, one Presbyterian, one Baptist, one Moravian, etc., those, in case of vacancy by death, were to fill it by election from among the contributors. The Moravian happen'd not to please his colleagues, and on his death they resolved to have no other of that sect. The difficulty then was, how to avoid having two of some other sect, by means of the new choice.

Several persons were named, and for that reason not agreed to. At length one mention'd me, with the observation that I was merely an honest man, and of no sect at all, which prevail'd with them to chuse me. The enthusiasm which existed when the house was built had long since abated, and its trustees had not been able to procure fresh contributions for paying the ground-rent, and discharging some other debts the building had occasion'd, which embarrass'd them greatly. Being now a member of both setts of trustees, that for the building and that for the Academy, I had a good opportunity of negotiating with both, and brought them finally to an agreement, by which the trustees for the building were to cede it to those of the academy, the latter undertaking to discharge the debt, to keep for ever open in the building a large hall for occasional preachers, according to the original intention, and maintain a free-school for the instruction of poor children. Writings were accordingly drawn, and on paying the debts the trustees of the academy were put in possession of the premises; and by dividing the great and lofty hall into stories, and different rooms above and below for the several schools, and purchasing some additional ground, the whole was soon made fit for our purpose, and the scholars remov'd into the building. The care and trouble of agreeing with the workmen, purchasing materials, and superintending the work, fell upon me; and I went thro' it the more cheerfully, as it did not then interfere with my private business, having the year before taken a very able, industrious, and honest partner, Mr David Hall, with whose character I was well acquainted, as he had work'd for me four years. He took off my hands all care of the printing-office, paying me punctually my share of the profits. The partnership continued eighteen years, successfully for us both.

The trustees of the academy, after a while, were incorporated by a charter from the governor; their funds were increas'd by contributions in Britain and grants of land from the proprietaries, to which the Assembly has since made considerable addition; and thus was established the present University of Philadelphia. I have been continued one of its trustees from the beginning, now near forty years, and have had the very great pleasure of seeing a number of the youth who have receiv'd their education in it, distinguish'd by their improv'd abilities, serviceable in public stations, and ornaments to their country.

When I disengaged myself, as above mentioned, from private business, I flatter'd myself that, by the sufficient tho' moderate fortune I had acquir'd, I had secured leisure during the rest of my life for philosophical studies and amusements. I purchased all Dr Spence's apparatus, who had come from England to lecture here, and I proceeded in my electrical experiments with great alacrity; but the publick, now considering me as a man of leisure, laid hold of me for their purposes, every part of our civil government, and almost at the same time, imposing some duty upon me. The governor put me into the commission of the peace; the corporation of the city chose me of the common council, and soon after an alderman; and the citizens at large chose me a burgess to represent them in Assembly. This latter station was the more agreeable to me, as I was at length tired with sitting there to hear debates, in which, as clerk, I could take no part, and which were often so unentertaining that I was induc'd to amuse myself with making magic squares or circles, or any thing to avoid weariness; and I conceiv'd my becoming a member would enlarge my power of doing good. I would not, however, insinuate that my ambition was not flatter'd by all these promotions; it certainly was; for, considering my low beginning, they were great things to me; and they were still more pleasing, as being so many spontaneous testimonies of the public good opinion, and by me entirely unsolicited.

The office of justice of the peace I try'd a little, by attending a few courts, and sitting on the bench to hear causes; but finding that more knowledge of the common law than I possess'd was necessary to act in that station with credit, I gradually withdrew from it, excusing myself by my being oblig'd to attend the higher duties of a legislator in the Assembly. My election to this trust was repeated every year for ten years, without my ever asking any elector for his vote, or signifying, either directly or indirectly, any desire of being chosen. On taking my seat in the House, my son was appointed their clerk.

The year following, a treaty being to be held with the Indians at Carlisle, the governor sent a message to the House, proposing that they should nominate some of their members, to be join'd with some members of council, as commissioners for that purpose.[1] The House named the speaker (Mr Norris) and myself; and, being commission'd, we went to Carlisle, and met the Indians accordingly.

As those people are extreamly apt to get drunk, and, when so, are very quarrelsome and disorderly, we strictly forbad the selling any liquor to them; and when they complain'd of this restriction, we told them that if they would continue sober during the treaty, we would give them plenty of rum when business was over. They promis'd this, and they

[1] See the votes to have this more correctly.—[*Marg. note.*]

kept their promise, because they could get no liquor, and the treaty was conducted very orderly, and concluded to mutual satisfaction. They then claim'd and receiv'd the rum; this was in the afternoon: they were near one hundred men, women, and children, and were lodg'd in temporary cabins, built in the form of a square, just without the town. In the evening, hearing a great noise among them, the commissioners walk'd out to see what was the matter. We found they had made a great bonfire in the middle of the square; they were all drunk, men and women, quarreling and fighting. Their dark-colour'd bodies, half naked, seen only by the gloomy light of the bonfire, running after and beating one another with firebrands, accompanied by their horrid yellings, form'd a scene the most resembling our ideas of hell that could well be imagin'd; there was no appeasing the tumult, and we retired to our lodging. At midnight a number of them came thundering at our door, demanding more rum, of which we took no notice.

The next day, sensible they had misbehav'd in giving us that disturbance, they sent three of their old counselors to make their apology. The orator acknowledg'd the fault, but laid it upon the rum; and then endeavored to excuse the rum by saying, "*The Great Spirit, who made all things, made every thing for some use, and whatever use he design'd any thing for, that use it should always be put to. Now, when he made rum, he said, 'Let this be for the Indians to get drunk with,' and it must be so.*" And, indeed, if it be the design of Providence to extirpate these savages in order to make room for cultivators of the earth, it seems not improbable that rum may be the appointed means. It has already annihilated all the tribes who formerly inhabited the sea-coast.

In 1751, Dr Thomas Bond, a particular friend of mine, conceived the idea of establishing a hospital in Philadelphia (a very beneficent design, which has been ascrib'd to me, but was originally his), for the reception and cure of poor sick persons, whether inhabitants of the province or strangers. He was zealous and active in endeavouring to procure subscriptions for it, but the proposal being a novelty in America, and at first not well understood, he met with but small success.

At length he came to me with the compliment that he found there was no such thing as carrying a public-spirited project through without my being concern'd in it. "For," says he, "I am often ask'd by those to whom I propose subscribing, Have you consulted Franklin upon this business? And what does he think of it? And when I tell them that I have not (supposing it rather out of your line), they do not subscribe, but say they will consider of it." I enquired into the nature and probable utility of his scheme, and receiving from him a very satisfactory explanation, I not only subscrib'd to it myself, but engag'd heartily in the design of procuring subscriptions from others. Previously, however, to the solicitation, I endeavoured to prepare the minds of the people by writing on the subject in the newspapers, which was my usual custom in such cases, but which he had omitted.

The subscriptions afterwards were more free and generous; but, beginning to flag, I saw they would be insufficient without some assistance from the Assembly, and therefore propos'd to petition for it, which was done. The country members did not at first relish the project; they objected that it could only be serviceable to the city, and therefore the citizens alone should be at the expense of it; and they doubted whether the citizens themselves generally approv'd of it. My allegation on the contrary, that it met with such approbation as to leave no doubt of our being able to raise two thousand pounds by voluntary donations, they considered as a most extravagant supposition, and utterly impossible.

On this I form'd my plan; and, asking leave to bring in a bill for incorporating the contributors according to the prayer of their petition, and granting them a blank sum of money, which leave was obtained chiefly on the consideration that the House could throw the bill out if they did not like it, I drew it so as to make the important clause a conditional one, viz., "And be it enacted, by the authority aforesaid, that when the said contributors shall have met and chosen their managers and treasurer, *and shall have raised by their contributions a capital stock of* ——— *value* (the yearly interest of which is to be applied to the accommodating of the sick poor in the said hospital, free of charge for diet, attendance, advice, and medicines), *and shall make the same appear to the satisfaction of the speaker of the Assembly for the time being*, that *then* it shall and may be lawful for the said speaker, and he is hereby required, to sign an order on the provincial treasurer for the payment of two thousand pounds, in two yearly payments, to the treasurer of the said hospital, to be applied to the founding, building, and finishing of the same."

This condition carried the bill through; for the members, who had oppos'd the grant, and now conceiv'd they might have the credit of being charitable without the expence, agreed to its passage; and then, in soliciting subscriptions among the people, we urg'd the conditional promise of the law as an additional motive to give, since every man's donation would be doubled; thus the clause work'd both ways. The subscriptions accordingly soon exceeded the requisite sum, and we claim'd and receiv'd the public gift, which enabled us to carry the design into execution. A convenient and handsome building was soon erected; the institution has by constant experience been found useful, and flourishes to this day; and I do not remember any of my political manœuvres, the success of which gave me at the time more pleasure, or wherein, after thinking of it, I more easily excus'd myself for having made some use of cunning.

It was about this time that another projector, the Rev. Gilbert Tennent, came to me with a request that I would assist him in procuring a subscription for erecting a new meeting-house. It was to be for the use of a congregation he had gathered among the Presbyterians, who were originally disciples of Mr Whitfield. Unwilling to make myself disagreeable to my fellow-citizens by too frequently soliciting their contributions, I absolutely refus'd. He then desired I would furnish him with a list of the names of persons I knew by experience to be generous and public-spirited. I thought it would be unbecoming in me, after their kind compliance with my solicitations, to mark them out to be worried by other beggars, and therefore refus'd also to give such a list. He then desir'd I would at least give him my advice. "That I will readily do," said I; "and, in the first place, I advise you to apply to all those whom you know will give something; next, to those whom you are uncertain whether they will give any thing or not, and show them the list of those who have given; and, lastly, do not neglect those who you are sure will give nothing, for in some of them you may be mistaken." He laugh'd and thank'd me, and said he would take my advice. He did so, for he ask'd of *everybody*, and he obtain'd a much larger sum than he expected, with which he erected the capacious and very elegant meeting-house that stands in Arch-street.

Our city, tho' laid out with a beautiful regularity, the streets large, strait, and crossing each other at right angles, had the disgrace of suffering those streets to remain long unpav'd, and in wet weather the wheels of heavy carriages plough'd them into a quagmire, so that it was difficult to cross them; and in dry weather the dust was offensive. I had liv'd near what was call'd the Jersey Market, and saw with pain the inhabitants wading in mud while purchasing their provisions. A strip of ground down the middle of that market was at length pav'd with brick, so that, being once in the market, they had firm footing, but were often over shoes in dirt to get there. By talking and writing on the subject, I was at length instrumental in getting the street pav'd with stone between the market and the brick'd foot-pavement, that was on each side next the houses. This, for some time, gave an easy access to the market dry-shod; but, the rest of the street not being pav'd, whenever a carriage came out of the mud upon this pavement, it shook off and left its dirt upon it, and it was soon cover'd with mire, which was not remov'd, the city as yet having no scavengers.

After some inquiry, I found a poor, industrious man, who was willing to undertake keeping the pavement clean, by sweeping it twice a week, carrying off the dirt from before all the neighbours' doors, for the sum of sixpence per month, to be paid by each house. I then wrote and printed a paper setting forth the advantages to the neighbourhood that might be obtain'd by this small expense; the greater ease in keeping our houses clean, so much dirt not being brought in by people's feet; the benefit to the shops by more custom, etc., etc., as buyers could more easily get at them; and by not having, in windy weather, the dust blown in upon their goods, etc., etc. I sent one of these papers to each house, and in a day or two went round to see who would subscribe an agreement to pay these sixpences; it was unanimously sign'd, and for a time well executed. All the inhabitants of the city were delighted with the cleanliness of the pavement that surrounded the market, it being a convenience to all, and this rais'd a general desire to have all the streets paved, and made the people more willing to submit to a tax for that purpose.

After some time I drew a bill for paving the city, and brought it into the Assembly. It was just before I went to England, in 1757, and did not pass till I was gone,[1] and then with an alteration in the mode of assessment, which I thought not for the better, but with an additional provision for lighting as well as paving the streets, which was a great improvement. It was by a private person, the late Mr John Clifton, his giving a sample of the utility of lamps, by placing one at his door, that the people were first impress'd with the idea of enlighting all the city. The honour of this public benefit has also been ascrib'd to me, but it belongs truly to that gentleman. I did but follow his example, and have only some merit to claim respecting the form of our lamps, as differing from the globe lamps we were at first supply'd with from London. Those we found inconvenient in these respects: they admitted no air below; the smoke, therefore, did not readily go out above, but circulated in the globe, lodg'd on its inside, and soon obstructed the light they were intended to afford; giving, besides, the daily trouble of wiping them clean; and an accidental stroke on one of them would demolish it, and render it totally useless. I therefore suggested the composing them of four flat panes, with a long funnel above to draw up the smoke, and crevices admitting air below, to facilitate the ascent of the smoke; by this means they were kept clean, and did not grow dark in a few hours, as the London lamps do, but continu'd

[1] See votes.

bright till morning, and an accidental stroke would generally break but a single pane, easily repair'd.

I have sometimes wonder'd that the Londoners did not, from the effect holes in the bottom of the globe lamps us'd at Vauxhall have in keeping them clean, learn to have such holes in their street lamps. But, these holes being made for another purpose, viz., to communicate flame more suddenly to the wick by a little flax hanging down thro' them, the other use, of letting in air, seems not to have been thought of; and therefore, after the lamps have been lit a few hours, the streets of London are very poorly illuminated.

The mention of these improvements puts me in mind of one I propos'd, when in London, to Dr Fothergill, who was among the best men I have known, and a great promoter of useful projects. I had observ'd that the streets, when dry, were never swept, and the light dust carried away; but it was suffer'd to accumulate till wet weather reduc'd it to mud, and then, after lying some days so deep on the pavement that there was no crossing but in paths kept clean by poor people with brooms, it was with great labour rak'd together and thrown up into carts open above, the sides of which suffer'd some of the slush at every jolt on the pavement to shake out and fall, sometimes to the annoyance of foot-passengers. The reason given for not sweeping the dusty streets was, that the dust would fly into the windows of shops and houses.

An accidental occurrence had instructed me how much sweeping might be done in a little time. I found at my door in Craven-street, one morning, a poor woman sweeping my pavement with a birch broom; she appeared very pale and feeble, as just come out of a fit of sickness. I ask'd who employ'd her to sweep there; she said, "Nobody, but I am very poor and in distress, and I sweeps before gentlefolkses doors, and hopes they will give me something." I bid her sweep the whole street clean, and I would give her a shilling; this was at nine o'clock; at 12 she came for the shilling. From the slowness I saw at first in her working, I could scarce believe that the work was done so soon, and sent my servant to examine it, who reported that the whole street was swept perfectly clean, and all the dust plac'd in the gutter, which was in the middle; and the next rain wash'd it quite away, so that the pavement and even the kennel were perfectly clean.

I then judg'd that, if that feeble woman could sweep such a street in three hours, a strong, active man might have done it in half the time. And here let me remark the convenience of having but one gutter in such a narrow street, running down its middle, instead of two, one on each side, near the footway; for where all the rain that falls on a street runs from the sides and meets in the middle, it forms there a current strong enough to wash away all the mud it meets with; but when divided into two channels, it is often too weak to cleanse either, and only makes the mud it finds more fluid, so that the wheels of carriages and feet of horses throw and dash it upon the foot-pavement, which is thereby rendered foul and slippery, and sometimes splash it upon those who are walking. My proposal, communicated to the good doctor, was as follows:

"For the more effectual cleaning and keeping clean the streets of London and Westminster, it is proposed that the several watchmen be contracted with to have the dust swept up in dry seasons, and the mud rak'd up at other times, each in the several streets and lanes of his round; that they be furnish'd with brooms and other proper instruments for these purposes, to be kept at their respective stands, ready to furnish the poor people they may employ in the service.

"That in the dry summer months the dust be all swept up into heaps at proper distances, before the shops and windows of houses are usually opened, when the scavengers, with close-covered carts, shall also carry it all away.

"That the mud, when rak'd up, be not left in heaps to be spread abroad again by the wheels of carriages and trampling of horses, but that the scavengers be provided with bodies of carts, not plac'd high upon wheels, but low upon sliders, with lattice bottoms, which, being cover'd with straw, will retain the mud thrown into them, and permit the water to drain from it, whereby it will become much lighter, water making the greatest part of its weight; these bodies of carts to be plac'd at convenient distances, and the mud brought to them in wheelbarrows; they remaining where plac'd till the mud is drain'd, and then horses brought to draw them away."

I have since had doubts of the practicability of the latter part of this proposal, on account of the narrowness of some streets, and the difficulty of placing the draining-sleds so as not to encumber too much the passage; but I am still of opinion that the former, requiring the dust to be swept up and carry'd away before the shops are open, is very practicable in the summer, when the days are long; for, in walking thro' the Strand and Fleet-street one morning at seven o'clock, I observ'd there was not one shop open, tho' it had been daylight and the sun up above three hours; the inhabitants of London chusing voluntarily to live much by candle-light, and sleep by sunshine, and yet often complain, a little absurdly, of the duty on candles, and the high price of tallow.

Some may think these trifling matters not worth minding or relating; but when they consider that tho' dust blown into the eyes of a single person, or into a single shop on a windy day, is but of small importance, yet the great number of the instances in a populous city, and its frequent repetitions give it weight and consequence, perhaps they will not censure very severely those who bestow some attention to affairs of this seemingly low nature. Human felicity is produc'd not so much by great pieces of good fortune that seldom happen, as by little advantages that occur every day. Thus, if you teach a poor young man to shave himself, and keep his razor in order, you may contribute more to the happiness of his life than in giving him a thousand guineas. The money may be soon spent, the regret only remaining of having foolishly consumed it; but in the other case, he escapes the frequent vexation of waiting for barbers, and of their sometimes dirty fingers, offensive breaths, and dull razors; he shaves when most convenient to him, and enjoys daily the pleasure of its being done with a good instrument. With these sentiments I have hazarded the few preceding pages, hoping they may afford hints which some time or other may be useful to a city I love, having lived many years in it very happily, and perhaps to some of our towns in America.

Having been for some time employed by the postmaster-general of America as his comptroller in regulating several offices, and bringing the officers to account, I was, upon his death in 1753, appointed, jointly with Mr William Hunter, to succeed him, by a commission from the postmaster-general in England. The American office never had hitherto paid any thing to that of Britain. We were to have six hundred pounds a year between us, if we could make that sum out of the profits of the office. To do this, a variety of improvements were necessary; some of these were inevitably at first expensive, so that in the first four years the office became above nine hundred pounds in debt to us. But it soon after began to repay us; and before I was displac'd by a freak of the ministers, of which I shall speak hereafter, we had brought it to yield *three times* as much clear revenue to the crown as the postoffice of Ireland. Since that imprudent transaction, they have receiv'd from it—not one farthing!

The business of the postoffice occasion'd my taking a journey this year to New England, where the College of Cambridge, of their own motion, presented me with the degree of Master of Arts. Yale College, in Connecticut, had before made me a similar compliment. Thus, without studying in any college, I came to partake of their honours. They were conferr'd in consideration of my improvements and discoveries in the electric branch of natural philosophy.

In 1754, war with France being again apprehended, a congress of commissioners from the different colonies was, by order of the Lord of Trade, to be assembled at Albany, there to confer with the chiefs of the Six Nations concerning the means of defending both their country and ours. Governor Hamilton, having receiv'd this order, acquainted the House with it, requesting they would furnish proper presents for the Indians, to be given on this occasion; and naming the speaker (Mr Norris) and myself to join Mr Thomas Penn and Mr Secretary Peters as commissioners to act for Pennsylvania. The House approv'd the nomination, and provided the goods for the present, and tho' they did not much like treating out of the provinces; and we met the other commissioners at Albany about the middle of June.

In our way thither, I projected and drew a plan for the union of all the colonies under one government, so far as might be necessary for defense, and other important general purposes. As we pass'd thro' New York, I had there shown my project to Mr James Alexander and Mr Kennedy, two gentlemen of great knowledge in public affairs, and, being fortified by their approbation, I ventur'd to lay it before the Congress. It then appeared that several of the commissioners had form'd plans of the same kind. A previous question was first taken, whether a union should be established, which pass'd in the affirmative unanimously. A committee was then appointed, one member from each colony, to consider the several plans and report. Mine happen'd to be preferr'd, and, with a few amendments, was accordingly reported.

By this plan the general government was to be administered by a president-general, appointed and supported by the crown, and a grand council was to be chosen by the representatives of the people of the several colonies, met in their respective assemblies. The debates upon it in Congress went on daily, hand in hand with the Indian business. Many objections and difficulties were started, but at length they were all overcome, and the plan was unanimously agreed to, and copies ordered to be transmitted to the Board of Trade and to the assemblies of the several provinces. Its fate was singular: the assemblies did not adopt it, as they all thought there was too much *prerogative* in it, and in England it was judg'd to have too much of the *democratic*. The Board of Trade therefore did not approve of it, nor recommend it for the approbation of his majesty; but another scheme was form'd, supposed to answer the same purpose better, whereby the governors of the provinces, with some members of their respective councils, were to meet and order the raising of troops, building of forts, etc., and to draw on the treasury of Great Britain for the expense, which was afterwards to be refunded by an act of Parliament laying a tax on America. My plan, with my reasons in support of it, is to be found among my political papers that are printed.

Being the winter following in Boston, I had much conversation with Governor Shirley upon both the plans. Part of what passed between us on the occasion may also be seen among those papers. The different and contrary reasons of dislike to my plan makes me suspect that it was really the true medium; and I am still of opinion it would have been happy for both sides the water if it had been adopted. The colonies, so united, would have been sufficiently strong to have defended themselves; there would then have been no need of troops from England; of course, the subsequent pretence for taxing America, and the bloody contest it occasioned, would have been avoided. But such mistakes are not new; history is full of the errors of states and princes.

> "Look round the habitable world, how few
> Know their own good, or, knowing it, pursue!"

Those who govern, having much business on their hands, do not generally like to take the trouble of considering and carrying into execution new projects. The best public measures are therefore seldom *adopted from previous wisdom, but forc'd by the occasion.*

The Governor of Pennsylvania, in sending it down to the Assembly, express'd his approbation of the plan, "as appearing to him to be drawn up with great clearness and strength of judgment, and therefore recommended it as well worthy of their closest and most serious attention." The House, however, by the management of a certain member, took it up when I happen'd to be absent, which I thought not very fair, and reprobated it without paying any attention to it at all, to my no small mortification.

In my journey to Boston this year, I met at New York with our new governor, Mr Morris, just arriv'd there from England, with whom I had been before intimately acquainted. He brought a commission to supersede Mr Hamilton, who, tir'd with the disputes his proprietary instructions subjected him to, had resign'd. Mr Morris ask'd me if I thought he must expect as uncomfortable an administration. I said, "No; you may, on the contrary, have a very comfortable one, if you will only take care not to enter into any dispute with the Assembly." "My dear friend," says he, pleasantly, "how can you advise my avoiding disputes? You know I love disputing; it is one of my greatest pleasures; however, to show the regard I have for your counsel, I promise you I will, if possible, avoid them." He had some reason for loving to dispute, being eloquent, an acute sophister, and, therefore, generally successful in argumentative conversation. He had been brought up to it from a boy, his father, as I have heard, accustoming his children to dispute with one another for his diversion, while sitting at table after dinner; but I think the practice was not wise; for, in the course of my observation, these disputing, contradicting, and confuting people are generally unfortunate in their affairs. They get victory sometimes, but they never get good will, which would be of more use to them. We parted, he going to Philadelphia, and I to Boston.

In returning, I met at New York with the votes of the Assembly, by which it appear'd that, notwithstanding his promise to me, he and the House were already in high contention; and it was a continual battle between them as long as he retain'd the government. I had my share of it; for, as soon as I got back to my seat in the Assembly, I was put on every committee for answering his speeches and messages, and by the committees always desired to make the drafts. Our answers, as well as his messages, were often tart, and sometimes indecently abusive; and, as he knew I wrote for the Assembly, one might have imagined that, when we met, we could hardly avoid cutting throats; but he was so good-natur'd a man that no personal difference between him and me was occasion'd by the contest, and we often din'd together.

One afternoon, in the height of this public quarrel, we met in the street. "Franklin," says he, "you must go home with me and spend the evening; I am to have some company that you will like"; and, taking me by the arm, he led me to his house. In gay conversation over our wine, after supper, he told us, jokingly, that he much admir'd the idea of Sancho Panza, who, when it was proposed to give him a government, requested it might be a government of *blacks*, as then, if he could not agree with his people, he might sell them. One of his friends, who sat next to me, says, "Franklin, why do you continue to side with these damn'd Quakers? Had not you better sell them? The proprietor would give you a good price." "The governor," says I, "has not yet *blacked* them enough." He, indeed, had labored hard to blacken the Assembly in all his messages, but they wip'd off his coloring as fast as he laid it on, and plac'd it, in return, thick upon his own face; so that, finding he was likely to be negrofied himself, he, as well as Mr Hamilton, grew tir'd of the contest, and quitted the government.

[1] These public quarrels were all at bottom owing to the proprietaries, our hereditary governors, who, when any expense was to be incurred for the defense of their province, with incredible meanness instructed their deputies to pass no act for levying the necessary taxes, unless their vast estates were

[1] My acts in Morris's time, military, etc.—[*Marg. note.*]

in the same act expressly excused; and they had even taken bonds of these deputies to observe such instructions. The Assemblies for three years held out against this injustice, tho' constrained to bend at last. At length Captain Denny, who was Governor Morris's successor, ventured to disobey those instructions; how that was brought about I shall show hereafter.

But I am got forward too fast with my story: there are still some transactions to be mention'd that happened during the administration of Governor Morris.

War being in a manner commenced with France, the government of Massachusetts Bay projected an attack upon Crown Point, and sent Mr Quincy to Pennsylvania, and Mr Pownall, afterward Governor Pownall, to New York, to solicit assistance. As I was in the Assembly, knew its temper, and was Mr Quincy's countryman, he appli'd to me for my influence and assistance. I dictated his address to them, which was well receiv'd. They voted an aid of ten thousand pounds, to be laid out in provisions. But the governor refusing his assent to their bill (which included this with other sums granted for the use of the crown), unless a clause were inserted exempting the proprietary estate from bearing any part of the tax that would be necessary, the Assembly, tho' very desirous of making their grant to New England effectual, were at a loss how to accomplish it. Mr Quincy labored hard with the governor to obtain his assent, but he was obstinate.

I then suggested a method of doing the business without the governor, by orders on the trustees of the Loan Office, which, by law, the Assembly had the right of drawing. There was, indeed, little or no money at that time in the office, and therefore I propos'd that the orders should be payable in a year, and to bear an interest of five per cent. With these orders I suppos'd the provisions might easily be purchas'd. The Assembly, with very little hesitation, adopted the proposal. The orders were immediately printed, and I was one of the committee directed to sign and dispose of them. The fund for paying them was the interest of all the paper currency then extant in the province upon loan, together with the revenue arising from the excise, which being known to be more than sufficient, they obtain'd instant credit, and were not only receiv'd in payment for the provisions, but many money'd people, who had cash lying by them, vested it in those orders, which they found advantageous, as they bore interest while upon hand, and might on any occasion be used as money; so that they were eagerly all bought up, and in a few weeks none of them were to be seen. Thus this important affair was by my means compleated. Mr Quincy return'd thanks to the Assembly in a handsome memorial, went home highly pleas'd with the success of his embassy, and ever after bore for me the most cordial and affectionate friendship.

The British government, not chusing to permit the union of the colonies as propos'd at Albany, and to trust that union with their defense, lest they should thereby grow too military, and feel their own strength, suspicions and jealousies at this time being entertain'd of them, sent over General Braddock with two regiments of regular English troops for that purpose. He landed at Alexandria, in Virginia, and thence march'd to Frederictown, in Maryland, where he halted for carriages. Our Assembly apprehending, from some information, that he had conceived violent prejudices against them, as averse to the service, wish'd me to wait upon him, not as from them, but as postmaster-general, under the guise of proposing to settle with him the mode of conducting with most celerity and certainty the despatches between him and the governors of the several provinces, with whom he must necessarily have continual correspondence, and of which they propos'd to pay the expense. My son accompanied me on this journey.

We found the general at Frederictown, waiting impatiently for the return of those he had sent thro' the back parts of Maryland and Virginia to collect waggons. I stayed with him several days, din'd with him daily, and had full opportunity of removing all his prejudices, by the information of what the Assembly had before his arrival actually done, and were still willing to do, to facilitate his operations. When I was about to depart, the returns of waggons to be obtained were brought in, by which it appear'd that they amounted only to twenty-five, and not all of those were in serviceable condition. The general and all the officers were surpris'd, declar'd the expedition was then at an end, being impossible, and exclaim'd against the ministers for ignorantly landing them in a country destitute of the means of conveying their stores, baggage, etc., not less than one hundred and fifty waggons being necessary.

I happen'd to say I thought it was pity they had not been landed rather in Pennsylvania, as in that country almost every farmer had his waggon. The general eagerly laid hold of my words, and said, "Then you, sir, who are a man of interest there, can probably procure them for us; and I beg you will undertake it." I ask'd what terms were to be offer'd the owners of the waggons; and I was desir'd to put on paper the terms that appeared to me necessary. This I did, and they were agreed to, and a commission and instructions accordingly prepar'd immediately. What those terms were will appear in the advertisement I publish'd as soon as I arriv'd at Lancaster, which being, from the great and sudden effect it produc'd, a piece of some curiosity, I shall insert it at length, as follows:

"ADVERTISEMENT.

"LANCASTER, *April* 26, 1755.

"Whereas, one hundred and fifty waggons, with four horses to each waggon, and fifteen hundred saddle or pack horses, are wanted for the service of his majesty's forces now about to rendezvous at Will's Creek, and his excellency General Braddock having been pleased to empower me to contract for the hire of the same, I hereby give notice that I shall attend for that purpose at Lancaster from this day to next Wednesday evening, and at York from next Thursday morning till Friday evening, where I shall be ready to agree for waggons and teams, or single horses, on the following terms, viz.: 1. That there shall be paid for each waggon, with four good horses and a driver, fifteen shillings per diem; and for each able horse with a pack-saddle, or other saddle and furniture, two shillings per diem; and for each able horse without a saddle, eighteen pence per diem. 2. That the pay commence from the time of their joining the forces at Will's Creek, which must be on or before the 20th of May ensuing, and that a reasonable allowance be paid over and above for the time necessary for their travelling to Will's Creek and home again after their discharge. 3. Each waggon and team, and every saddle or pack horse, is to be valued by indifferent persons chosen between me and the owner; and in case of the loss of any waggon, team, or other horse in the service, the price according to such valuation is to be allowed and paid. 4. Seven days' pay is to be advanced and paid in hand by me to the owner of each waggon and team, or horse, at the time of contracting, if required, and the remainder to be paid by

General Braddock, or by the paymaster of the army, at the time of their discharge, or from time to time, as it shall be demanded. 5. No drivers of waggons, or persons taking care of the hired horses, are on any account to be called upon to do the duty of soldiers, or be otherwise employed than in conducting or taking care of their carriages or horses. 6. All oats, Indian corn, or other forage that waggons or horses bring to the camp, more than is necessary for the subsistence of the horses, is to be taken for the use of the army, and a reasonable price paid for the same.

"Note. — My son, William Franklin, is empowered to enter into like contracts with any person in Cumberland county. B. FRANKLIN."

"*To the inhabitants of the Counties of Lancaster, York and Cumberland.*

"Friends and Countrymen,

"Being occasionally at the camp at Frederic a few days since, I found the general and officers extremely exasperated on account of their not being supplied with horses and carriages, which had been expected from this province, as most able to furnish them; but, through the dissensions between our governor and Assembly, money had not been provided, nor any steps taken for that purpose.

"It was proposed to send an armed force immediately into these counties, to seize as many of the best carriages and horses as should be wanted, and compel as many persons into the service as would be necessary to drive and take care of them.

"I apprehended that the progress of British soldiers through these counties on such an occasion, especially considering the temper they are in, and their resentment against us, would be attended with many and great inconveniences to the inhabitants, and therefore more willingly took the trouble of trying first what might be done by fair and equitable means. The people of these back counties have lately complained to the Assembly that a sufficient currency was wanting; you have an opportunity of receiving and dividing among you a very considerable sum; for, if the service of this expedition should continue, as it is more than probable it will, for one hundred and twenty days, the hire of these waggons and horses will amount to upward of thirty thousand pounds, which will be paid you in silver and gold of the king's money.

"The service will be light and easy, for the army will scarce march above twelve miles per day, and the waggons and baggage-horses, as they carry those things that are absolutely necessary to the welfare of the army, must march with the army, and no faster; and are, for the army's sake, always placed where they can be most secure, whether in a march or in a camp.

"If you are really, as I believe you are, good and loyal subjects to his majesty, you may now do a most acceptable service, and make it easy to yourselves; for three or four of such as can not separately spare from the business of their plantations a waggon and four horses and a driver, may do it together, one furnishing the waggon, another one or two horses, and another the driver, and divide the pay proportionably between you; but if you do not this service to your king and country voluntarily, when such good pay and reasonable terms are offered to you, your loyalty will be strongly suspected. The king's business must be done; so many brave troops, come so far for your defense, must not stand idle through your backwardness to do what may be reasonably expected from you; waggons and horses must be had; violent measures will probably be used, and you will be left to seek for a recompense where you can find it, and your case, perhaps, be little pitied or regarded.

"I have no particular interest in this affair, as, except the satisfaction of endeavoring to do good, I shall have only my labour for my pains. If this method of obtaining the waggons and horses is not likely to succeed, I am obliged to send word to the general in fourteen days; and I suppose Sir John St Clair, the hussar, with a body of soldiers, will immediately enter the province for the purpose, which I shall be sorry to hear, because I am very sincerely and truly your friend and well-wisher,

"B. FRANKLIN."

I received of the general about eight hundred pounds, to be disbursed in advance-money to the waggon owners, etc.; but that sum being insufficient, I advanc'd upward of two hundred pounds more, and in two weeks the one hundred and fifty waggons, with two hundred and fifty-nine carrying horses, were on their march for the camp. The advertisement promised payment according to the valuation, in case any waggon or horse should be lost. The owners, however, alleging they did not know General Braddock, or what dependence might be had on his promise, insisted on my bond for the performance, which I accordingly gave them.

While I was at the camp, supping one evening with the officers of Colonel Dunbar's regiment, he represented to me his concern for the subalterns, who, he said, were generally not in affluence, and could ill afford, in this dear country, to lay in the stores that might be necessary in so long a march, thro' a wilderness, where nothing was to be purchas'd. I commiserated their case, and resolved to endeavor procuring them some relief. I said nothing, however, to him of my intention, but wrote the next morning to the committee of the Assembly, who had the disposition of some public money, warmly recommending the case of these officers to their consideration, and proposing that a present should be sent them of necessaries and refreshments. My son, who had some experience of a camp life, and of its wants, drew up a list for me, which I enclos'd in my letter. The committee approv'd, and used such diligence that, conducted by my son, the stores arrived at the camp as soon as the waggons. They consisted of twenty parcels, each containing

6 lbs. loaf sugar.	1 Gloucester cheese.
6 lbs. good Muscovado do.	1 kegg containing 20 lbs. good butter.
1 lb. good green tea.	2 doz. old Madeira wine.
1 lb. good bohea do.	2 gallons Jamaica spirits.
6 lbs. good ground coffee.	1 bottle flour of mustard
6 lbs. chocolate.	2 well-cur'd hams.
1-2 cwt. best white biscuit.	1-2 dozen dry'd tongues.
1-2 lb. pepper.	6 lbs. rice.
1 quart best white wine vinegar.	6 lbs. raisins.

These twenty parcels, well pack'd, were placed on as many horses, each parcel, with the horse, being intended as a present for one officer. They were very thankfully receiv'd, and the kindness acknowledg'd by letters to me from the colonels of both regiments, in the most grateful terms. The general, too, was highly satisfied with my conduct in procuring him the waggons, etc., and readily paid my account of disbursements, thanking me repeatedly, and requesting my farther assistance in sending provisions after him. I undertook this also, and was busily employ'd in it till we heard of his defeat, advancing for the service of my own money, upwards of one thousand pounds sterling, of which I sent him an account. It came to his hands, luckily for me, a few days before the battle, and he return'd me immediately an order on the paymaster for the round sum of one thousand pounds, leaving the remainder to the next account. I consider this payment as good luck, having never been able to obtain that remainder, of which more hereafter.

This general was, I think, a brave man, and might probably have made a figure as a good officer in some European war. But he had too much self-confidence, too high an opinion of the validity of regular troops, and too mean a one of both Americans and Indians. George Croghan, our Indian interpreter, join'd him on his march with one hundred of those people, who might have been of great use to his army as guides, scouts, etc., if he had treated them kindly; but he slighted and neglected them, and they gradually left him.

In conversation with him one day, he was giving me some account of his intended progress. "After taking Fort Duquesne," says he, "I am to proceed to Niagara; and, having taken that, to Frontenac, if the season will allow time; and I suppose it will, for Duquesne can hardly detain me above three or four days; and then I see nothing that can obstruct my march to Niagara." Having before revolv'd in my mind the long line his army must make in their march by a very narrow road, to be cut for them thro' the woods and bushes, and also what I had read of a former defeat of fifteen hundred French, who invaded the Iroquois country, I had conceiv'd some doubts and some fears for the event of the campaign. But I ventur'd only to say, "To be sure, sir, if you arrive well before Duquesne, with these fine troops, so well provided with artillery, that place not yet completely fortified, and as we hear with no very strong garrison, can probably make but a short resistance. The only danger I apprehend of obstruction to your march is from ambuscades of Indians, who, by constant practice, are dexterous in laying and executing them; and the slender line, near four miles long, which your army must make, may expose it to be attack'd by surprise in its flanks, and to be cut like a thread into several pieces, which, from their distance, can not come up in time to support each other."

He smil'd at my ignorance, and reply'd, "These savages may, indeed, be a formidable enemy to your raw American militia, but upon the king's regular and disciplin'd troops, sir, it is impossible they should make any impression." I was conscious of an impropriety in my disputing with a military man in matters of his profession, and said no more. The enemy, however, did not take the advantage of his army which I apprehended its long line of march expos'd it to, but let it advance without interruption till within nine miles of the place; and then, when more in a body (for it had just passed a river, where the front had halted till all were come over), and in a more open part of the woods than any it had pass'd, attack'd its advanced guard by a heavy fire from behind trees and bushes, which was the first intelligence the general had of an enemy's being near him. This guard being disordered, the general hurried the troops up to their assistance, which was done in great confusion, thro' waggons, baggage, and cattle; and presently the fire came upon their flank: the officers, being on horseback, were more easily distinguish'd, pick'd out as marks, and fell very fast; and the soldiers were crowded together in a huddle, having or hearing no orders, and standing to be shot at till two-thirds of them were killed; and then, being seiz'd with a panick, the whole fled with precipitation.

The waggoners took each a horse out of his team and scamper'd; their example was immediately followed by others; so that all the waggons, provisions, artillery, and stores were left to the enemy. The general, being wounded, was brought off with difficulty; his secretary, Mr Shirley, was killed by his side; and out of eighty-six officers, sixty-three were killed or wounded, and seven hundred and fourteen men killed out of eleven hundred. These eleven hundred had been picked men from the whole army; the rest had been left behind with Colonel Dunbar, who was to follow with the heavier part of the stores, provisions, and baggage. The flyers, not being pursu'd, arriv'd at Dunbar's camp, and the panick they brought with them instantly seiz'd him and all his people; and, tho' he had now above one thousand men, and the enemy who had beaten Braddock did not at most exceed four hundred Indians and French together, instead of proceeding, and endeavoring to recover some of the lost honour, he ordered all the stores, ammunition, etc., to be destroy'd, that he might have more horses to assist his flight towards the settlements, and less lumber to remove. He was there met with requests from the governors of Virginia, Maryland, and Pennsylvania, that he would post his troops on the frontier, so as to afford some protection to the inhabitants; but he continu'd his hasty march thro' all the country, not thinking himself safe till he arriv'd at Philadelphia, where the inhabitants could protect him. This whole transaction gave us Americans the first suspicion that our exalted ideas of the prowess of British regulars had not been well founded.

In their first march, too, from their landing till they got beyond the settlements, they had plundered and stripped the inhabitants, totally ruining some poor families, besides insulting, abusing, and confining the people if they remonstrated. This was enough to put us out of conceit of such defenders, if we had really wanted any. How different was the conduct of our French friends in 1781, who, during a march thro' the most inhabited part of our country from Rhode Island to Virginia, near seven hundred miles, occasioned not the smallest complaint for the loss of a pig, a chicken, or even an apple.

Captain Orme, who was one of the general's aids-de-camp, and, being grievously wounded, was brought off with him, and continu'd with him to his death, which happen'd in a few days, told me that he was totally silent all the first day, and at night only said, "*Who would have thought it?*" That he was silent again the following day, saying only at last, "*We shall better know how to deal with them another time*"; and dy'd in a few minutes after.

The secretary's papers, with all the general's orders, instructions, and correspondence, falling into the enemy's hands, they selected and translated into French a number of the articles, which they printed, to prove the hostile intentions of the British court before the declaration of war. Among these I saw some letters of the general to the ministry, speaking highly of the great service I had rendered the army, and recommending me to their notice. David Hume, too, who was some years after secretary to Lord Hertford, when minister in France, and afterward to General Conway, when secretary of state, told me he had seen among the papers in that office, letters from Braddock highly recommending me. But, the expedition having been unfortunate, my service, it seems, was not thought of much value, for those recommendations were never of any use to me.

As to rewards from himself, I ask'd only one, which was, that he would give orders to his officers not to enlist any more of our bought servants, and that he would discharge such as had been already enlisted. This he readily granted, and several were accordingly return'd to their masters, on my application. Dunbar, when the command devolv'd on him, was not so generous. He being at Philadelphia, on his retreat, or rather flight, I apply'd to him for the discharge of the servants of three poor farmers of Lancaster county that he had enlisted, reminding him of the late general's orders on that head. He promised me that, if the masters would come to him at Trenton, where he should be in a few days on his march to New York, he would there deliver their men to them. They accordingly were at the expense and trouble of going to Trenton, and there he refus'd to perform his promise, to their great loss and disappointment.

As soon as the loss of the waggons and horses was generally known, all the owners came upon me for the valuation which I had given bond to pay. Their demands gave me a great deal of trouble, my acquainting them that the money was ready in the paymaster's hands, but that orders for paying it must first be obtained from General Shirley, and my assuring them that I had apply'd to that general by letter; but, he being at a distance, an answer could not soon be receiv'd, and they must have patience, all this was not sufficient to satisfy, and some began to sue me. General Shirley at length relieved me from this terrible situation by appointing commissioners to examine the claims, and ordering payment. They amounted to near twenty thousand pound, which to pay would have ruined me.

Before we had the news of this defeat, the two Doctors Bond came to me with a subscription paper for raising money to defray the expense of a grand firework, which it was intended to exhibit at a rejoicing on receipt of the news of our taking Fort Duquesne. I looked grave, and said it would, I thought, be time enough to prepare for the rejoicing when we knew we should have occasion to rejoice. They seem'd surpris'd that I did not immediately comply with their proposal. "Why the d—l!" says one of them, "you surely don't suppose that the fort will not be taken?" "I don't know that it will not be taken, but I know that the events of war are subject to great uncertainty." I gave them the reasons of my doubting; the subscription was dropt, and the projectors thereby missed the mortification they would have undergone if the firework had been prepared. Dr Bond, on some other occasion afterward, said that he did not like Franklin's forebodings.

Governor Morris, who had continually worried the Assembly with message after message before the defeat of Braddock, to beat them into the making of acts to raise money for the defense of the province, without taxing, among others, the proprietary estates, and had rejected all their bills for not having such an exempting clause, now redoubled his attacks with more hope of success, the danger and necessity being greater. The Assembly, however, continu'd firm, believing they had justice on their side, and that it would be giving up an essential right if they suffered the governor to amend their money-bills. In one of the last, indeed, which was for granting fifty thousand pounds, his propos'd amendment was only of a single word. The bill express'd "that all estates, real and personal, were to be taxed, those of the proprietaries *not* excepted." His amendment was, for *not* read *only:* a small, but very material alteration. However, when the news of this disaster reached England, our friends there, whom we had taken care to furnish with all the Assembly's answers to the governor's messages, rais'd a clamor against the proprietaries for their meanness and injustice in giving their governor such instructions; some going so far as to say that, by obstructing the defense of their province, they forfeited their right to it. They were intimidated by this, and sent orders to their receiver-general to add five thousand pounds of their money to whatever sum might be given by the Assembly for such purpose.

This, being notified to the House, was accepted in lieu of their share of a general tax, and a new bill was form'd, with an exempting clause, which passed accordingly. By this act I was appointed one of the commissioners for disposing of the money, sixty thousand pounds. I had been active in modelling the bill and procuring its passage, and had, at the same time, drawn a bill for establishing and disciplining a voluntary militia, which I carried thro' the House without much difficulty, as care was taken in it to leave the Quakers at their liberty. To promote the association necessary to form the militia, I wrote a dialogue,[1] stating and answering all the objections I could think of to such a militia, which was printed, and had, as I thought, great effect.

While the several companies in the city and country were forming, and learning their exercise, the governor prevail'd with me to take charge of our North-western frontier, which was infested by the enemy, and provide for the defense of the inhabitants by raising troops and building a line of forts. I undertook this military business, tho' I did not conceive myself well qualified for it. He gave me a commission with full powers, and a parcel of blank commissions for officers, to be given to whom I thought fit. I had but little difficulty in raising men, having soon five hundred and sixty under my command. My son, who had in the preceding war been an officer in the army rais'd against Canada, was my aid-de-camp, and of great use to me. The Indians had burned Gnaden-

[1] This dialogue and the militia act are in the Gentleman's Magazine for February and March, 1756.—[*Marg. note.*]

hut, a village settled by the Moravians, and massacred the inhabitants; but the place was thought a good situation for one of the forts.

In order to march thither, I assembled the companies at Bethlehem, the chief establishment of those people. I was surprised to find it in so good a posture of defense; the destruction of Gnadenhut had made them apprehend danger. The principal buildings were defended by a stockade; they had purchased a quantity of arms and ammunition from New York, and had even plac'd quantities of small paving stones between the windows of their high stone houses, for their women to throw down upon the heads of any Indians that should attempt to force into them. The armed brethren, too, kept watch, and reliev'd as methodically as in any garrison town. In conversation with the bishop, Spangenberg, I mention'd this my surprise; for, knowing they had obtained an act of Parliament exempting them from military duties in the colonies, I had suppos'd they were conscientiously scrupulous of bearing arms. He answer'd me that it was not one of their established principles, but that, at the time of their obtaining that act, it was thought to be a principle with many of their people. On this occasion, however, they, to their surprise, found it adopted by but a few. It seems they were either deceiv'd in themselves, or deceiv'd the Parliament; but common sense, aided by present danger, will sometimes be too strong for whimsical opinions.

It was the beginning of January when we set out upon this business of building forts. I sent one detachment toward the Minisink, with instructions to erect one for the security of that upper part of the country, and another to the lower part, with similar instructions; and I concluded to go myself with the rest of my force to Gnadenhut, where a fort was tho't more immediately necessary. The Moravians procur'd me five waggons for our tools, stores, baggage, etc.

Just before we left Bethlehem, eleven farmers, who had been driven from their plantations by the Indians, came to me requesting a supply of firearms, that they might go back and fetch off their cattle. I gave them each a gun with suitable ammunition. We had not march'd many miles before it began to rain, and it continued raining all day; there were no habitations on the road to shelter us, till we arriv'd near night at the house of a German, where, and in his barn, we were all huddled together, as wet as water could make us. It was well we were not attack'd in our march, for our arms were of the most ordinary sort, and our men could not keep their gun locks dry. The Indians are dextrous in contrivances for that purpose, which we had not. They met that day the eleven poor farmers above mentioned, and killed ten of them. The one who escap'd inform'd that his and his companions' guns would not go off, the priming being wet with the rain.

The next day being fair, we continu'd our march, and arriv'd at the desolated Gnadenhut. There was a saw-mill near, round which were left several piles of boards, with which we soon hutted ourselves; an operation the more necessary at that inclement season, as we had no tents. Our first work was to bury more effectually the dead we found there, who had been half interr'd by the country people.

The next morning our fort was plann'd and mark'd out, the circumference measuring four hundred and fifty-five feet, which would require as many palisades to be made of trees, one with another, of a foot diameter each. Our axes, of which we had seventy, were immediately set to work to cut down trees, and, our men being dextrous in the use of them, great despatch was made. Seeing the trees fall so fast, I had the curiosity to look at my watch when two men began to cut at a pine; in six minutes they had it upon the ground, and I found it of fourteen inches diameter. Each pine made three palisades of eighteen feet long, pointed at one end. While these were preparing, our other men dug a trench all round, of three feet deep, in which the palisades were to be planted; and, our waggons, the bodys being taken off, and the fore and hind wheels separated by taking out the pin which united the two parts of the perch, we had ten carriages, with two horses each, to bring the palisades from the woods to the spot. When they were set up, our carpenters built a stage of boards all round within, about six feet high, for the men to stand on when to fire thro' the loopholes. We had one swivel gun, which we mounted on one of the angles, and fir'd it as soon as fix'd, to let the Indians know, if any were within hearing, that we had such pieces; and thus our fort, if such a magnificent name may be given to so miserable a stockade, was finish'd in a week, though it rain'd so hard every other day that the men could not work.

This gave me occasion to observe, that, when men are employ'd, they are best content'd; for on the days they worked they were good-natur'd and cheerful, and, with the consciousness of having done a good day's work, they spent the evening jollily; but on our idle days they were mutinous and quarrelsome, finding fault with their pork, the bread, etc., and in continual ill-humor, which put me in mind of a sea-captain, whose rule it was to keep his men constantly at work; and, when his mate once told him that they had done every thing, and there was nothing further to employ them about, "*Oh*," *says he*, "*make them scour the anchor*."

This kind of fort, however contemptible, is a sufficient defense against Indians, who have no cannon. Finding ourselves now posted securely, and having a place to retreat to on occasion, we ventur'd out in parties to scour the adjacent country. We met with no Indians, but we found the places on the neighboring hills where they had lain to watch our proceedings. There was an art in their contrivance of those places that seems worth mention. It being winter, a fire was necessary for them; but a common fire on the surface of the ground would by its light have discover'd their position at a distance. They had therefore dug holes in the ground about three feet diameter, and somewhat deeper; we saw where they had with their hatchets cut off the charcoal from the sides of burnt logs lying in the woods. With these coals they had made small fires in the bottom of the holes, and we observ'd among the weeds and grass the prints of their bodies, made by their laying all round, with their legs hanging down in the holes to keep their feet warm, which, with them, is an essential point. This kind of fire, so manag'd, could not discover them, either by its light, flame, sparks, or even smoke: it appear'd that their number was not great, and it seems they saw we were too many to be attacked by them with prospect of advantage.

We had for our chaplain a zealous Presbyterian minister, Mr Beatty, who complained to me that the men did not generally attend his prayers and exhortations. When they enlisted, they were promised, besides pay and provisions, a gill of rum a day, which was punctually serv'd out to them, half in the morning, and the other half in the evening; and I observ'd they were as punctual in attending to receive it; upon which I said to Mr Beatty, "It is, perhaps, below the dignity of your profession to act as steward of the rum, but if you were to deal it out and only just after prayers, you would have them all about you." He liked the tho't, undertook the office, and, with the help of a few hands to measure out the liquor, executed it to satisfaction, and never were prayers more generally and more punctually attended; so that I thought this method preferable to the punishment inflicted by some military laws for non-attendance on divine service.

I had hardly finish'd this business, and got my fort well stor'd with provisions, when I receiv'd a letter from the governor, acquainting me that he had call'd the Assembly, and wished my attendance there, if the posture of affairs on the frontiers was such that my remaining there was no longer necessary. My friends, too, of the Assembly, pressing me by their letters to be, if possible, at the meeting, and my three intended forts being now compleated, and the inhabitants contented to remain on their farms under that protection, I resolved to return; the more willingly, as a New England officer, Colonel Clapham, experienced in Indian war, being on a visit to our establishment, consented to accept the command. I gave him a commission, and, parading the garrison, had it read before them, and introduc'd him to them as an officer who, from his skill in military affairs, was much more fit to command them than myself; and, giving them a little exhortation, took my leave. I was escorted as far as Bethlehem, where I rested a few days to recover from the fatigue I had undergone. The first night, being in a good bed, I could hardly sleep, it was so different from my hard lodging on the floor of our hut at Gnaden wrapt only in a blanket or two.

While at Bethlehem, I inquir'd a little into the practice of the Moravians: some of them had accompanied me, and all were very kind to me. I found they work'd for a common stock, eat at common tables, and slept in common dormitories, great numbers together. In the dormitories I observed loopholes, at certain distances all along just under the ceiling, which I thought judiciously placed for change of air. I was at their church, where I was entertain'd with good musick, the organ being accompanied with violins, hautboys, flutes, clarinets, etc. I understood that their sermons were not usually preached to mixed congregations of men, women, and children, as is our common practice, but that they assembled sometimes the married men, at other times their wives, then the young men, the young women, and the little children, each division by itself. The sermon I heard was to the latter, who came in and were plac'd in rows on benches; the boys under the conduct of a young man, their tutor, and the girls conducted by a young woman. The discourse seem'd well adapted to their capacities, and was deliver'd in a pleasing, familiar manner, coaxing them, as it were, to be good. They behav'd very orderly, but looked pale and unhealthy, which made me suspect they were kept too much within doors, or not allow'd sufficient exercise.

I inquir'd concerning the Moravian marriages, whether the report was true that they were by lot. I was told that lots were us'd only in particular cases; that generally, when a young man found himself dispos'd to marry, he inform'd the elders of his class, who consulted the elder ladies that govern'd the young women. As these elders of the different sexes were well acquainted with the tempers and dispositions of their respective pupils, they could best judge what matches were suitable, and their judgments were generally acquiesc'd in; but if, for example, it should happen that two or three young women were found to be equally proper for the young man, the lot was then recurred to. I objected, if the matches are not made by the mutual choice of the parties, some of them may chance to be very unhappy. "And so they may," answer'd my informer, "if you let the parties chuse for themselves;" which, indeed, I could not deny.

Being returned to Philadelphia, I found the association went on swimmingly, the inhabitants that were not Quakers having pretty generally come into it, formed themselves into companies, and chose their captains, lieutenants, and ensigns, according to the new law. Dr B. visited me, and gave me an account of the pains he had taken to spread a general good liking to the law, and ascribed much to those endeavors. I had had the vanity to ascribe all to my *Dialogue;* however, not knowing but that he might be in the right, I let him enjoy his opinion, which I take to be generally the best way in such cases. The officers, meeting, chose me to be colonel of the regiment, which I this time accepted. I forget how many companies we had, but we paraded about twelve hundred well-looking men, with a company of artillery, who had been furnished with six brass field-pieces, which they had become so expert in the use of as to fire twelve times in a minute. The first time I reviewed my regiment they accompanied me to my house, and would salute me with some rounds fired before my door, which shook down and broke several glasses of my electrical apparatus. And my new honour proved not much less brittle; for all our commissions were soon after broken by a repeal of the law in England.

During this short time of my colonelship, being about to set out on a journey to Virginia, the officers of my regiment took it into their heads that it would be proper for them to escort me out of town, as far as the Lower Ferry. Just as I was getting on horseback they came to my door, between thirty and forty, mounted, and all in their uniforms. I had not been previously acquainted with the project, or I should have prevented it, being naturally averse to the assuming of state on any occasion; and I was a good deal chagrin'd at their appearance, as I could not avoid their accompanying me. What made it worse was, that, as soon as we began to move, they drew their swords and rode with them naked all the way. Somebody wrote an account of this to the proprietor, and it gave him great offense. No such honor had been paid him when in the province, nor to any of his governors; and he said it was only proper to princes of the blood royal, which may be true for aught I know, who was, and still am, ignorant of the etiquette in such cases.

This silly affair, however, greatly increased his rancour against me, which was before not a little, on account of my conduct in the Assembly respecting the exemption of his estate from taxation, which I had always oppos'd very warmly, and not without severe reflections on his meanness and injustice of contending for it. He accused me to the ministry as being the great obstacle to the king's service, preventing, by my influence in the House, the proper form of the bills for raising money, and he instanced this parade with my officers as a proof of my having an intention to take the government of the province out of his hands by force. He also applied to Sir Everard Fawkener, the postmaster-general, to deprive me of my office; but it had no other effect than to procure from Sir Everard a gentle admonition.

Notwithstanding the continual wrangle between the governor and the House, in which I, as a member, had so large a share, there still subsisted a civil intercourse between that gentleman and myself, and we never had any personal difference. I have sometimes since thought that his little or no resentment against me, for the answers it was known I drew up to his messages, might be the effect of professional habit, and that, being bred a lawyer, he might consider us both as merely advocates for contending clients in a suit, he for the proprietaries and I for the Assembly. He would, therefore, sometimes call in a friendly way to advise with me on difficult points, and sometimes, tho' not often, take my advice.

We acted in concert to supply Braddock's army with provisions; and, when the shocking news arrived of his defeat, the governor sent in haste for me, to cousult with him on measures for preventing the desertion of the back counties. I forget now the advice I gave; but I think it was, that Dunbar should be written to, and prevail'd with, if possible, to post his troops on the frontiers for their protection, till, by re-enforcements from the colonies, he might be able to proceed on the expedition. And, after my return from the frontier, he would have had me undertake the conduct of such an expedition with provincial troops, for the reduction of Fort Duquesne, Dunbar and his men being otherwise employed; and he proposed to commission me as general. I had not so good an opinion of my military abilities as he profess'd to have, and I believe his professions must have exceeded his real sentiments; but probably he might think that my popularity would facilitate the raising of the men, and my influence in Assembly, the grant of money to pay them, and that, perhaps, without taxing the proprietary estate. Finding me not so forward to engage as he expected, the project was dropt, and he soon after left the government, being superseded by Captain Denny.

Before I proceed in relating the part I had in public affairs under this new governor's administration, it may not be amiss here to give some account of the rise and progress of my philosophical reputation.

In 1746, being at Boston, I met there with a Dr Spence, who was lately arrived from Scotland, and show'd me some electric experiments. They were imperfectly perform'd, as he was not very expert; but, being on a subject quite new to me, they equally surpris'd and pleased me. Soon after my return to Philadelphia, our library company receiv'd from Mr P. Collinson, Fellow of the Royal Society of London, a present of a glass tube, with some account of the use of it in making such experiments. I eagerly seized the opportunity of repeating what I had seen at Boston; and, by much practice, acquir'd great readiness in performing those, also, which we had an account of from England, adding a number of new ones. I say much practice, for my house was continually full, for some time, with people who came to see these new wonders.

To divide a little this incumbrance among my friends, I caused a number of similar tubes to be blown at our glass-house, with which they furnish'd themselves, so that we had at length several performers. Among these, the principal was Mr Kinnersley, an ingenious neighbor, who, being out of business, I encouraged to undertake showing the experiments for money, and drew up for him two lectures, in which the experiments were rang'd in such order, and accompanied with such explanations in such method, as that the foregoing should assist in comprehending the following. He procur'd an elegant apparatus for the purpose, in which all the little machines that I had roughly made for myself were nicely form'd by instrument-makers. His lectures were well attended, and gave great satisfaction; and after some time he went thro' the colonies, exhibiting them in every capital town, and pick'd up some money. In the West India islands, indeed, it was with difficulty the experiments could be made, from the general moisture of the air.

Oblig'd as we were to Mr Collinson for his present of the tube, etc., I thought it right he should be inform'd of our success in using it, and wrote him several letters containing accounts of our experiments. He got them read in the Royal Society, where they were not at first thought worth so much notice as to be printed in their Transactions. One paper, which I wrote for Mr Kinnersley, on the sameness of lightning with electricity, I sent to Dr Mitchel, an acquaintance of mine, and one of the members also of that society, who wrote me word that it had been read, but was laughed at by the connoisseurs. The papers, however, being shown to Dr Fothergill, he thought them of too much value to be stifled, and advis'd the printing of them. Mr Collinson then gave them to *Cave* for publication in his Gentleman's Magazine; but he chose to print them separately in a pamphlet, and Dr Fothergill wrote the preface. Cave, it seems, judged rightly for his profit, for by the additions that arrived afterward they swell'd, to a quarto volume, which has had five editions, and cost him nothing for copy-money.

It was, however, some time before those papers were much taken notice of in England. A copy of them happening to fall into the hands of the Count de Buffon, a philosopher deservedly of great reputation in France, and, indeed, all over Europe, he prevailed with M. Dalibard to translate them into French, and they were printed at Paris. The publication offended the Abbé Nollet, preceptor in Natural Philosophy to the royal family, and an able experimenter, who had form'd and publish'd a theory of electricity, which then had the general vogue. He could not at first believe that such a work came from America, and said it must have been fabricated by his enemies at Paris, to decry his system. Afterwards, having been assur'd that there really existed such a person as Franklin at Philadelphia, which he had doubted, he wrote and published a volume of Letters, chiefly address'd to me, defending his theory, and denying the verity of my experiments, and of the positions deduc'd from them.

I once purpos'd answering the abbé, and actually began the answer; but, on consideration that my writings contain'd a description of experiments which any one might repeat and verify, and if not to be verifi'd, could not be defended; or of observations offer'd as conjectures, and not delivered dogmatically, therefore not laying me under any obligation to defend them; and reflecting that a dispute between two persons, writing in different languages, might be lengthened greatly by mistranslations, and thence misconceptions of one another's meaning, much of one of the abbé's letters being founded on an error in the translation, I concluded to let my papers shift for themselves, believing it was better to spend what time I could spare from public business in making new experiments, than in disputing about those already made. I therefore never answered M. Nollet, and the event gave me no cause to repent my silence; for my friend M. le Roy, of the Royal Academy of Sciences, took up my cause and refuted him; my book was translated into the Italian, German, and Latin languages; and the doctrine it contain'd was by degrees universally adopted by the philosophers of Europe, in preference to that of the abbé; so that he lived to see himself the last of his sect, except Monsieur B——, of Paris, his *élève* and immediate disciple.

What gave my book the more sudden and general celebrity, was the success of one of its proposed experiments, made by Messrs Dalibard and De Lor at Marly, for drawing lightning from the clouds. This engag'd the public attention every where. M. de Lor, who had an apparatus for experimental philosophy, and lectur'd in that branch of science, undertook to repeat what he called the *Philadelphia*

Experiments; and, after they were performed before the king and court, all the curious of Paris flocked to see them. I will not swell this narrative with an account of that capital experiment, nor of the infinite pleasure I receiv'd in the success of a similar one I made soon after with a kite at Philadelphia, as both are to be found in the histories of electricity.

Dr Wright, an English physician, when at Paris, wrote to a friend, who was of the Royal Society, an account of the high esteem my experiments were in among the learned abroad, and of their wonder that my writings had been so little noticed in England. The society, on this, resum'd the consideration of the letters that had been read to them; and the celebrated Dr Watson drew up a summary account of them, and of all I had afterwards sent to England on the subject, which he accompanied with some praise of the writer. This summary was then printed in their Transactions; and some members of the society in London, particularly the very ingenious Mr Canton, having verified the experiment of procuring lightning from the clouds by a pointed rod, and acquainting them with the success, they soon made me more than amends for the slight with which they had before treated me. Without my having made any application for that honor, they chose me a member, and voted that I should be excus'd the customary payments, which would have amounted to twenty-five guineas; and ever since have given me their Transactions gratis. They also presented me with the gold medal of Sir Godfrey Copley for the year 1753, the delivery of which was accompanied by a very handsome speech of the president, Lord Macclesfield, wherein I was highly honoured.

Our new governor, Captain Denny, brought over for me the before-mentioned medal from the Royal Society, which he presented to me at an entertainment given him by the city. He accompanied it with very polite expressions of his esteem for me, having, as he said, been long acquainted with my character. After dinner, when the company, as was customary at that time, were engag'd in drinking, he took me aside into another room, and acquainted me that he had been advis'd by his friends in England to cultivate a friendship with me, as one who was capable of giving him the best advice, and of contributing most effectually to the making his administration easy; that he therefore desired of all things to have a good understanding with me, and he begg'd me to be assur'd of his readiness on all occasions to render me every service that might be in his power. He said much to me, also, of the proprietor's good disposition towards the province, and of the advantage it might be to us all, and to me in particular, if the opposition that had been so long continu'd to his measures was dropt, and harmony restor'd between him and the people; in effecting which, it was thought no one could be more serviceable than myself; and I might depend on adequate acknowledgments and recompenses, etc., etc. The drinkers, finding we did not return immediately to the table, sent us a decanter of Madeira, which the governor made liberal use of, and in proportion became more profuse of his solicitations and promises.

My answers were to this purpose: that my circumstances, thanks to God, were such as to make proprietary favours unnecessary to me; and that, being a member of the Assembly, I could not possibly accept of any; that, however, I had no personal enmity to the proprietary, and that, whenever the public measures he propos'd should appear to be for the good of the people, no one should espouse and forward them more zealously than myself; my past opposition having been founded on this, that the measures which had been urged were evidently intended to serve the proprietary interest, with great prejudice to that of the people; that I was much obliged to him (the governor) for his professions of regard to me, and that he might rely on every thing in my power to make his administration as easy as possible, hoping at the same time that he had not brought with him the same unfortunate instruction his predecessor had been hamper'd with.

On this he did not then explain himself; but when he afterwards came to do business with the Assembly, they appear'd again, the disputes were renewed, and I was as active as ever in the opposition, being the penman, first, of the request to have a communication of the instructions, and then of the remarks upon them, which may be found in the votes of the time, and in the Historical Review I afterward publish'd. But between us personally no enmity arose; we were often together; he was a man of letters, had seen much of the world, and was very entertaining and pleasing in conversation. He gave me the first information that my old friend Jas. Ralph was still alive; that he was esteem'd one of the best political writers in England; had been employ'd in the dispute between Prince Frederic and the king, and had obtain'd a pension of three hundred a year; that his reputation was indeed small as a poet, Pope having damned his poetry in the Dunciad; but his prose was thought as good as any man's.

[1] The Assembly finally finding the proprietary obstinately persisted in manacling their deputies with instructions inconsistent not only with the privileges of the people, but with the service of the crown, resolv'd to petition the king against them, and

[1] The many unanimous resolves of the Assembly—what date?—[*Marg. note.*]

appointed me their agent to go over to England, to present and support the petition. The House had sent up a bill to the governor, granting a sum of sixty thousand pounds for the king's use (ten thousand pounds of which was subjected to the orders of the then general, Lord Loudoun), which the governor absolutely refus'd to pass, in compliance with his instructions.

I had agreed with Captain Morris, of the paquet at New York, for my passage, and my stores were put on board, when Lord Loudoun arriv'd at Philadelphia, expressly, as he told me, to endeavor an accommodation between the governor and Assembly, that his majesty's service might not be obstructed by their dissensions. Accordingly, he desir'd the governor and myself to meet him, that he might hear what was to be said on both sides. We met and discuss'd the business. In behalf of the Assembly, I urg'd all the various arguments that may be found in the public papers of that time, which were of my writing, and are printed with the minutes of the Assembly; and the governor pleaded his instructions; the bond he had given to observe them, and his ruin if he disobey'd, yet seemed not unwilling to hazard himself if Lord Loudoun would advise it. This his lordship did not chuse to do, though I once thought I had nearly prevail'd with him to do it; but finally he rather chose to urge the compliance of the Assembly; and he entreated me to use my endeavours with them for that purpose, declaring that he would spare none of the king's troops for the defense of our frontiers, and that, if we did not continue to provide for that defense ourselves, they must remain expos'd to the enemy.

I acquainted the House with what had pass'd, and, presenting them with a set of resolutions I had drawn up, declaring our rights, and that we did not relinquish our claim to those rights, but only suspended the exercise of them on this occasion thro' *force*, against which we protested, they at length agreed to drop that bill, and frame another conformable to the proprietary instructions. This of course the governor pass'd, and I was then at liberty to proceed on my voyage. But, in the meantime, the paquet had sailed with my sea-stores, which was some loss to me, and my only recompense was his lordship's thanks for my service, all the credit of obtaining the accommodation falling to his share.

He set out for New York before me; and, as the time for dispatching the paquet-boats was at his disposition, and there were two then remaining there, one of which, he said, was to sail very soon, I requested to know the precise time, that I might not miss her by any delay of mine. His answer was, "I have given out that she is to sail on Saturday next; but I may let you know, *entre nous*, that if you are there by Monday morning, you will be in time, but do not delay longer." By some accidental hinderance at a ferry, it was Monday noon before I arrived, and I was much afraid she might have sailed, as the wind was fair; but I was soon made easy by the information that she was still in the harbor, and would not move till the next day. One would imagine that I was now on the very point of departing for Europe. I thought so; but I was not then so well acquainted with his lordship's character, of which *indecision* was one of the strongest features. I shall give some instances. It was about the beginning of April that I came to New York, and I think it was near the end of June before we sail'd. There were then two of the paquet-boats, which had been long in port, but were detained for the general's letters, which were always to be ready to-morrow. Another paquet arriv'd; she too was detain'd; and, before we sail'd, a fourth was expected. Ours was the first to be dispatch'd, as having been there longest. Passengers were engag'd in all, and some extremely impatient to be gone, and the merchants uneasy about their letters, and the orders they had given for insurance (it being war time) for fall goods; but their anxiety avail'd nothing; his lordship's letters were not ready; and yet whoever waited on him found him always at his desk, pen in hand, and concluded he must needs write abundantly.

Going myself one morning to pay my respects, I found in his antechamber one Innis, a messenger of Philadelphia, who had come from thence express with a paquet from Governor Denny for the General. He delivered to me some letters from my friends there, which occasion'd my inquiring when he was to return, and where he lodg'd, that I might send some letters by him. He told me he was order'd to call to-morrow at nine for the general's answer to the governor, and should set off immediately. I put my letters into his hands the same day. A fortnight after I met him again in the same place. "So, you are soon return'd, Innis?" "*Return'd!* no, I am not *gone* yet." "How so?" "I have called here by order every morning these two weeks past for his lordship's letter, and it is not yet ready." "Is it possible, when he is so great a writer? for I see him constantly at his escritoire." "Yes," says Innis, "but he is like St George on the signs, *always on horseback, and never rides on.*" This observation of the messenger was, it seems, well founded; for, when in England, I understood that Mr Pitt gave it as one reason for removing this general, and sending Generals Amherst and Wolfe, *that the minister never heard from him, and could not know what he was doing.*

This daily expectation of sailing, and all the three paquets going down to Sand Hook, to join the fleet there, the passengers thought it best to be on board, lest by a sudden order the ships should sail, and they be left behind. There, if I remember right, we were about six weeks, consuming our sea-stores, and oblig'd to procure more. At length the fleet sail'd, the General and all his army on board, bound to Louisburg, with intent to besiege and take that fortress; all the paquet-boats in company ordered to attend the General's ship, ready to receive his dispatches when they should be ready. We were out five days before we got a letter with leave to part, and then our ship quitted the fleet and steered for England. The other two paquets he still detained, carried them with him to Halifax, where he stayed some time to exercise the men in sham attacks upon sham forts, then alter'd his mind as to besieging Louisburg, and return'd to New York, with all his troops, together with the two paquets above mentioned, and all their passengers! During his absence the French and savages had taken Fort George, on the frontier of that province, and the savages had massacred many of the garrison after capitulation.

I saw afterwards in London Captain Bonnell, who commanded one of those paquets. He told me that, when he had been detain'd a month, he acquainted his lordship that his ship was grown foul, to a degree that must necessarily hinder her fast sailing, a point of consequence for a paquet-boat, and requested an allowance of time to heave her down and clean her bottom. He was asked how long time that would require. He answer'd, three days. The general replied, "If you can do it in one day, I give leave; otherwise not; for you must certainly sail the day after to-morrow." So he never obtain'd leave, though detained afterwards from day to day during full three months.

I saw also in London one of Bonnell's passengers, who was so enrag'd against his lordship for deceiv-ing and detaining him so long at New York, and then carrying him to Halifax and back again, that he swore he would sue him for damages. Whether he did or not, I never heard; but, as he represented the injury to his affairs, it was very considerable.

On the whole, I wonder'd much how such a man came to be intrusted with so important a business as the conduct of a great army; but, having since seen more of the great world, and the means of obtaining, and motives for giving places, my wonder is diminished. General Shirley, on whom the command of the army devolved upon the death of Braddock, would, in my opinion, if continued in place, have made a much better campaign than that of Loudoun in 1757, which was frivolous, expensive, and disgraceful to our nation beyond conception; for, tho' Shirley was not a bred soldier, he was sensible and sagacious in himself, and attentive to good advice from others, capable of forming judicious plans, and quick and active in carrying them into execution. Loudoun, instead of defending the colonies with his great army, left them totally expos'd while he paraded idly at Halifax, by which means Fort George was lost, besides, he derang'd all our mercantile operations, and distress'd our trade, by a long embargo on the exportation of provisions, on pretence of keeping supplies from being obtain'd by the enemy, but in reality for beating down their price in favor of the contractors, in whose profits, it was said, perhaps from suspicion only, he had a share. And, when at length the embargo was taken off, by neglecting to send notice of it to Charlestown, the Carolina fleet was detain'd near three months longer, whereby their bottoms were so much damaged by the worm that a great part of them foundered in their passage home.

Shirley was, I believe, sincerely glad of being relieved from so burdensome a charge as the conduct of an army must be to a man unacquainted with military business. I was at the entertainment given by the city of New York to Lord Loudoun, on his taking upon him the command. Shirley, tho' thereby superseded, was present also. There was a great company of officers, citizens, and strangers, and, some chairs having been borrowed in the neighborhood, there was one among them very low, which fell to the lot of Mr Shirley. Perceiving it as I sat by him, I said, "They have given you, sir, too low a seat." "No matter," says he, "Mr Franklin, I find *a low seat* the easiest."

While I was, as afore mention'd, detain'd at New York, I receiv'd all the accounts of the provisions, etc., that I had furnish'd to Braddock, some of which accounts could not sooner be obtain'd from the different persons I had employ'd to assist in the business. I presented them to Lord Loudoun, desiring to be paid the ballance. He caus'd them to be regularly examined by the proper officer, who, after comparing every article with its voucher, certified them to be right; and the balance due for which his lordship promis'd to give me an order on the paymaster. This was, however, put off from time to time; and, tho' I call'd often for it by appointment, I did not get it. At length, just before my departure, he told me he had, on better consideration, concluded not to mix his accounts with those of his predecessors. "And you," says he, "when in England, have only to exhibit your accounts at the treasury, and you will be paid immediately."

I mention'd, but without effect, the great and unexpected expense I had been put to by being detain'd so long at New York, as a reason for my desiring to be presently paid; and on my observing that it was not right I should be put to any further trouble or delay in obtaining the money I had advanc'd, as I charged no commission for my service, "O, Sir," says he, "you must not think of persuading us that you are no gainer; we understand better those affairs, and know that every one concerned in supplying the army finds means, in the doing it, to fill his own pockets." I assur'd him that was not my case, and that I had not pocketed a farthing; but he appear'd clearly not to believe me; and, indeed, I have since learnt that immense fortunes are often made in such employments. As to my ballance, I am not paid it to this day, of which more hereafter.

Our captain of the paquet had boasted much, before we sailed, of the swiftness of his ship; unfortunately, when we came to sea, she proved the dullest of ninety-six sail, to his no small mortification. After many conjectures respecting the cause, when we were near another ship almost as dull as ours, which, however, gain'd upon us, the captain ordered all hands to come aft, and stand as near the ensign staff as possible. We were, passengers included, about forty persons. While we stood there, the ship mended her pace, and soon left her neighbour far behind, which prov'd clearly what our captain suspected, that she was loaded too much by the head. The casks of water, it seems, had been all plac'd forward; these he therefore order'd to be mov'd further aft, on which the ship recover'd her character, and proved the sailer in the fleet.

The captain said she had once gone at the rate of thirteen knots, which is accounted thirteen miles per hour. We had on board, as a passenger, Captain Kennedy, of the Navy, who contended that it was impossible, and that no ship ever sailed so fast, and that there must have been some error in the division of the log-line, or some mistake in heaving the log. A wager ensu'd between the two captains, to be decided when there should be sufficient wind. Kennedy thereupon examin'd rigorously the log-line, and, being satisfi'd with that, he determin'd to throw the log himself. Accordingly some days after, when the wind blew very fair and fresh, and the captain of the paquet, Lutwidge, said he believ'd she then went at the rate of thirteen knots, Kennedy made the experiment, and own'd his wager lost.

The above fact I give for the sake of the following observation. It has been remark'd, as an imperfection in the art of ship-building, that it can never be known, till she is tried, whether a new ship will or will not be a good sailer; for that the model of a good-sailing ship has been exactly follow'd in a new one, which has prov'd, on the contrary, remarkably dull. I apprehend that this may partly be occasion'd by the different opinions of seamen respecting the modes of lading, rigging, and sailing of a ship; each has his system; and the same vessel, laden by the judgment and orders of one captain, shall sail better or worse than when by the orders of another. Besides, it scarce ever happens that a ship is form'd, fitted for the sea, and sail'd by the same person. One man builds the hull, another rigs her, a third lades and sails her. No one of these has the advantage of knowing all the ideas and experience of the others, and, therefore, can not draw just conclusions from a combination of the whole.

Even in the simple operation of sailing when at sea, I have often observ'd different judgments in the officers who commanded the successive watches, the wind being the same. One would have the sails trimm'd sharper or flatter than another, so that they seem'd to have no certain rule to govern by. Yet I think a set of experiments might be instituted, first, to determine the most proper form of the hull for swift sailing; next, the best dimensions and properest place for the masts; then the form and quantity of sails, and their position, as the wind may be; and, lastly, the disposition of the lading. This is an age of experiments, and I think a set accurately made and combin'd would be of great use. I am persuaded, therefore, that ere long some ingenious philosopher will undertake it, to whom I wish success.

We were several times chas'd in our passage, but outsail'd every thing, and in thirty days had soundings. We had a good observation, and the captain judg'd himself so near our port, Falmouth, that, if we made a good run in the night, we might be off the mouth of that harbor in the morning, and by running in the night might escape the notice of the enemy's privateers, who often crus'd near the entrance of the channel. Accordingly, all the sail was set that we could possibly make, and the wind being very fresh and fair, we went right before it, and made great way. The captain, after his observation, shap'd his course, as he thought, so as to pass wide of the Scilly Isles; but it seems there is sometimes a strong indraught setting up St George's Channel, which deceives seamen and caused the loss of Sir Cloudesley Shovel's squadron. This indraught was probably the cause of what happened to us.

We had a watchman plac'd in the bow, to whom they often called, "*Look well out before there,*" and he as often answered, "*Ay, ay*"; but perhaps had his eyes shut, and was half asleep at the time, they sometimes answering, as is said, mechanically; for he did not see a light just before us, which had been hid by the studding-sails from the man at the helm, and from the rest of the watch, but by an accidental yaw of the ship was discover'd, and occasion'd a great alarm, we being very near it, the light appearing to me as big as a cart-wheel. It was midnight, and our captain fast asleep; but

Captain Kennedy, jumping upon deck, and seeing the danger, ordered the ship to wear round, all sails standing; an operation dangerous to the masts, but it carried us clear, and we escaped shipwreck, for we were running right upon the rocks on which the light-house was erected. This deliverance impressed me strongly with the utility of light-houses, and made me resolve to encourage the building more of them in America, if I should live to return there.

In the morning it was found by the soundings, etc., that we were near our port, but a thick fog hid the land from our sight. About nine o'clock the fog began to rise, and seem'd to be lifted up from the water like the curtain at a play-house, discovering underneath, the town of Falmouth, the vessels in its harbor, and the fields that surrounded it. This was a most pleasing spectacle to those who had been so long without any other prospects than the uniform view of a vacant ocean, and it gave us the more pleasure as we were now free from the anxieties which the state of war occasion'd.

I set out immediately, with my son, for London, and we only stopt a little by the way to view Stonehenge on Salisbury Plain, and Lord Pembroke's house and gardens, with his very curious antiquities at Wilton. We arrived in London the 27th of July, 1757.[1]

[1] Here terminates the Autobiography, as published by Wm. Temple Franklin and his successors. What follows was written in the last year of Dr Franklin's life, and was first printed (in English) in Mr Bigelow's edition of 1868.—Ed.

As soon as I was settled in a lodging Mr Charles had provided for me, I went to visit Dr Fothergill, to whom I was strongly recommended, and whose counsel respecting my proceedings I was advis'd to obtain. He was against an immediate complaint to government, and thought the proprietaries should first be personally appli'd to, who might possibly be induc'd by the interposition and persuasion of some private friends, to accommodate matters amicably. I then waited on my old friend and correspondent, Mr Peter Collinson, who told me that John Hanbury, the great Virginia merchant, had requested to be informed when I should arrive, that he might carry me to Lord Granville's, who was then President of the Council and wished to see me as soon as possible. I agreed to go with him the next morning. Accordingly Mr Hanbury called for me and took me in his carriage to that nobleman's, who receiv'd me with great civility; and after some questions respecting the present state of affairs in America and discourse thereupon, he said to me: "You Americans have wrong ideas of the nature of your constitution; you contend that the king's instructions to his governors are not laws, and think yourselves at liberty to regard or disregard them at your own discretion. But those instructions are not like the pocket instructions given to a minister going abroad, for regulating his conduct in some trifling point of ceremony. They are first drawn up by judges learned in the laws; they are then considered, debated, and perhaps amended in Council, after which they are signed by the king. They are then, so far as they relate to you, the *law of the land*, for the king is the LEGISLATOR OF THE COLONIES." I told his lordship this was new doctrine to me. I had always understood from our charters that our laws were to be made by our Assemblies, to be presented indeed to the king for his royal assent, but that being once given the king could not repeal or alter them. And as the Assemblies could not make permanent laws without his assent, so neither could he make a law for them without theirs. He assur'd me I was totally mistaken. I did not think so, however, and his lordship's conversation having a little alarm'd me as to what might be the sentiments of the court concerning us, I wrote it down as soon as I return'd to my lodgings. I recollected that about 20 years before, a clause in a bill brought into Parliament by the ministry had propos'd to make the king's instructions laws in the colonies, but the clause was thrown out by the Commons, for which we adored them as our friends and friends of liberty, till by their conduct towards us in 1765 it seem'd that they had refus'd that point of sovereignty to the king only that they might reserve it for themselves.

After some days, Dr Fothergill having spoken to the proprietaries, they agreed to a meeting with me at Mr T. Penn's house in Spring Garden. The conversation at first consisted of mutual declarations of disposition to reasonable accommodations, but I suppose each party had its own ideas of what should be meant by *reasonable*. We then went into consideration of our several points of complaint, which I enumerated. The proprietaries justify'd their conduct as well as they could, and I the Assembly's. We now appeared very wide, and so far from each other in our opinions as to discourage all hope of agreement. However, it was concluded that I should give them the heads of our complaints in writing, and they promis'd then to consider them. I did so soon after, but they put the paper into the hands of their solicitor, Ferdinand John Paris, who managed for them all their law business in their great suit with the neighbouring proprietary of Maryland, Lord Baltimore, which had subsisted 70 years, and wrote for them all their papers and messages in their dispute with the Assembly. He was a proud, angry man, and as I had occasionally in the answers of the Assembly treated his papers with some severity, they being really weak in point of argument and haughty in expression, he had conceived a mortal enmity to me, which discovering itself whenever we met, I declin'd the proprietary's proposal that he and I should discuss the heads of complaint between our two selves, and refus'd treating with any one but them. They then by his advice put the paper into the hands of the Attorney and Solicitor-General for their opinion and counsel upon it, where it lay unanswered a year wanting eight days, during which time I made frequent demands of an answer from the proprietaries, but without obtaining any other than that they had not yet received the opinion of the Attorney and Solicitor-General. What it was when they did receive it I never learnt, for they did not communicate it to me, but sent a long message to the Assembly drawn and signed by Paris, reciting my paper, complaining of its want of formality, as a rudeness on my part, and giving a flimsy justification of their conduct, adding that they should be willing to accommodate matters if the Assembly would send out *some person of candour* to treat with them for that purpose, intimating thereby that I was not such.

The want of formality or rudeness was, probably, my not having address'd the paper to them with their assum'd titles of True and Absolute Proprietaries of the Province of Pennsylvania, which I omitted as not thinking it necessary in a paper, the intention of which was only to reduce to a certainty by writing, what in conversation I had delivered *viva voce*.

But during this delay, the Assembly having prevailed with Gov'r Denny to pass an act taxing the proprietary estate in common with the estates of the people, which was the grand point in dispute, they omitted answering the message.

When this act however came over, the proprietaries, counselled by Paris, determined to oppose its receiving the royal assent. Accordingly they petition'd the king in Council, and a hearing was appointed in which two lawyers were employ'd by them against the act, and two by me in support of it. They alledg'd that the act was intended to load the proprietary estate in order to spare those of the people, and that if it were suffer'd to continue in force, and the proprietaries who were in odium with the people, left to their mercy in proportioning the taxes, they would inevitably be ruined. We reply'd that the act had no such intention, and would have no such effect. That the assessors were honest and discreet men under an oath to assess fairly and equitably, and that any advantage each of them might expect in lessening his own tax by augmenting that of the proprietaries was too trifling to induce them to perjure themselves. This is the purport of what I remember as urged by both sides, except that we insisted strongly on the mischievous consequences that must attend a repeal, for that the money, £100,000, being printed and given to the king's use, expended in his service, and now spread among the people, the repeal would strike it dead in their hands to the ruin of many, and the total discouragement of future grants, and the selfishness of the proprietors in soliciting such a general catastrophe, merely from a groundless fear of their estate being taxed too highly, was insisted on in the strongest terms. On this, Lord Mansfield, one of the counsel rose, and beckoning me took me into the clerk's chamber, while the lawyers were pleading, and asked me if I was really of opinion that no injury would be done the proprietary estate in the execution of the act. I said certainly. "Then," says he, "you can have little objection to enter into an engagement to assure that point." I answer'd, "None at all." He then call'd in Paris, and after some discourse, his lordship's proposition was accepted on both sides; a paper to the purpose was drawn up by the Clerk of the Council, which I sign'd with Mr Charles, who was also an Agent of the Province for their ordinary affairs, when Lord Mansfield returned to the Council Chamber, where finally the law was allowed to pass. Some changes were however recommended and we also engaged they should be made by a subsequent law, but the Assembly did not think them necessary; for one year's tax having been levied by the act before the order of Council arrived, they appointed a committee to examine the proceedings of the assessors, and on this committee they put several particular friends of the proprietaries. After a full enquiry, they unanimously sign'd a report that they found the tax had been assess'd with perfect equity.

The Assembly looked into my entering into the first part of the engagement, as an essential service to the Province, since it secured the credit of the paper money then spread over all the country. They gave me their thanks in form when I return'd. But the proprietaries were enraged at Governor Denny for having pass'd the act, and turn'd him out with threats of suing him for breach of instructions which he had given bond to observe. He, however, having done it at the instance of the General, and for His Majesty's service, and having some powerful interest at court, despis'd the threats and they were never put in execution. . . . [Unfinished].

SOME ACCOUNT OF

FRANKLIN'S LATER LIFE

PRINCIPALLY IN RELATION TO THE

HISTORY OF HIS TIME

BY

W. MACDONALD

BENJAMIN FRANKLIN

THERE are a multiplicity of standpoints from which we must view the many-sided Franklin if we would have more than a meagre misconception of that rich and varied personality; but I think his life, regarded somewhat objectively, falls readily into three periods which have a historical quite as much as they have a biographic character. If we look upon him, as surely we must look upon him, as the greatest type and example of the Citizen which modern history knows, and recognise that it was evidently Benjamin Franklin's business and affair upon this earth to be a citizen, and only his trade and livelihood to be a printer, and his casual occupation and pastime to be, amongst many other things, a celebrated man of science—then we shall also recognise that his life is divisible into his Apprenticeship, his Journeyman-years, and the great period of his Mastership in the practical art and mystery, which he made so completely his own, in all its branches and at all its levels, of being the Complete Citizen—of his city, his country, and the world. And upon further consideration we shall find that the three great stages of his life are marked by such a progressive enlargement of the scene and the character of his civic activity as these three words—city, country, world—may stand for.

Already in his twenty-second year we have the spectacle of a certain ingenious, purposeful young man called Franklin, a citizen of Philadelphia, whom, young as he is, Philadelphia is peculiarly conscious of possessing. He is but a working printer, newly set up in a small way of business with another man, has no position worth speaking of, and really ought to count for nothing with his neighbours. But his practical turn and his genius for thriving on a very little, which one must respect, and his searching and humorous sort of mind, which is perhaps not quite so pleasant to live beside, have made him a marked man among them. A stranger coming into that part, and taking his ease at his inn, would (we feel) be sure to hear him spoken of, not in every case with approbation, within the next twenty-four hours. Benjamin Franklin is already an asset of the place, though nobody there sees that he is on his way to become a power in the land. He does not see it himself; and if he has already done some things, and is daily exercising some faculties, that must tend to carry him into a large sphere of activity, he does those things and exercises those faculties strictly with regard to the day's purposes and to the sphere of activity in which he actually finds himself. Whatever his defects—for he has been self-educated and has lived as a kind of orphan, runaway or castaway, in two hemispheres—he is singularly lucid, singularly alive: and has drawn a wonderful number of moral inferences, considering his years, from his own experience and his own thought. But perhaps his simple and axiomatic desire to be as little as possible either an incompetent, a fool, or a rogue in his passage through this world, affords the only, as it is a quite sufficient token, that he is an original genius and a man in five millions.

Having begun at the beginning, and having a long way to go, he must needs travel at a great rate through the earlier stages of the journey; and by his twenty-seventh or his thirtieth year he has covered the whole course usually comprised in the biographies of successful men and eminently exemplary citizens. At twenty-one he had organised the

Junto, and was himself, we cannot doubt, equal to half the entire intellectual strength of that famous body and its branches. At twenty-two he has become partner in a business, his intelligence and character being reckoned a contribution amply equivalent to the other parties' capital. At twenty-three he improvises and publishes a pamphlet upon a difficult currency question concerning which opinion was fiercely agitated, and so does much to determine the colonial legislature's decision on that matter. This "Modest Inquiry into the Nature and Necessity of a Paper Currency" is now looked upon as having been an extraordinary production for its place and time, anticipating the method and some of the positions of Adam Smith—who was then, however, an urchin six years old. In this same year our young printer takes over the *Pennsylvania Gazette*, of which he is manager, editor, and by far the wisest and most humorous contributor to its columns; and he makes of it in a day such a newspaper as America had not hitherto known. In his twenty-fourth year he has become sole proprietor of the growing business by an honourable arrangement with his partner, who has decided that town-work is not his vocation and wants to get back to husbandry. For Franklin, the only difficult point is to choose his creditor in making the necessary arrangements, more than one friend having spontaneously pressed upon him the offer of financial facilities for a venture of his own, if he would make it. Next year, at the age of twenty-five, he has, "acting with some friends"—who would not have acted at all in the matter but for his ingenuity in making them believe that they cared for these things far more than he did—brought into being and started on a prosperous career the Philadelphia Library, the parent of the subscription libraries in America, and to-day a flourishing institution of which that country is justly proud. In his twenty-seventh year he has begun to publish the most famous popular annual which ever came from the press. *Poor Richard's Almanack* was indeed influential as well as famous, and is perhaps the one secular work in the world which has educated a people and formed the character of a nation. Yet the voice that spoke in it was always the voice of Ben Franklin, printer in Philadelphia, and expressed his mind even when the words were those of other men. We might legitimately, therefore, look on his apprentice period in the art of citizenship as ending at this point, where Poor Richard begins, or earlier. But though he has already, in this so-called apprentice period, done work which would be achievement enough for an ordinary excellent citizen's lifetime, yet the more historical view justifies us in dating his second period from about his thirty-third year.

What is worth noting in his first period is less what he has done, notable as that is, than the way in which he has done it, the motives by which he has been impelled. His progress towards being a philosopher and even a person of some social importance, is neither the issue of any expansive ideologies nor the realisation of any ambitious dreams. It seems to come about, naturally and almost unperceived, from the everyday applications of common-sense to the things immediately in view, the little situations of the day and the hour. As he is a Man, he wishes to be an intelligent one, and therefore takes the trouble of thinking; and that he may think to better purpose, he seeks information wherever he can find it. As he is a Printer, he attends to his business; and he differs from the majority in that and all other trades in recognising that his business has claims upon him, and that those claims include not only industry and intelligence but also character. He is one of the half-dozen optimists who have firmly believed that moral worth is worth something even in the most desperate circumstances, such as the conduct of a thriving business. Finally, as a Philadelphian, he is interested in all the things and the people immediately around him; and he has his own thought, and presently his own word to say, on all the little politics of the place and the province. His pamphlet on paper currency has been spoken of; but it is less useful, for an understanding of Franklin, to exclaim about its precocity and its argumentative value than to recognise its immediately practical genesis and aim. It is not a treatise by a young thinker, but the printed reasonings of a townsman, which he thinks may help. It is, in a word, but an instance of that civic handiness, that immediate unprofessional competence in all the things upon which good sense could have a word to say, or character a point of view to advocate, which by-and-by carried Franklin forward into the ranks of the foremost men of his age. Yet he laid down nothing, emerged from no limitations, in issuing from the smaller sphere; he took up no new fashion or faculty or knowledge in entering into the larger one—but was just the same Benjamin Franklin, reasoning and reasonable, whether as citizen of Philadelphia taking home his purchases of paper in a wheelbarrow, or as the representative man of a whole people, placed prominently in the eye of all the world. At any time in his third period he could have returned to the scenes and occupations of his first—to his daily work as a colonial printer, and his limited concernments as a citizen of Philadelphia — without any change of that habit of mind and that level of intellect and character which won him such esteem from the learned men of the French enlightenment and such confidence and respect, amounting to a moral ascendancy, in the minds of the ministers of Louis XVI. And we may say that if Franklin was always the right man in the right place, it was because, more than any man who ever moved through such a range of activity and experience, he was always the same man wherever he found himself. It is this which has made it seem worth while to linger thus over what was meant to be but a passing reference to the beginning of his career. For, not to say that in the beginning all things were, we may opine at least that Franklin's life affords an extraordinary example of the value of an unpretending disposition and an axiomatic mind; and that all his career seems, as we read it in greatest detail, but the matter-of-fact consequence of being alive, and having a home like one's neighbour, and a business to attend to, and a city to care for and serve. That is why I have called him the greatest Citizen in modern history.

From what has been said above it follows that the difference between his first and his second period is expresssed rather by a change in the sphere of his activities or of his effective interests than in the character of the man or the range of his competence. The marked Philadelphian, much commented on by his neighbours, and sometimes spoken of even in the country places, has imperceptibly, and without perceiving it, become transformed into the leading Pennsylvanian. His home is in Philadelphia still, but the whole province has become his city; and the wider neighbourhood, beyond that province, through which his name is becoming quoted and familiar, coincides with the area of English settlement on the Atlantic seaboard. But during the first part of this period, though he counts for more and more in the life of the community to which he belongs, it is still almost entirely as a private individual that he exercises a felt influence. He is, more than any other, the man from whom people receive suggestions, or to whom they come for counsel in moments of difficulty or impending failure of their own efforts. Even when a very good man has laboured hard at a very good scheme—as did Dr Bond at his project for a Pennsylvania Hospital—the thing cannot make headway with the public until the public is assured that their townsman Franklin has looked into and approves of it. His good sense, his good humour, his more than good wits in a case requiring them, his aptness to initiate improvements, his admirable moral faculty of never claiming the chief credit when they have been achieved—in a word, his instinct for well-doing, his knowledge of men, and his control over the common littlenesses of human nature in himself—have made him the most helpful man in Pennsylvania for all sorts of occasions. And the occasions on which Pennsylvania availed herself of the services of this private citizen led to public results of enduring consequence, and mark important steps in the evolution of the city and the province. The paving, cleaning, and lighting of the streets; the introduction of new trees, new cereals, and of fertilisers; the invention of the famed American stove; the formation of a citizens' fire brigade; the founding of that academy which became in no long time the University of Pennsylvania; the organisation of the defences both of the city and the province—these are some of the favours, and there were many more, for which Pennsylvania was indebted to Franklin, and, for the most part, not to Franklin as a public man, but only as a private man of incomparable public spirit.

All this time, too, we might say that he was mainly minding and extending his own private business, were it not that, as we have already agreed, his business was really to be a citizen, and his occupation to make himself useful. Even his pastimes subserved that end. If he went out of doors one day, attended only by his son, to fly a kite in a thunderstorm and snatch the lightning from the clouds, it was less out of an abstract desire to verify his theory of the identity of the lightning flash and the so-called electric fluid than because he felt that the home life of mankind would be practically benefited by the conquest of that knowledge. In the four years between 1749 and 1753, he suddenly became the most famous scientific discoverer of his time. The letters in which he had described his surmises and experiments, as so much news sent to a friend in England, were translated in the course of a few years into the principal European languages (including Latin), and were universally admired; not only for the "results" which they communicated, but for their many qualities of matter and form, which ranked them as classics of scientific exposition. This philosopher of the backwoods was the wonder of the world in the middle of that century. And there was that about the very subject-matter of his reputation which caused him to be regarded by the simpler public of many nations as a man of weird knowledge and power, if not exactly as a wizard: in an earlier age he would have had his legend, like Michael Scot, rather than a scientific recognition, like Newton. Nevertheless, all this time the aforesaid private business — the business of Benjamin Franklin, printer and stationer in Philadelphia — was prospering and extending, so that the head of it was now a man of wealth and substance, drawing from this source alone two thousand pounds a year. But Franklin valued money only for the degree in which it made him master of his own time, and so enabled him to prosecute his proper occupation of growing wise and being useful. To further this end he made, about the time that we speak of (in 1748), one of the most generously arranged retirements from business on record. That is to say, he handed over the whole business with all its branches to his foreman David Hall—a former fellow-workman whom he had taken into his employment a few years previously, having a high respect for his qualities of character and intelligence—handed over the entire business to Hall on an agreement that Hall should pay to him *one-half of the present profits* for a term of eighteen years, and then become absolute and sole proprietor, doing with the business as he liked. At the same time it was arranged that neither *Poor Richard's Almanack* nor the *Pennsylvania Gazette* was to be deprived of the strength and fascination which the sagacity, the knowledge, and the humour of Benjamin Franklin could alone impart to their pages.

The actual consequences of this retirement were very different from those looked forward to by the magnanimous printer, who, in taking this great step, had dreamt of securing "leisure during the rest of my life for philosophical studies and amusements." Leisure he had indeed secured, ample leisure in which to wear himself out in the service of his country almost to within an hour of his death forty-two years later. And as to his amusements, if any man might draw amusement from observing the inner springs of great events and studying the behaviour of our little human nature at the elevated plane of *la haute politique*, it should be one who to a profound acquaintance with the realities of life, as only poor and common folk for the most part know them, has added the intellect of a philosopher and the discernment of a humourist. And to Franklin, who was practical man and philosopher and humourist in their happiest and most intimate combination, these opportunities were to be afforded, or forced upon him, in consequence of this said retirement from business and of some other happenings which were less within his control. To refer to this, however, is to anticipate. The point to be noted here is that Franklin's retirement from business meant his entry into the sphere of what, at the risk of appearing paradoxical, I shall call official usefulness. Of course it is the aim and reason-for-being of officials, as such, to prevent anything useful from being done by anybody, and to do as little harm themselves as they can with the remainder of their time. At any rate, in Franklin's own words:—

"The publick now considering me as a man of leisure, laid hold of me for their purposes, every part of our civil government, and almost at the same time, imposing some duty upon me. The governor put me into the commission of the peace; the corporation of the city chose me of the common council, and soon after an alderman; and the citizens at large chose me a burgess to represent them in Assembly."

Thus the leading Pennsylvanian was a leading Pennsylvanian still, only more full of works than ever. But he is now rendering services to the province upon a scale and of a kind that would not have been possible to a private member of the community, however distinguished, influential, and honoured. Of these occupations—such as his improvement of the postal system of the entire colonies; his Plan of Union, submitted to the Congress at Albany in 1754; his co-operation with General Braddock (by which he averted an impending risk of Pennsylvania being dragooned if not devastated by that iracund defender of colonial safeties); his brief but creditable career as a military commander and builder of wooden frontier fortresses—of these he has given in the latter part of the Autobiography a summary which is sufficient in regard to the historical events, but which makes too little of his own part and merit in the things that took place. But it was as leader of the popular party in the constitutional conflict with the Penns, proprietaries of Pennsylvania, that his powers were now (from about 1850 onwards) most signally developed and used to most far-reaching effect. It is, finally, in the course of this provincial conflict that he arrives at the further limit of what I have called his second stage: when, at the crossing of an invisible line, the leading Pennsylvanian becomes the Representative American—because the most absolutely and comprehensively American man on that continent—and as such is planted forward, outside his own country, and upon the universal platform of the world, to be the intellectual and moral protagonist of a new nation, and the advocate of his distressed people to the hearts of the peoples of Europe.

Now regarding the first of these periods, the Philadelphian period, the Autobiography gives a sufficient and a famous account. Regarding the second, the Pennsylvanian period, it speaks with less fulness, and the record is abruptly broken off. Regarding the third—the American or Continental period, when he became so conspicuously a citizen of the world, just because he loved his native country best—the Autobiography tells us nothing at all, ceasing as it does at a point some twenty years earlier. That is a loss which can never be made good, even by the longest and best biography, and the biographies of Franklin are amongst the longest and best in the English language. Within the limits of this appendix all that can be attempted is a brief summary, indicating the part played by Franklin in the history of the Revolutionary era. But even this may be serviceable to some readers of the present reprint, to whom, as few of them can have had the advantage of being born American citizens, knowledge of these things may not have come by nature. First, however, something must be said in order to make more intelligible to English readers that struggle against the proprietors which engaged Franklin's energies during the latter part of his Pennsylvanian period.

The Province was named after Admiral William Penn, to whose son—a more famous William—Charles II. conveyed it in 1681, in lieu of a monetary settlement of the large claim against the Crown which the said son had inherited from the Admiral. Under the title of Proprietor (or Proprietary) of Pennsylvania, William Penn was invested with the functions of a captain-general over this vast region, with power to make treaties with the Indians and to purchase lands from them; and while retaining the status of an English gentleman at home, was virtually created a prince beyond the seas.

"He was to appoint judges and magistrates; could pardon all crimes, except murder and treason; and whatever things he could lawfully do himself he could appoint a deputy to do, he and his heirs for ever. *But* he could lay no impost, no customs, no tax, nor enact a law, without the consent of the freemen of the province in Assembly represented. Of the land he was absolute proprietor; nor would he dispose of any of it absolutely. He sold great tracts at forty shillings per hundred acres, all subject to an annual quit-rent of one shilling per hundred acres. He also reserved manors, city lots, and various portions of territory, either holding them against a rise in value or letting them to tenants."

The history of the province is not our proper topic, so it will be sufficient if the reader takes note of two things that had happened in the interval between, say, 1681 and 1753. In the first place the province of Pennsylvania had grown wonderfully in all senses, by the addition of lands purchased from the Indians, and by the rapid incoming and thriving of settlers. Thus Philadelphia, a garden city with over fourteen thousand inhabitants, was also a great place of trade and shipping, and the business and marketing centre for a provincial population of nearly two hundred thousand. In the second place, the proprietorship had passed to Thomas and Richard Penn, the surviving sons of the founder. Thomas Penn possessed three-fourths of the entire estate; and was in all respects so much the leading personality in this brotherhood that Franklin frequently speaks of "the proprietary," as if there were only one to be reckoned with. The proprietaries were not, in an absolute sense, legislators of Pennsylvania. But through their right of appointment they had a predominant influence, and by their power of veto on all acts of Assembly they were in a position to hinder the conduct of public business to any extent they pleased. They were pleased to do so on all occasions when their prerogatives or their private interest seemed to be either immediately or remotely impinged upon or imperilled. The resident governor of the province was but the nominee and political man-of-business of the Penns, the factor and watch-dog of what was to them merely an enormous private estate. The more that estate became developed by the intelligence and industry, the character and courage of other men—religious men from all the world who had made their homes there, on the confines of the wilderness and with the savage for their neighbour—the more did the Penn interests seem worth fostering and looking after with the closest vigilance and the most jealous foresight. Governor after governor was sent out, each with his secret instructions to this end; and the effect of these instructions was that the history of each governorship is a story of protracted wrangles between the representatives of the people and the deputy of the proprietors. The governor could refuse to sign the bills of the Assembly if the Assembly showed a disposition to encroach or no disposition to comply; and sometimes a whole table-load of these inhibited acts of parliament awaited his pleasure to become law. The Assembly could retaliate by refusing or deferring to "consider the question of the governor's support"—in plain English to pay him his salary, which was optional and honorary and of unfixed amount. Meanwhile the man must live, and bills of another kind than those forwarded by the Assembly were apt to accumulate upon his table. Thus the situation tended to resolve itself into a question of who could hold out longest: the Assembly under the inconveniences of an arrest of public business, or the governor under the discomforts and the privations due to a stoppage of supplies. On one occasion at least the comedy was played out to the point at which the curtain came down upon the historic tableau of a governor receiving his salary with the one hand while with the other he appended his signature to the Assembly's bills. Latterly, however, the proprietors had bethought them to safeguard their interests against the risks of such a surrender by taking a bond of the new governor before sending him out; so that for him to give way upon any point contrary to the spirit or letter of his instructions, would now mean not only ignominious recall, but more or less financial damage for himself or his guarantors.

The antagonism between Proprietors and People that was inherent in the system of government led to a succession of minor disputes, having a merely local interest. But about the time when Franklin entered public life the questions at issue began to take a broader character, entitling them to be considered constitutional rather than local ones. This new phase began with a dispute in regard to the expences of what were called Indian Affairs; by which was meant the expence of keeping up friendly relations with the Indians, and especially of making the considerable presents that were always incidental to negotiations for the purchasing of land from the tribes. The Assembly, as the other charges of administration grew, now submitted that the Proprietors ought to bear a share of this particular burden. How reasonable the request was, will be understood when it is explained that the people had at an earlier time conceded to the Proprietors an exclusive right—which does not seem to have belonged to them originally—of purchasing lands from the Indians. How valuable, also, that right was, will be understood when it is added that, on one occasion alone, the Penns bought for £700 a stretch of lands which they valued at £3,000,000 in their own land-selling negotiations with the colonists. Nevertheless, they stoutly and angrily resisted the demand that they should help to pay the expences incurred in securing for them such vast advantages. If there were such expences, the people, and not they, must be taxed to pay them. This chapter of the dispute was still unclosed when the second and greater one opened. By this second one, Pennsylvania is brought into connection with the great currents of history and the rivalries of mighty nations. England and France were technically at peace with one another from 1748 to 1756; but in North America a war, in which much was achieved and more was suffered, was in active progress from about 1752. Such a war not only threatened England with the loss of her colonies, but threatened the colonists with more than the loss of their homes. For war in that part of the world, in those days, brought the Indian, and all the horrors that Indian warfare meant. No colony was more exposed to the visitations of this unchristian foe than the Quaker colony of Pennsylvania. Therefore the inhabitants hardly needed the commands of the Home Government, which were emphatic and urgent enough, that they (and all other loyal subjects in America) should put themselves in a state of defence. But the Proprietors regarded such conditions of public peril as but favourable opportunities for getting the Assembly to abandon some claim of its own, or to ratify some claim of theirs, which might at the moment be in dispute; and the method was, to permit nothing to be done until they had their way. So bill after bill, appropriating money for war purposes—or, as it was called, "for the King's use"—was now vetoed by the Governor, because the estates of the Penns had not been exempted from the taxation imposed for the defence of their property and everyone else's. The story cannot be followed out in these pages. Suffice it, that the Assembly conducted its disputation with these arrogant and foolish Proprietors in a way that would have been creditable to a greater Parliament, in not its meanest ages; and knew how to be forcible and trenchant without loss of moderation, and constitutionally respectful without abating a tittle of the respect which it very properly had for itself. This strong quality was introduced into the deliberations and the documents of Assembly by Benjamin Franklin; who, as leader of the popular party, and the most gifted writing-man in America, was virtually Secretary for the People during ten years of ever-renewed controversy. In his Autobiography he understates, as usual, the extent to which his personality was a prevailing power, an inspiration and a defence, to the province in those days. Even the Proprietors at last recognised that he was of some importance; and if this knowledge only prompted them to approach him with a bribe, the blunder was quite in character and did him no damage. The colonists expressed their recognition of his value in a more worthy way. For when a point had been reached at which the alternatives presented to them were, either, to accept finally a position of legal vassalage to the Penns, or else allow the defenceless province to go under altogether—then they decided that Benjamin Franklin, their wisest and strongest, was the man to take their cause across the seas for settlement, and submit it to the judgment of greater powers in the English world than even Thomas and Richard Penn.

The last pages of the Autobiography tell of his arrival in England, and indicate rather than explain what he effected. To explain fully would require more space than is available here, but his account may be supplemented a little. In the first place he had come upon a more unwelcome errand than he was aware of when he set out. Colonial affairs had lately begun to receive a good deal of attention from the Home Government, but the tendency of that attention was by no means favourable to colonial ideas. Ministers and officials had discovered that matters were rather confused in that part of the world, and had decided very wisely that they must be put in better order. Unfortunately, the putting in order was to consist in the colonies being taken in hand and "put in their places;" which they were supposed to have wandered away from in dreams of unqualified self-government and such like delusions. In a word, governmental and bureaucratic ideas were having their turn just then in what we may call, by courtesy, official thought. It was likely to be an ill turn for Pennsylvania in particular, since that colony was not a favourite with official thinkers. In the second place, special steps were presently taken by the Proprietors to secure a pronouncement in favour of their own claims as against the Assembly; which were just the kind of claims the Home Government was itself inclined to set up against Assemblies one and all. The occasion was this. Governor Denny, not being at a safe distance in England while the French were marching and the Indians prowling about the frontier of every colony, was in a position to realise what the course which he was commanded to take was likely to lead to. He had, therefore, as became a soldier and a man of sense, broken his instructions and given his assent to bills involving taxation of the Proprietary estates. When this was known in England, a new Governor was at once despatched to take his place. But alas! Governor Hamilton did what Governor Denny had done; so the only remedy remaining was for the poor Penns to invoke the King of England to protect their pockets against the tax-gatherer. The custom of the constitution required that all colonial Acts of Assembly, after being duly passed, should be forwarded to England for the King's assent. The Penns now made a test case of one of those above referred to, and appealed to the King in Council to disallow it. In June 1760 the committee to which the matter was referred rendered a report such as the brothers Penn might themselves have written; so emphatic it was in its vindication of their claims and its denunciation of the Assembly. And not of the Pennsylvania Assembly alone. For, going out into general reflections that were intended as a reprimand and a warning to all other Assemblies in America, it contained much about "attempts to set up a democracy in place of His Majesty's Government"; about the constitution being "brought back to its proper principles"; about "restoring to the Crown, in the person of the Proprietaries, its just prerogatives"—in a word, the note of the time resounded menacingly throughout the dread and decisive document. Franklin was in the act of setting out for a holiday when a copy of this report, or precise information as to its character, reached him. He at once turned back and addressed himself to the task of getting the thing set aside before its stupid thunders had raised, as they would have raised, a real storm. By what means he wrought during the next three months we do not know; but by the time when the King in Council sat to dispose of this matter on September 2, 1760, wisdom and Franklin had prevailed to such effect that the points at issue between Assembly and Proprietors were decided almost without qualification in the Assembly's favour. As for the interview with Lord Mansfield in a back room (referred to in the last lines of the Autobiography), it seems to have been a little theatrical manœuvre by which the Council "saved its face," as the modern diplomatic slang expresses it. The Council also saved in this way the feelings of its over-hasty committee, by affecting to believe that in securing such guarantees as Franklin was now giving it was securing something *quite new and important*, something that entirely changed the aspect of the dispute!

Thus after three years of waiting, he was able to bring to a prosperous conclusion the main business on which he had come. He was detained in England two years longer by other colonial business; but this five years' absence from home was a time pleasantly and usefully spent. Usefully, even from the point of view of imperial affairs; for it would seem that to Franklin, in a degree, we are indebted for the addition of Canada to the British Empire. He shared keenly in the public interests of that time, and was very emphatically what would be called nowadays an Imperialist. Being struck by the futility of England carrying on her war against France in the heart of Germany—where nothing could be gained by her in the end, and not much lost by France, save the winning and losing of battles—he pointed to Canada as a more eligible field of operations: since it was a field which England, should she be victorious, would be able to add permanently to her own estate when the fighting was done. His views and arguments on the subject were laid before Pitt by confidential intermediaries; and whether prompted by Franklin's intelligence or his own, the great War-Minister put this plan in execution, with memorable consequences. But as the end of the war drew near, and when journalists and pamphleteers began to occupy themselves in forecasting the probable terms of peace, Canada became a leading topic. The question was agitated whether England, since she could hardly expect to retain all the spoils that had fallen to her in the course of the struggle, should elect to restore to France the valuable sugar-islands of Guadaloupe, or the dearly-won province of Canada. On such a question Franklin could not be indifferent. He who had been the first to recommend that conquest was naturally the last man to like the idea of its being nullified. And he had better reasons, based upon longer views. "I have long been of opinion," he wrote to Lord Kames, "that the foundations of the future grandeur and stability of the British Empire lie in America; and though, like other foundations, they are low and little now, they are, nevertheless, broad and strong enough to support the greatest political structure that human wisdom ever yet erected." With Canada added, they would be broader and stronger still; and he was led to forecast the expansion of the British race in that part of the world, and thereby the increase of English power in the world at large, in a very optimistic sense. To influence public opinion and the councils of state in favour of his views, he published a voluminous pamphlet setting forth the advantages likely to accrue to England from her new possession in

America. And doubtless the pamphlet had its influence, for he had a good case, and, at all times, a knack of convincing writing. At any rate, by the Treaty of Paris (1763) Guadaloupe was restored to France, and Canada remained, and remains to this day, with England.

Turning from these public concerns to the more personal life of Franklin in England, we may say that if he had not much work to do, every day of the time was well filled. His electrical studies were not neglected. He had experimental apparatus, mostly of his own invention and his own building, set up in his London rooms; and of the many visitors who travelled thither most came to see the man, but not a few came to see the Wonder-worker. A great many of the best papers contained in his Collected Works were written for the amusement or the instruction of the daughter of Mrs Stevenson, the lady whose house at 7 Craven Street, Strand, was his home and headquarters in England now and later. He was accompanied on this visit by his son William, a young man in all senses well formed to make his way in the social and official world; and father and son made many little journeys into different parts of England, and even as far as to Scotland. In the latter country, it is pleasing to know, Franklin found the welcome which he looked back to with the greatest pleasure of all, and avowed that if he were to choose his life-abode anew, it was there he would choose to be and to abide. They also explored the Northamptonshire countryside whence his own and his wife's forbears had come; and he found some new relations who, albeit in a humble station of life, were worthily maintaining the Franklin tradition of health, intelligence, and character. He also sought the printing-house in which he had worked as a lad, and, standing by the old case, which he himself had used, chatted long and curiously with the compositors about how things were in *his* day. On this occasion he derogated so far alas! from the virtues of the Water-American as to send out for a plentiful supply of beer, that he and his fellow-craftsmen might celebrate this reunion in the spirit of true British happiness. On a visit to Cambridge he was received with a great deal of distinction by the learned men of that place, as he was by all learned and thoughtful men wherever he went. Franklin's visit to England was indeed a sort of five-years'-long event, and broken records of the profound impression which his personality made upon all who met him are scattered throughout the social, political, and literary memoirs of that time. He was the subject of a wide curiosity. Great expectations, which it was hard for any man to live up to, everywhere preceded him. Yet none who met him were disappointed, and many were surprised; so wise he was, and so various, so much a perfect man at every point. More notable, perhaps, than the admiration everywhere accorded him was the warm feeling of friendship which he inspired in so many of his contemporaries. And those friendships stood the test of time as few friendships do; not only of time, but of historical circumstances that seldom fail to compel estrangement even between brother and brother, or father and son. To refer to this, however, is to anticipate. What has to be said here is that the enthusiasm of some of his friends would be content with nothing less than his settling in England for good. And had it lain only with him to decide, he was more than half willing. But he well knew that no power on earth could ever induce his good wife to face the horrors of a sea-voyage; so he made his preparations for getting home. The feelings with which he left these shores are happily expressed in a letter to Lord Kames, written from Portsmouth in August

1762. "I am now waiting here only for a wind to waft me to America, but cannot leave this happy island and my friends in it without extreme regret, though I am going to a country and a people that I love. I am going from the Old world to the New; and I fancy I feel like those who are leaving this world for the next: grief at the parting; fear of the passage; hope of the future."

On arriving at Philadelphia, at the beginning of November, he was enthusiastically welcomed by his fellow-citizens. He was, indeed, so much called upon by congratulating friends, and so greatly in request for public business, that he said, in a letter to Miss Stevenson, he would have to come back to England for a little repose. Little as he guessed it, he was to be back in England very soon; and there was not much repose for him in the interval. Almost the whole of the year 1763 was given to a laborious post-office pilgrimage through the colonies, and on his return to Philadelphia he found plenty to do. The whole province was in a state of commotion and dread, the condition of things being between anarchy and civil war. It arose in this way. At the conclusion of the war between France and England, the Indians had not been sufficiently taken into account. Besides being demoralised by their late participation in the white man's doings, they were in a bad temper at the loss of what had been for some years a sort of livelihood. So they continued the war on their own account and in their own way; to such effect that all along the western frontier, "men loathed the very name of Indian" in the year 1763. Among the wild, if godly, Scoto-Irish Calvinists of Paxton, a western county of Pennsylvania, this feeling of morbid repugnance was reinforced by religious fanaticism. In the eyes of these, Indians were "Canaanites," and as such ought righteously to be put to the sword wherever found. Going to find them, they began conveniently by massacring a small group of harmless (apparently Christianised) Indians, who for about two generations had lived in close neighbourhood and in daily intercourse with the white settlers. Them the "Paxton Boys" killed and scalped on one December dawn, and burned their village to the ground. Those who escaped on this occasion fell victims a few days later, when the same band broke into the building at Lancaster in which the poor fugitives had been placed by the local magistrate for safety. Young and old, women and children, all were put to the hatchet. These outrages created a profound horror throughout the province; yet the ruffians were not without their discreet sympathisers and their smug priestly apologists. Franklin, who had just returned from his tour, virtually took the province into his private charge at this juncture, and carried it, as nobody else could have done, through a most ominous passage of its history. He first used his pen and press to admirable purpose in rallying to the cause of humanity the ineffective virtues of the quieter people, and in putting the respectable sympathisers and apologists of massacre out of countenance. He next, as the need arose, improvised a civil guard of a thousand men, for the defence of a terrified congregation of Christian Indians who had come, led by their Moravian pastor, to seek protection in Philadelphia. By and by the Paxton people advanced, heavily armed and in hunting gear, breathing wrath and tags of Scripture, to take these refugees in the heart of the city and scalp them where they stood. Franklin and his men were prepared to fight to the death if need be; yet he was loath to shed the blood even of a

"Paxton Boy" if he could help it. So when the rabble of terrorists was within a mile or two of the city, he went out, accompanied only by a couple of citizens, to meet and confer with them. The effect of that conference, in which he took a very high and severe tone, such as these wild but vigorous-minded men would respect, was that they recognised the odds as well as the argument against them, and went home. So there was an end of that trouble, thanks to the courage and character of a single man.

Troubles of a more familiar sort speedily ensued. In October 1763, a new governor had arrived in the person of a nephew of the Proprietors. A nephew of the Proprietors meant a grandson of the revered Founder, so no appointment could have been more pleasing to Pennsylvanian feelings. The sending of a member of the family to reside among them was taken to be an augury that the days of conflict were at an end; that an era of conciliation, good understanding, and co-operation between Proprietors and people, was about to begin. Governor Penn was received in Pennsylvania as an English royal prince would be received in any English colony to-day; and in this instance, at least, the gratified Assembly made all haste to "consider the question of the Governor's support." Unfortunately this enthusiasm was misplaced, and these hopes were illusory. During the Paxton affair, the new Governor played a very weak part, and was fain to take up his abode in Franklin's house till the trouble was over. When business was resumed, it began to appear that he had his "instructions," like any other. The result was such a series of vetoes and interferences that by the middle of March 1764 the Assembly was brought into a state of sheer paralysis or arrest of its functions as a legislative body. After this disappointment of such generous hopes, a sort of desperation prevailed. It seemed that nothing could be done at all with that family. The obvious alternative, then, was to do without it; if only it could be got rid of. So the Assembly adjourned until May 14th. The recess was devoted to a political campaign concerned with only one point: namely "Whether an humble address should be drawn up and transmitted to his Majesty; praying that his Majesty would be graciously pleased to take the people of this province under his immediate protection and government." It was found that an overwhelming majority of the freeholders was in favour of the change of constitution which this pointed to. It had been powerfully advocated by Franklin in a timely pamphlet which was widely read throughout Pennsylvania during the recess. In this he had reviewed, not for the first or last time, the history of their constitutional conflict, and argued cogently that there was something wrong in the system which led to such results.

"For though it is not unlikely that in these as well as other disputes there are faults on both sides, every glowing coal being apt to inflame its opposite; yet I see no reason to suppose that all proprietary rulers are worse men than other rulers, nor that all people in proprietary governments are worse people than those in other governments. I suspect, therefore, that the cause is radical, interwoven in the constitution, and so become the very nature, of proprietary governments; and will therefore produce its effects so long as such government continue."

That was a very exciting year in the political history of Pennsylvania, and Franklin's pen was very busy, to good literary as well as controversial purpose. Suffice it, however, to say here that when a new Assembly met in October the business of appointing an agent to carry the petition to the King was at once taken up. For this duty Franklin was chosen, in spite of an impassioned endeavour of the small but influential proprietary party in the House to have someone "less dangerous"—that is, less likely to succeed—employed in the hateful and fateful business. November 7 found Franklin setting out for Chester, on the Delaware, where he was to embark for England. A cavalcade of five hundred citizens brought him on the way, who was crossing the seas to serve them all. With good weather to help, the ship made a quick voyage, and on December 9 he was delivered (delivered, indeed! for a sea voyage in those days was a hard imprisonment, from which he was especially apt to suffer) on to kindly English ground. Posting from Portsmouth to London he was soon established at his old quarters in Craven Street, receiving his delighted, astonished, thrice-welcoming friends once more.

From this point the Pennsylvanian question ceases to have actuality, even for the biographer of Franklin. It has henceforth only a retrospective interest, as it is seen to have supplied a kind of rehearsal in little of that larger constitutional conflict with which the Great Pennsylvanian was to be so memorably associated. In this new conflict, the place of Pennsylvania is taken by the whole of the American colonies; and the place of the Proprietors, infatuated in their assertion of unjust and impossible prerogatives, is taken by our good King George the Third. The historic course of events which solved the greater question disposed of the lesser one by a sort of immediate inference, since the privileges of the vassal-despot in a distant dependency could not well survive the deposition of his sovereign. It needs only to be said here that Franklin, once arrived in England, was soon advised how unfavourable the moment was for pressing the business on which he had come. And although the petition of the Assembly was duly presented, and references to the probability or improbability of some impending result thereof appear from time to time in Franklin's correspondence, we may practically consider the question as having been in abeyance from now until the Fourth of July 1776: when an end was made of that old song, and of an older and better one.

The new and greater question referred to above, was, of course, that of England's right to tax the colonies by Act of Parliament. The idea had been mooted more than once during the first part of the century, but no responsible politician had ever deigned to take it seriously. In recent years, however, several circumstances had co-operated in disposing statesmen to accord more respectful consideration to what had been hitherto a scouted project. There was, in the first place, that general strengthening of the ideals of what one may call governmentalism, already alluded to, which began to be effective on the accession of George the Third. About that time there also began to be felt a great need for new sources of revenue; partly owing to the cost of the war, and partly because the territorial expansion which that war led to, carried with it a heavy increase in the charges of Empire. Finally, the war itself had shown the resources of the colonists, even their resources in ready money, to be far greater than had hitherto been supposed. When, therefore, Mr Charles Townshend prepared in 1763 his extensive plan for organising and governing the colonies: and when it was known that the said plan would have for its immediate result and visible token the raising of a revenue there by taxation imposed from England, and the planting of a standing army in the heart of the country, to keep everything and everybody in good order—of course he had with him at once the implicit approbation of every man in England who was by way of being in the current of prevailing ideas: that is to say, who was well-informed without knowledge, and intelligent without thought. As it happened, Mr Townshend and his particular set were somewhat abruptly unseated from the place of authority; but the spirit of the time being what I have said, this displacement made little difference in the plans of government. His successors promptly took up his unfinished work. Some months before Franklin sailed for England, news reached the colonies that Mr George Grenville had intimated his intention of introducing a bill into Parliament at an early date, to provide for the raising of a revenue in America by means of a stamp duty. Colonists were almost as much astonished as alarmed at this talk of the English Parliament imposing taxation upon them; who conceived themselves to be within the British Empire, indeed, but outside that particular realm which Parliament represented and made laws for. They were not represented there: therefore they could not be taxed there. The Assemblies, that of Pennsylvania among the rest, took steps to formulate the colonial view, and appealed to the Common Law of England, the provisions of their charters, and the custom of the constitution, in support of it. These views were embodied in loyal and dutiful Resolutions, to be transmitted to England, deprecating an innovation which was felt to be fraught with the most evil consequences. Franklin brought over the Resolution of his Assembly, and was further instructed to co-operate with the other colonial agents in trying to get the Ministry to abandon its ill-considered scheme. And try they did; but, for all the effect they could produce, they might as well have been at home. An interview with Grenville on February 2, 1765, only showed how little common ground, whether of opinion or feeling, there was to the two sides, and how little the best of arguments were likely to influence the action of Government. Eleven days later the bill was read a first time in the House of

Commons; and, despite the brave resistance of a very small band who stood for sense and liberty, its passage through both Houses was so easy and rapid that by the 22nd of March it had received the royal assent and become law. So that matter was settled, it seemed. The principle of taxation by Act of Parliament had been asserted beyond recall. The only question now open, in the minds of English politicians and people, was, "How shall we next apply that principle—what new taxes shall we impose?" It was a question that all were asking, and very many were hastening to answer.

One answer as good as all came from America, like the muttering of far-off thunder, about six months later. News of the passing of the Stamp Act had arrived there at the beginning of July: the returning packets which reached England at the beginning of November reported the result. The whole country was swayed by one universal indignation. The separate colonies were drawn together as they had never been before. Resolutions denouncing the new law as tyrannical and unconstitutional had been passed by the leading Assemblies. The people had made a bond with each other to use no articles of English manufacture, or articles imported from England, until the injustice was undone. If they had not the cloth with which to make their own clothes, they would wear their old ones until the new were ready. And in the meantime no lamb was to be killed for food, but all reared for their wool, until the country should be supplied with the material of the textile and clothing industries. This, and much else like this, was strange news to English ears. Even Franklin seems to have been surprised at the vigour and unanimity of protest. Without waiting for this encouragement, however, he had been hard at work since July trying whether the disastrous measure of the late government (for Grenville and his colleagues, they also in turn, had been thrown out of office by the caprice of their sovereign) could not be cancelled, even yet. While he was thus employed in England his fellow-countrymen in America were denouncing him as the worst of traitors, and rioters were surrounding his house in Pennsylvania, where his good wife was for a while in a state of siege. The explanation of this curious phenomenon is simple enough. When the Stamp Act was passed Grenville had sent for the colonial agents and asked them to help him, for their country's sake as well as the King's, in a matter of some delicacy. He was unwilling to send persons from England to be collectors of the revenue arising under the Stamp Act, since the appearance of these strangers as tax-gatherers could not but be hurtful to colonial feelings. He therefore begged that the agents would give him the names of men of good repute and liking, in their several parts of the country, whom he might take steps to have appointed collectors of this revenue. For Pennsylvania, Franklin submitted the name of Mr John Hughes, but in doing so he neither signified his own approval of the Act nor his opinion that Mr Hughes would accept the post if it were offered him. Folk in America, however, gathered only that Hughes had been appointed collector under the hateful Act, and that his nomination, if not the Act itself, was Franklin's work. Hence the emotion and the riot aforesaid. The riot did no great harm to him or his, and the emotion gave place to more worthy feelings when the truth of the matter came home, as it did, by a later ship.

Meanwhile Franklin was working away, interviewing ministers and other public men—"explaining, consulting, disputing, in a continual hurry from morning till night"—during all the second half of that year and the first weeks of the next one. The new government consisted mainly of friends of America, many of them personal friends of his. The most powerful friend of all, however, was the enormous section of the British mercantile and manufacturing class, which found itself being ruined by the sudden disappearance of America as a market for British goods. These good men passed from astonishment to dismay, and from dismay to desperation; and before the end was reached, their clamours filled the lobbies of the House of Commons. Ministers saw that there was nothing for it but to repeal the unfortunate Act, at all costs to the pride of the people, or the self-will of the King. To strengthen its hands before attempting to do so, the Ministry held a famous Enquiry at the beginning of the year 1766. A Committee of the whole House sat for many days receiving evidence from men of every class, occupation, and description, who had any, even the remotest, experience of, or connection with, America or American affairs. The Enquiry is famous, however, mainly on account of the evidence given in the course of it by one witness, whose testimony was of so remarkable a character, and covered so completely the whole ground of the Committee's reference, that it has extinguished for us, and really rendered superfluous at the time, that of all the other witnesses together. Needless to say, this witness was Benjamin Franklin. Of this celebrated "Examination of Dr Franklin before the House of Commons," it would be impossible to overstate the significance and value, whether regarded as a contribution to a great historic question, or as a revelation of the many powers of the man himself. In both respects it was surprising, and in both respects it created a profound impression both in this country and in America. In America, it put new heart and patriotism even into the most fervent; in England, it informed those who were already most deeply informed in American affairs; and to those who had long known and admired Franklin it revealed a compass of qualities, a faultless fulness of knowledge, and a control equally of his knowledge and his powers, which went beyond all that they expected even from him. They were men of affairs, and some of them men of talent, who examined him; and the questions were subtly and searchingly put, for the purpose of placing him in at least a momentary difficulty. Yet Edmund Burke could only compare the whole scene to that of a schoolmaster submitting to be catechised by his pupils. When Franklin withdrew from the Bar of the House, the apologists of the Stamp Act had not a solid inch of ground to stand upon. Ministers were ready to hug themselves for joy, and him also. And indeed he had done their business for them, as all of them combined could not have done it. His examination closed on February 13. Just eight days later a Repealing Bill was introduced into Parliament, and, after a debate of which the eloquence has perished but the glory and splendour yet somehow abide, as though it had been fully reported—the bill was carried through both Houses, and on March 8 it received the royal and unwilling assent. When the good news reached America, there was such rejoicing as that side of the world had never seen, and everywhere honour and acclamation attended the name of Franklin.

But that was a time of quick changes in the political world. They were seldom changes for the better, and that which now followed proved one of the most disastrous in English history. Within four months of its passing the Repealing Act, the Rockingham Ministry was wrecked by

Court influences. Its place was taken, after a time, by a famous cabinet, of some of the talents and all the contradictions; a cabinet which had been put together by Lord Chatham, but was never presided over by him. In the absence of any effective head of the Government, the different departments of state policy now went their different ways; and those concerned with American affairs soon took a direction as contrary to all that Lord Chatham considered wise or right as well could be. The dispute with the Colonies was wantonly revived at once, never to be quieted again till England had lost these colonies for good, and the world had thereby gained a new nation. The series of events which led to this result was initiated by the Mr Charles Townshend referred to some pages back, who had entered the new cabinet as Chancellor of the Exchequer. As such, it was his business to propose schemes of taxation; and the nature of the man himself, as well as the character of the influences continually brought to bear upon him, made it inevitable that he should use his position in order to raise again the question of getting a revenue out of America and—what was of infinitely more concern to the feelings, both of the King and People of this country—of getting it from taxation imposed upon Americans by the English Parliament. He addressed himself to this task with vigour, promptness and ingenuity. On March 13, 1767, he laid before the House of Commons a general view of extensive plans with regard to America. The nature of the policy then unfolded is sufficiently indicated by the fact that the parliamentary door-keepers had orders not to admit the colonial agents within the precincts on that day. The House approved heartily of the plans submitted to it, and directed that bills embodying them should be drafted forthwith and introduced. They were drafted, introduced, and passed, within a month;

and two months later all America was in a ferment.

In the banquet of discord which the obliging Mr Townshend now " set before the King," the Revenue Act may be considered as the grand piece of provocation, the veritable *pièce de résistance.* It was ingeniously concocted, but I must refer the Reader to the pages of Burke for a description of the many ingredients of contradictory motive which it embodied without managing to blend them. Three chief things are to be noted about it. It was an Act of Parliament, imposing taxation, a thing which Americans abhorred; and its preamble asserted the general principle which they had contested so famously. But then, what it imposed was a duty on imports from Britain. So, it had an affinity with the duties already being paid under the Navigation Act; the principle of which had been admitted as constitutional and just by Franklin in his examination before the House. But again, the scene of collection was now to be in America; so that there should be no question any more as to the jurisdiction of Parliament, or the validity of its Acts, in that country. The inhabitants would see the tax-gatherer in their midst, and they would know who had sent him. Further, the proceeds of the taxes were to go to form a Civil List; out of which the governors of colonies, and presently other officials, were to receive their salaries *from the King.* This innovation would make the relation of the people to the Governors that of a subject population in a conquered province to officials set over them by a distant despot: to whom, and to whom alone, these Governors would feel that they owed either respect or kindness. Finally, it was indicated clearly that this was not the end, but that more would follow as occasion served or the need arose.

Small wonder, then, if the resistance opposed to

this new attack was fierce and general. As the commotion exceeded that created by the Stamp Act, so the measures of retaliation proposed were of a more drastic and defiant kind. Not only was the non-consumption of British goods again resolved upon, but the different colonies now decided to set up all sorts of manufactures for themselves; not for the occasion only, but for the rest of time. It is scarcely possible for us nowadays to conceive how extreme, how unnatural, how monstrous almost, this decision of Americans to make for themselves the pins, nails, beaver hats and cutlery which they needed, seemed to honest, home-staying English folk in those days. Even friends of America felt that the colonists were going very far indeed! And since "all minds were now employed in considering, all pens in defending, the rights which Mr Townshend's Acts invaded," there presently resulted an immense intellectual development of the whole subject, a development of all its bearings in the consciousness and daily thoughts of men. This in itself was fast creating an entirely new situation, not to be nullified by the half-hearted undoing, on the part of the mother-country, of that which it had been an insult as well as a wrong to do at all. The history of the six or eight years that followed might be set forth as an illustration of this text, and very full of moral interest it would be. This, however, is not the place for it, so the Reader can only be reminded of two or three important dates. One day in September 1768 — eighteen months after the passing of the Revenue Act—fourteen British men-of-war lay with their broadsides towards the town of Boston, to cover the landing of 700 British soldiers. "With muskets charged, bayonets fixed, drums beating, fifes playing, and a complete train of artillery," these took possession of the Common, the State-house, the Court-house, and the Fanueil Hall, where those famous town-meetings of the Boston citizens had been held. An apparition like this did not bode reconciliation: but the people being helpless, the peace was kept for a time. About eighteen months later, however (March 1770), occurred the affair between soldiers and populace, known as the Boston Massacre; a trivial affair in itself, but immensely dynamic in its moral effects. A little after this came an incomplete, and therefore ineffective repeal of the Revenue Act; the tax on tea being retained for the sake of asserting the principle. But as Americans, strange to say, still gave no orders for this taxed tea (though they were really going to have it cheaper than they had ever had it before) the King induced ministers to have four ship-loads sent into American ports, thus bringing temptation very near the door. From New York and Philadelphia the ships were ignominiously sent back. At Charleston the people unloaded the tea, and stored it in cellars, where it perished. But at Boston the Governor would not permit the ship to clear out again, as the people demanded that it should; so a lawless band, disguised as Red Indians, went aboard and emptied the cargo into the harbour. This was in December, 1773; and both in England and America the state of popular feeling was now such as to leave small prospect of a speedy, if indeed of any, renewal of kindness between colonies and mother-country. To such a pass had it come, in so few years. But though the years were few, the time seemed an era to those who had to bear the burden and the strain of them; to those who, like Franklin, called to the difficult part of mediators, had to deal with each day's difficulties as they could, every new day in all that time bringing its own changes of hope and fear.

To treat of Franklin's life during this period with sufficient fulness to make the account interesting would be to write not a biographical sketch but a very long chapter in general history. The effect of it all would be to show that, apart from any particular transaction in which he may have been concerned, the mere fact of his presence in England during those years was a historical factor of the first importance. And it was a factor which, so long as it counted for anything, counted for preservation of the peace between England and her colonies. His great intellectual and moral prestige dignified in the eyes of all, and especially in the eyes of Ministers, the cause which he stood for; a cause which might else have been more summarily dealt with, as official contempt for the claims of a troublesome pack of people on the fringe of the Empire might have dictated. It was impossible to regard in that way the people who had a Benjamin Franklin for their advocate and representative man. Franklin's many social qualities also, which gained him friendships even in circles least sympathetic to the American cause, enabled him to exercise an influence which cannot be verified in detail, it is true, but the absence of which for a single season would, we cannot doubt, have greatly affected the course of events. And, as a fact, it was not until the hour when that influence was withdrawn—until the hour when Franklin, giving up the long struggle with the forces of arrogance and blindness, bade farewell to these shores and sailed for home—that England gave a head to the counsels of final rigour which changed her children into enemies and lost her an Empire. While he remained here, also, his influence with his countrymen, which was very great in spite of the distance and in spite of the tendency of the colonists to suspect ever and again that they were being sold to the enemy, was of great effect in the service of moderation. He was as much a patriot as any man in America, and few in America had such a reasoned faith as he in the justice of his country's claims and her power to make them ultimately prevail. But at the same time he knew also the greatness of England, and was acquainted with those good qualities of the English people which were not apparent for the moment in its political relations to America. Therefore, while urging his countrymen not to grow faint in maintaining their rights by all constitutional means — and especially by persisting in their non-importation resolutions with a unanimity which would leave no doubt of their being in earnest—he was none the less explicit in his disapprobation of all those (they were a small but dangerous band) whose idea of patriotism tended to express itself in words of provocation and acts of violence, whereby conciliation would be made more difficult. Thus it came, that while some in England, finding that Franklin, for all his reasonableness, was as firm as bed-rock on the great principles at issue, described him regretfully as being "too much of an American" for their purposes—at this very time the more forward set among his countrymen were apt to insinuate that, after all, Franklin was "too much of an Englishman" to be really heart and soul with the patriots in America. This absurdity, however, which was the property of a few, belongs to the later and more morbid stages of the disagreement. Upon the whole, his prestige was as high amongst his countrymen at this time as it was in Europe, and by the year 1770 he found himself invested with the Agentship for four of the colonies. The Agentship for Massachusetts, especially, gave him a good deal of difficult work to do, owing to the great part played by that province in the events which developed the Revolution. For a time, indeed, he was able to do little in the matter, since that self-conscious, vain, and vacillating would-be martinet of office, Lord

Hillsborough,[1] refused to recognise his appointment as valid. Franklin has left a most dramatically-written minute of their famous interview, in which the whole man Hillsborough, both the individual and the type, is set before us with almost creative talent. Franklin's studies of the course of action in the years of Lord Hillsborough's management of colonial affairs are all summed up in an essay called "Rules for Reducing a Great Empire to a Small One." This had an immense success at the time, and was at once so matterful and so spirited in composition that Franklin himself was very well pleased to have been the author of it. It was reprinted as a pamphlet in London twenty-six years later, in order to meet a steady public demand for copies, when the things it referred to were very ancient history indeed. Another literary *jeu d'esprit* of this period (1770-3) was "An Edict by the King of Prussia:" a very sly composition, in which that German potentate was represented as claiming to impose upon England (a country long ago colonised by emigrants from *his* dominions) those duties and burdens of obedience and tribute which England was actually seeking to impose on America. This thing was cast in the form of an exciting piece of newspaper intelligence, enclosing a verbatim version of the alleged startling edict. Scores of well-informed folk were deceived by it for something more than a moment, and thousands were amused for at least a week. As for Lord Hillsborough, Franklin was instrumental in having him removed from office, in July 1772; and had some influence in the choice of Lord Dartmouth as his successor. A better choice could not have been made, if good-disposition towards all parties, and an honest desire to be useful, and to conciliate, had

[1] Appointed, at the end of 1768, head of the newly-created department called the Colonial Office.

been qualifications enough for the post. But Dartmouth, as it proved, had not that independence of judgment and that force of character that would have been needed to undo, and to undo quickly enough, the evil which had been done during Hillsborough's four years' term of office. Though there was now better ground for hope, fulfilment somehow tarried; and meantime matters were moving apace at the other side of the world. At this critical juncture it was that England, in a momentary indulgence of all that is worst in her national temper, saw fit to deprive herself of the services of the one man whose presence here made conciliation still possible, the one man who was capable, even yet, of holding the Empire together.

One day towards the close of 1772, Franklin was talking to a friend, a member of Parliament, about American affairs. He spoke with some warmth of the recklessness of ministers in persisting as they did in a policy of provocations and reprisals; to which he could see no end save a complete change and alienation of American feeling towards England. It was possible for him, he said, residing in this country and knowing the people, to view the various ill-advised acts of policy as merely the acts of politicians, and to allow a great deal for personal character and for personal purposes. But in America, men could take little account of such considerations, even if they were in the temper to do so. They would only see, in all that had been attempted or done in the name of this country during recent years, an expression of the feelings towards them of the British people. His friend replied that Franklin was in error in assuming that ministers were entirely to blame, or that the policy which had worked so badly had been originated solely by them. He could assure him that the measures which he more particularly complained of—the introduction of an

English soldiery to overawe the people, and the rendering of Governors, Judges, and other officials, dependent on the King for their salaries—had been first urged upon ministers by natives of that country, resident in the country, and held in the highest respect there. In proof of what he then said, he brought to Franklin some days later the batch of correspondence known to history as the Hutchinson Letters.

These were a series of letters which had been written, during the years 1768 and 1769, by Thomas Hutchinson and Andrew Oliver, to a correspondent in this country. The name of this correspondent had been carefully erased before the documents were placed in Franklin's hands; but the general drift and subject-matter of the letters indicated clearly enough that they were meant to meet the eyes of someone in a position to influence the plans of Government towards America. It may be explained at once (what Franklin did not know till later) that they had been addressed to Mr William Whately, a member of Parliament, then lately deceased. At the time when the letters were written, Hutchinson was Lieutenant-Governor and Chief-Justice, and Oliver was Secretary, of the colony of Massachusett's Bay; while Whately was then private secretary to Mr George Grenville, of Stamp Act renown. Though ostensibly addressed to Whately, the letters had really been written for Grenville's information and misguidance. That gentleman was not himself in the Government in 1768-9, but many of his friends were; and to him and those friends the writers looked to have the policy which they recommended brought into force. As a fact, they had not looked in vain. There was a strong family resemblance between the recommendations of Messrs Hutchinson and Oliver and the recent measures of the British Government; nor could any bureaucrat seated at the heart of an Empire have greater faith in the blessed efficacy of vigour and rigour, rigour and vigour, than those denaturalised natives of a distant province. Lieutenant-Governor Hutchinson is here found bravely declaring his conviction that "there must be some abrogation of English liberties" in that part of the world; while Mr Oliver has an ingenious scheme for getting rid, in some degree, of the prevailing prejudice in favour of social equality, and so arresting that democratic tendency which is such a lamentable feature of colonial life. It is urged again and again that a sufficient stand of imperial troops ought to be kept in the country, to support the governors in enforcing whatever new laws might be imposed *invito populo*. Perhaps the most mischievous feature of these letters, however, was the fact that they so seriously misrepresented to the home authorities the state of public feeling in America. That there was any general or national sentiment in the country was ignored or explicitly denied. The opposition to the Revenue Act, it seemed, was limited to a prominent minority of the population; and behind the recent display of resistance there was nothing but the personal influence of a few agitators. These, of course, could be removed by the exercise of a little proper vigour—and then! Altogether of this nature, in a word, were the Hutchinson Letters. That they had a considerable influence cannot be doubted, even though one may hold that things would have gone almost equally astray without the misdirections which they afforded. We know, as a fact, that King George, who had so great a part in all that was attempted in those years in regard to America, attached particular value to the opinions of Mr Hutchinson. That gentleman had now been advanced to the Governorship, with Oliver succeeding him in the lieutenancy. Thus the pair were still undivided. Governor Hutchinson was at that moment (end of 1772) in high conflict with the Assembly and people of Massachusetts, and was indeed making no little trouble for the home Government by the provocative attitude which he maintained.

But our concern is with Franklin. The reading of these letters produced upon him an impression at first startling and painful, and yet in the end restorative and cheering. It was painful indeed to discover that such counsels as these had been secretly sent to England by men who were Americans born; to know that the forces of coercion had received not only support but persistent prompting from those who, by ancestry, birth-place, up-bringing, social standing, and official position, were called upon, more than most others, to be the sympathetic interpreters of their countrymen's views to the English Government. In making themselves the mouthpiece of views so adverse, they had done evil to their country. And the evil had been done in a clandestine way which invested the whole correspondence, in the eyes of a patriot like Franklin, with an additional character of baseness, of conspiracy, almost of treason. But then, just in proportion as Hutchinson and Oliver were to be condemned, in that degree, also, was the English Government to be exonerated. It was liable enough to go wrong of its own initiative; and the English character is more prone than others, the world admits, to arrogance and self-righteousness. But it was somewhat to be excused, surely, for not doubting its own justice and reasonableness, in relation to the recalcitrant colonists, when it found native Americans, of the standing of Hutchinson and Oliver, hastening to recommend just the kind of foolish strong measures towards which it was spontaneously carried by its own share and portion in the original sin of all governing Powers. For Franklin, these letters threw a flood of light upon the political events of the past few years, and it is possible he may even have over-estimated their significance and influence. They showed, at any rate, that those measures which were most bitterly resented by the Colonists had been long advocated and preached in the secret ear of Government by responsible Americans, whose opinions could not but carry great weight with English ministers. From this discovery it followed, that there was at once less cause for anger and less reason for despair than there had lately seemed to be, even to Franklin. His own vast patience had begun to feel the strain and the wear of those years; and across the ocean English injustice, as it was considered, was fast creating a new America, an America very full of anti-British feeling. This was very unlike that land as he had known it, and the change was to him sincerely regrettable. It was also a menace; for it might presently gather sufficient force to make the pace in that country, and then the hopes of reconciliation would be small indeed. To avert this, and to neutralise the growing sense of a national animosity, Franklin considered that no means would serve so powerfully as the conveying to the leaders of opinion in America that new knowledge, that new side-light upon the whole situation, which had just come to him, and had affected his own feelings so favourably, so forgivingly, towards those who were responsible in this country. He begged permission to send these letters to America. After some delay, permission was granted; and on December 2, 1772, he enclosed them in his usual official dispatch, addressed to the secretary of the committee of correspondence of Massachusetts Assembly. He was not at liberty to explain whom he had them from: they were not to be copied or printed: and when they had been shown to the leading men of the popular party, they were to be returned to this country. On all these points he had, and transmitted to his correspondent, explicit instructions.

There is not space here to follow the letters in their wanderings. Suffice it, that they were shown to many men and some women, and that their presence in America, if not their precise import, was soon the secret of a whole continent. The effect was everywhere what Franklin had anticipated: rage against Hutchinson; kindlier feelings towards England than had prevailed for many months. They were duly returned after a time; but, Franklin's instructions notwithstanding, they had got into print in America. Copies found their way over here, the newspapers gave them in full, there was a great deal of annoyance in the official world, a great deal of talk about the matter everywhere. In all of which there was nothing that called for Franklin's intervention. But just when the nine-days' wonder was ready to die down, it suddenly started off into a new and untoward career of thrilling interest. Mr Thomas Whately announced in the newspapers that the letters so much spoken of had been written to his late brother; and as good as said that they had been stolen from the executors by Mr John Temple. Mr Temple thereupon challenged Mr Whately to fight. Fight they did at dawn of a December day, in Hyde Park, and Whately was badly wounded. On returning to town (he had been in the country for a few days) Franklin heard of this duel, and heard also that the gentlemen were going to fight again. He therefore sat down and promptly wrote the following letter:—

"To the Printer of the Public Advertiser.

"Sir,—Finding that two gentlemen have been unfortunately engaged in a duel, about a transaction and its circumstances, of which both of them are totally ignorant and innocent, I think it incumbent upon me to declare (for the prevention of farther mischief, as far as such a declaration may contribute to prevent it) that I alone am the person who obtained and transmitted to

Boston the letters in question. Mr W. could not communicate them, because they were never in his possession; and, for the same reason, they could not be taken from him by Mr T. They were not of the nature of *private* letters between friends. They were written by public officers to persons in public stations, on public affairs, and intended to procure public measures; they were therefore handed to other public persons, who might be influenced by them to produce those measures. Their tendency was to incense the mother-country against her Colonies, and, by the steps recommended, to widen the breach; which they effected. The chief caution expressed with regard to privacy was, to keep their contents from the Colony agents, who, the writers apprehended, might return them, or copies of them, to America. That apprehension was, it seems, well founded; for the first Colony agent who laid his hands on them thought it his duty to transmit them to his constituents.

"B. FRANKLIN,

"*Agent for the House of Representatives of Massachusetts Bay.*

"Craven Street, December 25th, 1773."

By this announcement, a new surprise sprang out of this surprising, if not sensational, subject. But the greatest sensation was yet to come. Franklin had not expected his letter to have any other effect than the preventing of possible homicide, and everybody thought he had acted with spirit and propriety in the matter. He was soon to find that he had delivered himself into the hands of enemies. Personal enemies, it is true, he had none in England, and of friends he had a great many. But the cause which he represented was becoming more and more obnoxious and exasperating to those in power. Which means that a growing sense of their own incapacity to deal with the situation which they had made for themselves, against all wise advice, had begun already to render them morbid. Those who were disappointed at finding Franklin "too much of an American," were apt also to tell themselves, when matters came to this stage, and as their troubles thickened, that if it were not for that disobliging, therefore ill-disposed Franklin, those troubles would not exist at all. It is natural to the human mind to hate a just man; and equally natural to those who find themselves vainly battling against a moral principle and the wishes of a people, to assume that the interpreter and spokesman of the insurgent moral will is the sole maker of all the mischief. These and other determinants may have been at work. Certain it is that official England now thought it saw a possibility of damaging the American cause in the person of its most illustrious exponent; and, no kind god preventing, it hurriedly took the foolish business in hand.

It had been Franklin's duty some months previously to present a Petition from the Massachusetts Assembly, praying that his Majesty would be graciously pleased to remove from their official positions Governor Hutchinson and Lieutenant-Governor Oliver, as being men who had wrought to make misunderstanding and dispeace between the different parts of his Majesty's dominions. Months passed, and no result of this petition was forthcoming. But now Franklin received on Saturday, January 8, 1774, a brief and sudden intimation that this petition was to be considered by the Lords of Committee (to whom it had been referred by the King) on the following Tuesday; when he, as agent for the Assembly, was commanded to attend. Late on Monday afternoon it was intimated to him that Messrs Hutchinson and Oliver were to be heard by counsel. This was short notice of an unusual procedure, not to say a startling fact. At the meeting he at once raised that point, submitting that the matter before their Lordships was "a question of civil or political prudence," upon which their Lordships were "already perfect judges, and could receive no assistance in it from the arguments of counsel." If counsel was heard on the one side, however, it ought also to be heard on the other. He therefore craved their Lordships to appoint a further day for the hearing, that he might have an opportunity of instructing counsel on behalf of his clients. A further hearing was accordingly appointed for Saturday the 29th of that month.

Brief as the proceedings at this meeting had been, they left little room for doubt that some very bad intentions towards himself were preparing their hour. An inkling that this was so became curiously diffused; and the Press of this country hastened to assume an exceedingly sympathetic attitude towards these intentions, whatever they might be. Franklin suddenly found himself an object of general attack, and very precise reports reached him as to the nature and upshot of the performance which had been arranged for the 29th.

After some difficulty in finding a suitable counsel, he secured the famous John Dunning, afterwards Lord Ashburton; a lawyer of the highest intellectual power, but too often unable to do himself justice owing to his many physical frailties. Dunning promptly set aside the elaborate brief which Franklin's solicitor had prepared, and decided that their case could not be better argued than on the ground taken up by Franklin himself at the first meeting of the Committee.

On the morning of the 29th there was a general movement of high political London towards the Cockpit, as the building was called, in which these Privy Council meetings were held. The attendance of Privy Councillors on this occasion was almost unprecedented: thirty-five in all sat round the table, which extended down the middle of the large oblong room. There was, besides, a large gathering of members of Parliament and other public men, and a few private persons whose distinction or connections had gained them admittance. Amongst the former was Edmund Burke, amongst the latter Dr Priestley and Jeremy Bentham. Everyone except the Privy Councillors had to stand during the whole proceedings. Franklin stood near the fireplace at the upper end of the room, motionless and erect, for a space of three hours. A few paces off, by the Lord President's chair, stood the hero of the occasion, Alexander Wedderburn, whom Mr Israel Mauduit, the solicitor for Hutchinson and Oliver, had engaged as counsel. He had been engaged for his special talents, which though not of the kind that make men honoured, were of the kind that may render them useful for purposes of a sort. By the exercise of these talents in the support of evil causes he rose ultimately to be a peer and the Lord Chancellor of England. Then he died, hated and despised even by those who had used him longest. No human being in his own or subsequent times has had a good word to say for Alexander Wedderburn. Even Mr Doyle, who writes American history from an English, not to say a Georgian, point of view, freely gives Wedderburn to the dogs. Even Mr Lecky, who is astonishingly unjust to Franklin in his account of this affair, calls Wedderburn the Belial of his profession. Even George the Third, whom he served so well—until he ratted from him in turn—said, upon hearing of his death, as first Earl of Rosslyn, twenty-four years later: "Then he has not left a worse man behind him." This was the creature who had been put forward on this public occasion to browbeat and insult one of the most illustrious and most honoured characters of that age—an old man, and one doubly entitled to respect not only on account of his own great qualities and his services to humanity, but because he was one in whom an entire people was proud to see itself represented to the world. Aged just forty-one years at this time, Wedderburn had already made more than a beginning of his career of contemptible success, being now Solicitor-General in succession to Thurlow, that other infamy of the woolsack.

The preliminaries having been gone through, Dunning opened his case. In a very brief speech—in which he aimed chiefly at placing the question at issue upon a ground where it would not be necessary to touch the dangerous topic of political rights and wrongs as between colonies and mother-country—he submitted that "the Assembly did not come before the throne demanding justice; they appealed to the wisdom and goodness of their Sovereign. They asked a *favour*, which the King could grant or refuse." The Governor and Lieutenant-Governor had lost the confidence of the people; the petition was there as the expression of that feeling. But, "no cause was thereby instituted, no prosecution was intended. . . . As the Assembly had no impeachment to make, so they had no evidence to offer." Though this was one of Dunning's bad days, and he could scarcely speak so as to be heard, the impression created by this unexpected line of argument was distinctly favourable. Yet in proportion as the spirit of it was magnanimous and wise, it really gave the case into the hands of the unscrupulous Wedderburn. That hero advanced to his task as to a scenic display, a declamation, or a prize-fight. The speech which he proceeded to deliver showed the highest abilities of the lowest kind, and is worthy of a more careful analysis than can be given to it here. It began with a passage in which he magnified the legal and constitutional importance of his case, and at the same time contrived to appeal powerfully at the very outset to the prejudices, political and national, of the auditory which he addressed. He then passed to a laudation of Governor Hutchinson, from which that gentleman issued in an anointed condition, with a brevet of utter blamelessness, that would have astonished himself. His ancestry, his training, his own inherent virtues, his studies, his experience, his disposition towards the people of Massachusetts—all conspired to make him, it seemed, the ideal of what a governor should be. A review of his career in that office justified these expectations, exemplified these virtues. At this point the speaker cleverly availed himself of Dunning's admission that no impeachment was made by the Assembly, that no evidence was offered. "All that the members of this hostile Assembly can say is that they do not *like* Governor Hutchinson!" It would have required less cleverness than Wedderburn's to make this point tell, as he did. He was now able to make a transition to the subject of the letters, a subject which was, nevertheless, entirely foreign to the business of that meeting. If it *was* the case, he said, that the Governor and his colleague had in some degree lost that *universal confidence* which had hitherto belonged to them, the fact was due solely to the mischievous sending of their letters to Boston by Franklin. "Dr Franklin therefore," he said, "stands in the light of the first mover and prime conductor of this whole contrivance against his Majesty's two governors;" and he went on to describe Franklin as having come to that meeting with the sinister purpose of putting the finishing touches to his diabolical work. He next enlarged with astounding effrontery upon the alleged private character of the famous letters. "How those letters," he said, "came into the possession of anyone but the right owners, is a mystery for Dr Franklin to explain." After speaking with emotion of his own intimate acquaintance with the lamented Whately—and of that gentleman's exceptional discreetness, especially in regard to all his correspondence—and of the profound pain of his brothers at finding the said Letters had fallen into evil hands—he continued thus: "These Letters, I believe, were in his custody at his death; and I as firmly believe that without fraud they could not have been got out of the custody of the person whose hands they fell into. The Letters, I say, could not have come to Dr Franklin by fair means. The writers did not give them to him; nor yet did the deceased correspondent. Nothing then will acquit Dr Franklin of the charge of obtaining them by fraudulent or corrupt means, for the most malignant purposes: *unless he stole them from the person who stole them.*" Then the orator, his indecency accumulating momentum as he went, half turned towards the venerable philosopher and thundered thus: "I hope, my lords, you will mark and brand the man, for the honour of this country—of Europe—and of mankind! He has forfeited all the respect of societies and of men. Into what company will he hereafter go with an unembarrassed face, or the honest intrepidity of virtue? Men will watch him with a jealous eye. They will hide their papers from him, and lock up their escritoires. He will henceforth esteem it a libel to be called a Man-of-Letters: this Man of Three Letters!" This classical allusion,[1] by which he publicly called Franklin a *Thief* in the presence of half the political and social power of England—it was reckoned the intellectual triumph of that great display! And perhaps we should come away from the feast with the taste of that sweet morsel in our mouths. One famous passage, however, must be quoted. After having descanted, with overflowing unction, upon the injury done to the memory of Mr Whately—the unhappiness caused to the surviving members of that affectionate family by the desecration of their archives — the subsequent confusions which had

[1] To a well-known tag of learning, taken from Plautus: in one of whose plays a thief (Latin, *fur*) is called *Homo trium litterarum* ("A man of three letters").

almost involved the lives of other men—the peril of *murder* which his own respected friend had barely, very barely, escaped—he then proceeded to set Franklin's letter to the *Morning Advertiser* in a surprising new light: as the act of a gloating fiend. "After the mischiefs of this concealment had been left for five months to have their full operation . . . at length comes out *a letter*, which it is impossible to read without horror, expressive of the coolest and most deliberate malevolence. My lords, what poetic fiction only had penned for the breast of a cruel African, Dr Franklin has realised and transcribed from his own. His, too, is the language of a Zanga.

> "'Know then, 'twas—*I*!
> *I* forged the letter—*I* disposed the picture
> *I* hated—*I* despised—and I *destroy*!'"

The remaining passages were equally worthy, and some of them more subtle, but none had the arresting and terrific character of this great outburst. What is of more importance to record is that no one arrested the orator in his flagrant career. No one took exception to the irrelevance, the gross impropriety, of intruding the subject of the Letters into the business of that place and hour, and of giving the proceedings the complexion of an impeachment of Dr Franklin. Least of all did any of these representatives of the King and the Law, the Constitution and the honour of England, resent the astonishing indecency and brutality of this attack upon a man so eminent, and who, had he been the lowest of criminals, was not *there* upon his trial.[1] The assembled Privy Councillors, from the Lord President downwards, manifested the utmost pleasure

[1] As a fact, the question of the Letters was then strictly *sub judice*, a Chancery suit with regard to them having been instituted by Whately. The suit was not persevered in; those who had instigated the bringing of it having, as it turned out, managed to get their business done sufficiently well at the Cockpit.

in the whole entertainment, and accompanied their creature through all his grosser passages with a chorus of encouragements, laughter and applause. Of all the members of the Court and Coercion party in that room, Lord North himself, it is recorded, was the only man who behaved becomingly throughout, short of actually interfering. The Privy Councillors, however, were the more worthy representatives of their country, as its temper and feeling were then: for the enthusiasm with which men read the printed speech a few days later was absolute and national. To return, however. When Wedderburn ceased, the proceedings were at an end. Dunning essayed some kind of reply; but the fatigues of standing three hours were alone enough to have rendered him, as he now was, physically non-effective. The meeting broke up in a buzz of excitement. Franklin moved from the place in which he had stood—motionless, statuesque, attentive—during all that time. In passing out, he clasped the hand of an old friend, but said nothing, and went home alone. That was about one o'clock on Saturday. At the hour of breakfast on Monday, he received a curt and formal intimation that the King "had found it necessary" to dismiss him from the office of Postmaster-General for America. So no time had been lost! Nay, the report of the Committee was dated on Saturday, and had, likely enough, been draughted and ready before the hearing took place. It was a fitting sequel and souvenir of that well-arranged and admirably carried-out performance. It condemned the Petition and the petitioners in tumid and aggressive terms, and went aside to make a cowardly attack upon Dr Franklin. The hearing had been a farce; the report was a falsehood. But both were intended for the Public; and both reached their mark and made their impression. Which is the highest and happiest success of state-craft among a people delighting to think itself free.

Franklin had shown an astonishing self-command during the whole of the scene just described; nor did his strength or dignity forsake him for a moment in the days that followed. He made no pretence of not being moved, but how deeply he was moved we can only guess. He was, at least, as much astounded as shocked, he was more concerned than angry; for he thought of what it all meant, what it was meant to mean for his country. It was America that was insulted in him; and the temper signified by Wedderburn's speech, and still more by the delight with which that speech was heard, promised little consideration for any new petitions or protests that might be forwarded to England. As to the attack upon himself, he set about preparing a reply to it; but the serious aspect which public affairs soon developed, and the rate at which things began to move, soon drew off his attention from what was a comparatively personal and negligible wrong. He felt sure that time would right him. And it has done so, long ago, in the judgment of all the world, except a few good men in this country who still cherish the political views and the personal dislikes which were an anchronism and a misfortune when George the Third was King. Make the best of it that we may, the 29th of January 1774 was a disgraceful day for England. Whether it was also a fateful day, is a question quickly asked, but not to be answered in a word. I do not think myself that Franklin really became, on that day and in his secret soul—neither on that day nor for long afterwards—that which he was called later, not without merit, the arch-rebel of the Revolution. What took place at that time was this: his inherited, compulsive, active, much-contriving love for England received a blow, from which it never again recovered. There remained only, to carry him through his task as mediator, that general benevolence of intention, that desire to save and to serve, which he had towards all the human family. So he worked for a while longer, as we shall see; but perhaps the strength of the heart was not in these labours. One somehow regards the twelvemonth which he was still to pass in England as being merely an empty interval between his issuing from the Cockpit and his stepping on board the ship that was to carry him home. Still more did it seem so to his contemporaries, who knew nothing of the secret labours which engaged him during that interval. Their imagination leapt the space separating the Privy Council outrage and the Declaration of Independence, and saw these two events as a dramatic sequence of historic cause and effect, historic crime and punishment. And there is a sense in which they were right. There is a sense in which there is literal truth in the famous epigram of Horace Walpole:

> Sarcastic Sawney, swoll'n with spite and prate,
> On silent Franklin poured his venal hate.
> The calm philosopher, without reply,
> Withdrew, and gave his country liberty!

But, as already indicated, before he withdrew he assisted loyally in some further efforts to avert the rupture that was fast becoming "inevitable." For a study of his character these months are worthy of close attention; but as nothing of historical importance came of all that was attempted, we may pass quickly here. After the Privy Council affair, Franklin kept as much as possible aloof from ministers and their social circle, though going into general society as much as formerly. The effect of his abstention was soon felt, and ere the year was out both sides in politics were seeking his aid. To the latter half of 1774 and the beginning of 1775 belongs Chatham's memorable intervention, when he threw off the load of sickness and came to the rescue, if rescue there still might be, of the State. He worked hard and studiously at the great problem for several months ere coming forward with his solution; and during that time he had frequent long consultations with Franklin, both at his own place in Kent and at Franklin's lodging in Craven Street. On January 31, 1775, he submitted to the House of Lords the resolution which he considered was the necessary first step in any overtures of conciliation: "That the troops be withdrawn from Boston." It was rejected with scorn and anger. Undeterred by this rebuff, and unwarped from his patriotic purpose by feelings of pique, the great statesman introduced, about a fortnight later, his Conciliation Bill. It was thrown out without consideration. In the course of that sitting, one noble speaker went aside to make an attack upon Franklin (who was in the House at the time), and called him "one of the bitterest and most mischievous enemies this country had ever known." In his reply, Chatham rebutted this slander with eloquence and magnanimity, and spoke of Franklin ("the gentleman alluded to, and so injuriously reflected on") as one "whom all Europe held in high estimation for his knowledge and wisdom, and ranked with our Boyles and Newtons—one who was an honour not to the English nation only, but to human nature." To have been previously vilified by a Wedderburn was perhaps a small price to pay for the privilege of being so vindicated by a Chatham. But the scene is important because of the deep impression which it left on Franklin's mind. When he saw that even this great man, who had done such mighty things for England, could yet scarce secure a decent hearing, could certainly not secure a moment's respectful consideration for his proposals, when he attempted to establish a possibility of conciliation with America—then, indeed, for the first time, Franklin thought of England and the English, in so far as the governing classes represented either, with hopelessness and contempt. Such a House of tetchy, childish, puffy Lords pompously scowling out such a man as Chatham—it was indeed a sight to make a cynic. Yet if there was anything to choose between the Lords and the Commons, the former, he recognised, had the greater claim upon his respect. For they were the more honest, as being, upon the whole, less needy.

When the noble Sandwich permitted himself to speak of Franklin as "one of the bitterest and most mischievous enemies this country had ever known," his lordship may not have been aware that .his own colleagues were even then, and had been for months past, engaged in continual secret negotiations with the said bitter and mischievous enemy. Of these negotiations, however, since they were secret, and since nothing came of them, and especially since the story would require a score or two of pages for its proper telling, I shall not attempt to give any account here.[1] Nevertheless, it is curious and worth remembering that while responsible supporters of the Government were referring to Franklin, in Parliament and in the Press, as one who was walking the streets of London when his proper place was a cell in Newgate, at that very time Government (and a Higher Power, in those days, than the ostensible Government) were actually doing what Chatham had bravely said that he would do if he were in their position: they were "calling to their assistance the gentleman so injuriously reflected on." But they were not

[1] Following the example of Mr Morse, who, although he writes a book, and his subject is Franklin the Statesman, yet rightly pleads that "the story will not bear curtailment nor admit of being related at length" within his limits. Readers may be referred to Bigelow's "Life of Franklin," ii. 256-338; or (for an abridgment about half as long as this Memoir) to the second volume of Parton.

doing it *publicly*, as he said that he would do. That qualification, to what had else been a sign of saving wisdom, was vital, and meant much. The same half-will to reason the matter out; the same conflict of anxiety and pride, pride having always the last word; the same desire to secure the future without recanting the past or making just the present; the same reluctance to cancel a wrong or to acknowledge a right—all worked to ensure that of these negotiations, which lasted from November till March, nothing should come in the end. Their interest is now mainly moral and psychological, and here Franklin is seen to be very great. More than his precision, his strong grasp, his broad view, one is astonished, as the time goes on, at his patience with those people, who clearly do not know their own minds, and display not a little of that famous British inability to understand the mind of others, or to believe, at least, that there can be much in it. The impossibility of doing anything with them seems to have saddened rather than disgusted him. He had presently a more personal reason for being sad. For just when it was possible at last for him to leave England, after having again and again deferred his departure for yet another season, and another, at the entreaty of the well-wishers to both countries—just when he saw that the day of his usefulness, if not of his safety, was nearly done in this country, and that it was time to be getting back among his own folk, who might still have use for him—came the sudden news of his good wife's death. Every spring and every autumn since he set sail, ten years ago, she had hoped to welcome him home. In 1774 she had written that if he did not get back that autumn, she felt that he would never see her alive again. And so it proved; for though a hale woman, she fell away suddenly, and died after a few days' illness at the beginning of the year. Whatever the patriot may have thought, the man and the husband must have regretted a little that last season of all, that one season too many, taken from their lives together, to give to the service of his country; to the service also, had they had the grace or sense to see it, of those in this country who were even then making him the daily mark of their ill words and their worse intentions. But at any rate his term was now almost done, and his ship would soon sail. He respectfully took leave to close the time-wasting business with their various negotiating lordships, and placed the affairs of the Massachusetts Assembly in the hands of his successor-designate, the famous Arthur Lee. Then, posting from London to Portsmouth, he embarked for Philadelphia on March 21, 1775. Little as he expected it, he was to find, on arriving there, a scene of things which would engage him in a new life of labours, with an object very different from the one which he had hitherto cherished and served. But at least it is true, as his biographer[1] says, that "Down to the packing of his last trunk, he had still striven, with all the might of his genius, his wisdom, his patience, and his wrath, to save entire the great empire of his pride and love."

THE SHIP dropped anchor in the Delaware, opposite Philadelphia, on the evening of May 5, and Franklin slipped quietly home before information of his arrival had got about. But in a few hours the news was over the whole city and was speeding through the province. It was everywhere received with joy, a joy heightened by some circumstances of the hour that were news to him when he came ashore. While the ship that brought him was still sixteen days from home, hostilities had broken out between the King's

[1] Parton, vol. ii. p. 65.

troops and the colonists! The affair of Lexington, the battle of Concord, had thrown the whole country into a thrill of amazement and expectancy. The appearance of Franklin among them at such a moment was dramatic, opportune, auspicious; it was heartening beyond words. The country was like to have need of all her sons, the strong in council, and the strong in arms; and here was her greatest of all, alighted, as it were, from the clouds at this juncture! Early on the morning after his arrival, the Pennsylvania Assembly hastened to appoint him one of its delegates to the second Continental Congress, which was to meet in that city a few days later; and Congress, when it met, hastened to appoint him to almost every separate business which it took in hand. A mere catalogue of the committees he served upon would take up too much of our space, and to describe his operations and interests fully would be to write the history of the colonies during the next eighteen months. A few of these must be mentioned; and something must be said to explain that development of his feelings which changed him, hitherto as convinced an Imperialist as Cecil Rhodes or the great Lord Chatham himself, into the arch-separatist and the chief agent—always excepting the good King George—in wresting her colonies from England.

One of the first things the new Congress had to take thought for was the reorganising of the Post Office, with a view both to facility and to safety. Government in those days had small respect, either in England or the colonies, for the alleged sacredness of private correspondence even in times of peace. No added sanctity, to say the least, would belong in its eyes to the correspondence of those who were already described as "rebels." Congress therefore took possession of that service, and placed at the head of it Benjamin Franklin, with the title of

Postmaster-General. He did his work as an organiser so well that the system which he then instituted did not need to be recast, in any essential respect, in a hundred years of unparalleled national expansion and progress. Another scene in which he did redoubtable service was the Pennsylvania Committee of Safety, of which he was chairman. The business of this committee was "to arm and defend Pennsylvania; to call out, drill, and organise the militia; to provide supplies and ammunition; and to issue bills of credit to pay for the same." Here he appears in a new character, as the Vauban of the Quaker colony; for some of the most effective defences, especially a famous marine *chevaux-de-frise*, to keep the British from coming up the Delaware, were expressly designed by the chairman himself. At a later time he presided over the Convention which framed the Constitution of Pennsylvania, and no man better fitted for such a function ever lived. As to the committees of Congress he served upon, their number seems legion, and their business "Whatever men do" who are in the act, the hope, or the peril, of waging war. The earliest met at six in the morning, and he would carry the energy of his great calm mind from one to another till nightfall. Although he took as little part in mere debates as he could, and made no oratorical displays, the country was full of a sense of his presence and his value, and was proud of the one and grateful for the other. There was no subject upon which his work or his word was not of value, so he was wanted for all subjects. Thus, when General Washington wrote a lamentable tale of how his extemporised army was melting away and he saw no means, on the present lines, of continuing any kind of military operations, Franklin must needs be one of the Commission of Three sent by Congress to consult with him, and to frame a plan for putting the defence of the country upon a permanent basis. From Philadelphia to Cambridge was a thirteen days' ride (begun on October 4), and the conference lasted four days. The result was that scheme of a continental army, speedily put into execution, by which Washington was able to carry on a seven years' war. But Franklin came back from that conference an altered man.

When he left England he was far from considering the old cause as lost. Its state was indeed serious, and there was like to be further trouble; but there was no necessity to assume that the trouble would be different in kind from that which had been more or less continuous since the passing of the Stamp Act. He saw that nothing but a display of unanimity, firmness, and strength on the part of the colonists, and the loss to English commerce which the non-importation policy would go on to make increasingly felt, was likely to bring England to a sense of the folly of being on bad terms with her sons across the sea. That she should decide to enforce her point and settle this family disagreement off-hand by starting to destroy buildings, burn towns, and slaughter men—it was a contingency which he may have contemplated, as he contemplated every other, but he regarded it as a very remote one. On arriving, he found that a sort of beginning on these lines had actually been made, and that the country was organising to resist the invasion of its liberties which such acts portended. He was at once with the fighting party in such a cause. It was, however, only a fight for freedom as yet, the English freedom of English subjects, not a war for the independence of Americans. There were a few, a very few in the entire country, who looked towards that goal; and Franklin was not of them. Just as little, however, was he of that timorous band, headed by John Dickenson of Pennsylvania, who anxiously deprecated, even after midsummer of 1775, even after Bunker Hill and Charlestown, any measures which might "have a bad effect" upon the minds of people in England. *These* were for sending petitions to the King, even at that time of day; whereas Franklin put more faith in a permanent Union of the colonies, and drew up a plan for effecting it. The plan was reserved for a later time, however, since it was deemed advisable, Franklin himself consenting, that the futile and stultifying petition to the King—yet another of these disgraced and disregarded petitions to the King!—should go forth in the name of Congress. This was done, that the "moderate" men should not seem to have been overborne in the National Council, and that the fate of the petition might convince them when the arguments of their compatriots and colleagues had failed. And the event was according to the forecast: the almost dramatic and spectacular contempt with which that petition was treated in England made up the minds of thousands in America. And meantime, as one scene of slaughter succeeded another, the royal troops always taking the initiative, it grew more apparent to the colonists that what had occurred earlier in the year was no affair of an unfortunate rencontre or an administrative blunder, but the carrying out of a steady policy of haughty subjection; of a determination to bear them to the ground and then dictate to them on what terms they were to live. So these months, the summer and autumn of 1775, saw a heightening of feeling that was preparing the way for a momentous general change of mind and policy. Thus it was with Franklin more than most men. No man then living knew both countries so well as he, and none could judge so securely the waste, the gratuitousness, and the wrong. The absurdity also, the outrage upon common sense it must have seemed, when he thought of who they were, those governing persons so far away, who claimed to dispose of the property and make forfeit the lives of those industrious Americans around him, who were not indebted to *them* for life, nor for a crumb of bread. But those fatuous governing persons could send armies into this distant country; and though they could not reason, nor understand reason, they could destroy, and destroy, and destroy. Many expedients—he had proved it at the cost of his own patience—had seemed insuperably difficult to them; but the last, the most brutal, and, to a humane mind, the most difficult of all—into *that* they could throw themselves with a light heart. So he reasoned, remembering the past and looking round at the present; and to him, reasoning so, Bunker Hill and the burning of Charlestown left, of his old allegiance for England, but a very slender filament of remembered feeling by the time October of that year had come. Then he went to the conference with Washington. When setting out to return home, accounts reached him of the wanton destruction of Falmouth in Maine, by British men-of-war; neither church nor school spared; the houses which had escaped the cannonade deliberately fired by the torch, marines being landed to carry out that splendid exploit; all the shipping burned, so that the poor people should neither have the means of restoring their fortunes nor of finding food—and all this done on the verge of a northern winter! Such was the wisdom and mercy of the King, whom some folk were still for petitioning; such were the rights of sovereignty and, to Americans, the blessings of the English connection. Whatever others might think of it, Franklin resolved at once that rights like these were to be warred against by all good men, and that the sooner the egregious connection ceased to exist, the less anomalous the world would be. If he had doubted at all before, he had done with doubting now. From this moment he devoted himself utterly—every power of his mind, every fibre of his body—to the cause which he now publicly declared for, the Independence of America.

My topic not being the history of the Revolution, I can do little more than name rapidly the three or four chief events with which he was connected during the next twelvemonth. In the winter of 1775-6, the Colonists, accepting what was a tacit declaration of war against them by the Mother-Country, had begun military operations against the British forces in Canada. After opening well, these operations became inglorious, if they did not bring disgrace. Congress decided early in the spring to send a commissioner to see if its affairs could not be retrieved somewhat; and in spite of his seventy years and two months, it chose to send Franklin. Never sparing himself in his country's service, he did not refuse the duty now imposed upon him; but the journey into these Polar regions went near to killing him; and though he came back alive, he felt for many a day afterwards the effect of the hardships then undergone. As to the situation there, it was fairly irretrievable, and he reported to that effect. Two pieces of good news gladdened his heart on getting back. The first was that a plentiful supply of gunpowder was now on hand. The second was that during the past two months *Independence* had been gaining new adherents by the hundred every day. It was no longer the whispered word of two or three, but the war-cry of a growing host. This was good hearing; and he threw himself with a will into making that disposition prevail more and more. In June the great issue was fought out in Congress and the momentous Resolution carried. Franklin was one of a committee of five appointed to draw up a Declaration; but *the* Declaration was the work of Thomas Jefferson alone. A few days later came the first Fourth of July in universal history. Eight days later still, arrived off Sandy Hook Franklin's esteemed friend Lord Howe, bringing overtures of conciliation; and a fleet and an army (a second army) to enforce them with. On September 11, there took place, in a hut on Staten Island, a picturesque conference between Lord Howe and a commission consisting of Franklin, John Adams, and Edward Rutledge, who had been sent by Congress in compliance with Lord Howe's request, to hear what his lordship had to offer. The Commissioners sat very tight, and his lordship was bound by his instructions, so between the two parties matters got no forarder. His lordship, indeed, had nothing ready for immediate offer, save the King's pardon for those who would give in their submission. Pardon, submission!—these were not the things that Americans were asking or giving eight weeks after the Fourth of July. So the Commissioners withdrew; and Lord Howe continued his negotiations with the help of two armies and a fleet. Against such arguments one needed to have a strong case; and the eyes of Congress looked across the world for signs of aid. Better than watching and waiting, was to go and seek for it, go and ask it. So, on an evening towards the end of October, there slipped secretly out of Philadelphia an old man of seventy-one accompanied by two boys, his grandsons. Early next morning they rode from Chester on the Delaware to Marcus Hook, three miles beyond, and embarked on board a sloop of war—the *Reprisal* sixteen guns—which was waiting out of sight to receive them. Then the sloop stole down the river and put out into a wintry sea. The old man was Benjamin Franklin, accredited Envoy to the Court of Versailles.

Franklin was not venturing into a strange world in going to France for aid, nor into one where an interest in the American cause had yet to be created. During his residence in England he had paid visits to the French capital, and had been received with the distinction which his fame as a savant, and his European prestige as a practical moralist, could not but ensure for him in that city of the philosophers and the economists. He made also many friendships of that kind, that fervour and fastness through life, which he had the gift of making wherever he went. These, like every other power or acquisition of his, were now at the service of his country. When a Committee of Secret Correspondence was formed in November 1775, he had written at once to men on the continent of Europe who would have moved the world, or tried to, at his request. And some of them had effected much, before the following summer was come. There was indeed a very general social and popular interest in the subject of American insurgency throughout all Europe, but especially in France: an interest sympathetic in the highest degree. In France there was also an interest felt by statesmen, an interest of special vivacity, in the progress and upshot of England's quarrel with her colonies. For if the colonists were to shake themselves free, as they well might, then the balance of power as between England and France would be more comfortable to contemplate than the issue of the last war had left it. Those two kinds of interest in the question—that of popular enthusiasm and that of political deliberation—met and fused in the mind of Caron de Beaumarchais. As a privileged person at court and almost a statesman (on occasion) without an office, he maintained for some months his parable that the historic juncture involved almost a call of destiny to the Most Christian King, to come to the aid of the insurgent colonists and so, by breaking the power of an insulting enemy, secure the safety of France for generations. His eloquence and ingenuity, however, made no headway against the reluctance of the King and the wisdom of Turgot. But when Turgot was dismissed, Beaumarchais' views received the qualified support of the new Foreign Minister, the Comte de Vergennes, and the King complied in part. Direct intervention was on all grounds out of the question, but some degree of aid might be extended to the Colonists. For this benevolent purpose, a comic-opera scheme of the Enthusiast's own conceiving was put into execution about the middle of June 1776. With a capital of a million livres (advanced by the court) Beaumarchais opened a commercial house with a Spanish style and title. Its business (a mystery to passers-by) was really to ship to the English colonies all sorts of military supplies, receiving as payment consignments of American produce. The operations of the house were for a few months most successful, several ships laden with contraband having been got safely away. But as no return consignments appeared, the operations of the house began to be hampered owing to overtrading or lack of funds. They were still more hampered presently owing to the repeated remonstrances of the British Ambassador, angrily calling attention to the kind of business being done by Roderique Hortalez & Company. The innocent French Government, surprised and shocked, promptly put the ships of that firm under lock and key. But though some would manage, somehow, to get away, yet no consignments of produce came to off-set the account. Towards the end of the year, all life was gone out of the venture. The head of the house was dejected; not so much at being insolvent as at being out of favour at court. It was alleged that but for his gross imprudence in certain places, the

BENJAMIN FRANKLIN (IN 1783).

From an engraving by J. Thomson, after the portrait by Duplessis.

British lion would not have roared in that painful way. Now since July he had been acting along with Mr Silas Deane, who had been sent to Europe early in the year by Congress (or by Franklin) with somewhat vague powers and purposes as a commercial and political agent and envoy to the world at large. While things went well with Beaumarchais, they went well with Silas Deane. But when the former became insolvent and fell into disgrace, the latter lost at once his only means of subsistence and his one influential ally. I cannot sing here the Iliad of the woes of Silas Deane; a good man not heroically strong, who was marooned on a populous strange continent, the unsalaried representative of a pack of rebels, and who heard, as the months went by, no news nor report of his country but the rumour of her downfall, and who expected to find himself some fine morning placed beyond the frontier at the request of the British Ambassador, or handed over, a recreant traitor, to the tender mercies of his sovereign. To him thus besieged by distress and perplexity and fear, and ready to capitulate, came news on December 7 that Dr Franklin had arrived at Nantes. And to Silas Deane it was as if an army had come to his relief, an army with banners!

And if it was not at once followed by such a display of reversing power as the metaphor seems to imply, it is none the less true that his coming had a moral effect almost as striking and as instantaneous as its spectacular value. The latter could hardly be exaggerated. No piece of news in those years so arrested the attention of mankind as the news that Dr Franklin—who but yesterday had been in Philadelphia, and the day before in the midst of a Canadian winter outside of the world—had suddenly appeared in Paris, the intellectual and diplomatic centre of Europe. It was more than a nine days' wonder; and nobody doubted it might portend immensities. To Paris, and to the French people, it was not more a wonder than a joy. The American cause, in which all minds were interested and so many hearts engaged, had now for its defender and representative in their own midst a man so famous that hardly any name in the world at that time commanded such a universal respect as his. Amongst the learned, the wise or the intellectual he was regarded as an elder and chief; amongst the mass of the people he was conceived of as a benefactor of the race, a parent by adoption of the whole human family. "Franklin's reputation," says John Adams, speaking of what he saw, on coming to France a year later, and what was little to his liking, "was more universal than that of Leibnitz or Newton, Frederick or Voltaire; and his character more beloved and esteemed than any or all of them." And not only the many friendships which he had already formed there, and to which he returned as to the enjoyment of an estate, but also that comprehensiveness of his, that humane universality for which he was unmatched among men, went to render his sojourn in a strange land seem but an exchange of country-seats, each equally in his native air. Amongst his fellow-men, whatever language they spoke, he lived always at home, as among a nation of friends and kinsmen: whereas all other Americans were acutely conscious of the fact that Englishmen were British, and that Frenchmen were Foreigners, and were *not* so conscious as they might have been that they themselves were Provincials. And the longer Franklin's friends in any country knew him, the deeper became their admiration and the warmer their esteem. Even on the plane of high politics, as in social relations and in private life, the personal qualities of Franklin were effective, and made a way for him through many an *impasse*. It would have gone hard with his country, in the years that were now to follow, had not many an effort been made, had not many a point been stretched, for the sake of the man, which would scarcely have been undertaken, so willingly, for the cause alone. Thus, while the whole course of his past life, and the secular growth of his fame, went to invest him with such an interest for the imagination as rendered him virtually Ambassador to the People of France, his authentic personal qualities secured for him in time, as longer acquaintance made them better known, a second privilege and ascendency as one who was an esteemed friend, and almost a colleague, rather than a foreign envoy, in the eyes of the Ministers of Louis XVI.

The terrible shaking of that voyage through thirty days of November storm had left Franklin very feeble; so that though he reached Nantes on December 6, he did not continue the journey to Paris till about a fortnight later. With his arrival there on December 21, the external history of the American Revolution begins to have an official character. He found Deane in Paris, and on the following day they were joined by Arthur Lee. Both of these were joint-envoys with him, Deane being already in France, and Lee in England, when the Commission of Legation was appointed. On the 28th, the envoys had an audience of the Foreign Minister, the Comte de Vergennes. The most notable gain from this audience was an assurance that the hospitality of France would in no case be withdrawn from them: that the King was resolved to protect them while they chose to reside in his dominions. For the rest, there was a hint or two for their guidance in the diplomatic system of things, and a request that they should prepare a statement of their proposals, to be placed in the hands of M. Gérard, the Secretary of the Council. This was soon done; and within a few days after its delivery,

M. Gérard came with a verbal reply. The tone of the reply was friendly in the extreme, but the general effect was non-compliance with the specific proposals. This was hardly wonderful, seeing that compliance with almost any one of them would have been equivalent to an instant declaration of war with England: and it was yet to be seen whether the Colonists were worth anything to themselves—to say nothing of their allies—in so great a venture. Nevertheless, the friendly disposition of the King and his advisers was as good as admitted, the Envoys being told that whatever countenance it might be possible to afford them, without impairing the neutrality of France, would always be gladly given. As a token of this good feeling, an unsolicited loan of two million francs, free of interest and not repayable till the end of the war, was at the service of the Commission. These were not small mercies, all things considered; and they gave a basis for large hopes. It must be remembered that the current omens, as seen from Europe at that actual hour, were not auspicious for the Rebels or for those whom they might contrive to associate with their sin. The last public news was of American defeats, the latest official information was of yet greater English armies getting ready to sail; and here, in Paris, was Lord Stormont again remonstrating. All which things notwithstanding, it somehow happened that, not long after the interview just spoken of, two of Beaumarchais' ships—Beaumarchais, again in some miraculous way made solvent—managed, in spite of severest orders and strictest vigilance, to get safe to sea!

The year Seventy-seven, regarded as a whole, was essentially the waiting time of the Revolution. Yet in Europe, as in America, it was a time of brisk action as well as of grave anxiety and deadly lull. Franklin directed the one or endured the other, so far as they belonged to this hemisphere, in the quiet of a house within a garden, situated in Passy, at that time a semi-rural suburb of Paris. A large part of a great mansion there, the Hôtel Valentinois, had been placed at his disposal, and that of his colleagues if they would share his occupancy of it, by the owner, M. Le Ray de Chaumont, one of Franklin's most fervid admirers and warmest friends. So thither he migrated early in the year, and here set up his establishment as became an Envoy; far enough from Paris to secure quiet, and to seem but a private dweller in a land which could not officially recognise his presence in any other character.

This rural seclusion and private innocence notwithstanding, Franklin was very full of work of a public and even death-dealing kind. That is, he soon found himself in the position of Admiralty to a little fleet of privateersmen who waged war upon England in the narrow sea and in neighbouring waters. Their operations were so successful that England, or at least English merchants, began to feel that these islands were in a state of blockade. Lord Chatham spoke in Parliament of "our commerce" being "torn to pieces" by them. So dire were the doings, or at least the impressions created, by three or four such tiny craft. Tiny as they were, they gave almost as much trouble and anxiety to their admiral on land as to their enemies at sea. For the brave commanders would assume that they might bring their prizes into French ports, as into Boston or Falmouth, and sell them there; and it was Franklin's weary task to awaken in them some small respect for the law of nations or (oftener still) to obviate the perilous consequences of their transgression thereof. Before the end of February they had collected about a hundred British seamen, prisoners of war. With these victims on hand, the Envoys thought well to approach the English Ambassador on the subject of an *exchange*. After some eight or ten weeks' interval, and in reply to a second letter, they heard at last from his lordship. That is, they received a piece of official notepaper, undated, unsigned, and containing only these great words: "The King's Ambassador receives no applications from rebels, unless they come to implore his Majesty's mercy." The retort of the Envoys was more severe than this was crushing, and quite as dignified. "In answer to a letter," it ran, "which concerns some of the most material interests of humanity, and of the two nations, Great Britain and the United States of America, now at war, we received the enclosed indecent paper as coming from your Lordship, which we return for your Lordship's more mature consideration." But though Lord Stormont was a little unfortunate in his style, and was considered to have rendered himself ridiculous, his attitude was correct enough and implied a view of the situation which was, to say the least, excusable in a British Ambassador. At any rate it was a view from which the British Government could not be induced to recede by any argument, save the argument of triumphing arms.

And as the year wore on, it grew less and less likely that the envoys would have that argument in their favour. The career of the good captains, if bright, was brief, and as autumn turned towards winter the seas that had known their renown knew them no more. From America came no direct news, and if any rumours came, they were only of defeat. Intelligence from England was all to that effect; the hands of Government strengthened, armies victorious, the American cause regarded as lost by those who had wished it well. On the continent, and even in France, the same conviction gaining ground. And with this darkening of prospects, an ebb of resource. No prizes were being brought in now;

even that good ally, Beaumarchais, was at the end of his efforts. Towards the close of October the envoys were fain to ask the French Government to buy from them a frigate which was then being built to their order in Holland: so little chance did there seem of its being allowed to sail. And such melancholy tokens. Yet even at this time, in a lull that was heavy with hopelessness, and when the outlook was into sheer darkness, Franklin did not for a moment lose his calm, or even his confidence in the ultimate—nay, in the proximate—success of his country's fortunes. He was not only steady himself, but he made others steadfast: he impressed even Arthur Lee with a sense of his greatness. And when, upon the back of this, came news that Philadelphia was taken, and the good Silas Deane was thereupon for going to the French Ministry to demand an alliance at once, under a threat of their making terms, else, with England—Franklin stood firm against that counsel of panic also, as being inconsistent with the dignity and the interests of his country. Seldom in history has there been such sublime and unshakable confidence as this: and never perhaps was such confidence so dramatically and swiftly justified. For it was but a week later (December 4, 1777), that a carriage dashed into the courtyard of the Hôtel Valentinois, and there sprang from it a young man who had travelled hard over land and sea, all the way from Massachusetts, to announce to the representatives of America in Europe that General Burgoyne and his whole army were prisoners of war.

Whether the victory at Saratoga had definitely secured American Independence for the rest of time, was a matter not to be ascertained in half an hour; and its probability might have been comfortably discussed for a good part of a year, without anybody being proved completely in the wrong, in those days before the telegraph. But the fact that so signal, and by all tokens so decisive, a success had been achieved by the colonists at the end of a two years' resistance to the forces of an Empire, afforded ground enough to go upon for a Government that was already prepared to recognise the independence and sovereignty of the United States, as soon as the situation of affairs gave any colourable pretext for doing so. It was not war against England that the French Court relucted from, but the somewhat delicate act of intervention. Saratoga removed those scruples; and the Government, having promptly come to a decision, acted upon that decision with simplicity, directness and speed. On December 6, the envoys received, along with the congratulations of the Ministry, a request that they would now renew their application for an alliance. The application was soon put in form and delivered, and soon reported upon. On December 17 M. Gérard came to Passy to announce that the French Government had decided to make a treaty with the United States. In the crowded days then following, there was much unprofitable activity of smaller wits, much quiet, swift and sure *work* of one calm and comprehensive mind, in the neighbourhood of the Hôtel Valentinois. The effects of the former being eliminated, those of the latter remained; and appeared when, on February 6, 1778, there were signed and sealed Three Treaties between the King of France and the Congress of the United States. The first was a *Treaty of Amity and Commerce*, which bound the two nations to be good friends, to trade fairly, and to allow no superior advantages to any other nation. The second was a *Treaty of Alliance*, and had reference to the events likely to arise out of the action of France in thus according international recognition to the revolted colonists.

Recognition was intervention, and intervention would probably mean war. France here bound herself never to withdraw from that war, should war be made upon her, till the Independence of the United States had been achieved; the States in turn bound themselves not to make peace on any terms short of Independence; and neither party to the treaty was to make a separate peace or a separate truce without the consent of the other first obtained. The third, or *Secret Treaty*, merely provided for the entry of Spain into this compact at a later time. All three treaties, indeed, must be secret treaties for the next few days, because of certain ships then at sea. But the mask was laid aside, the position of affairs revealed to the world, on March 20,[1] the date of the famous reception of the American Envoys by the King at Versailles. One ought rather to say, the reception of Dr Franklin and his Associates; for that is how that memorable function phrased itself to the imagination of contemporaries. Everybody has read, somewhere or other, references to the profound impression his appearance there created; his serenity and benevolence of aspect, his dignity, and yet portentous audacity; his own personal white locks worn instead of the wig proper and imperative, an oaken staff in his hand in lieu of the sword of ceremony! Neverthless, there was too much ceremony in all this for the British Ambassador, who departed next morning without taking leave. Franklin remained to make up for the void thus left in the hearts of all Paris; and perhaps all Paris was never so full of Franklin as now. To this spring of 1778, it may be noted, belongs another

[1] It had been revealed to the British Ministry a week earlier, in a rescript handed in by the French Ambassador in London on March 13. In this document the United States were declared to be in full possession of Independence, the Treaty of Amity and Commerce "between the two nations" was formally announced, and the Treaty of Alliance was not obscurely indicated.

appearance of his, which had an immense appeal for the hearts aforesaid: namely, his appearance upon the same platform with Voltaire at a meeting of the Academy of Sciences on April 27. The great concourse of scientists and philosophers which filled the room, becoming possessed by one feeling and one wish, refused to be satisfied until these two—a Solon and a Sophocles, as they were in *their* eyes—had been made to approach from their respective seats and embrace each other—"*à la française!*"—to the universal delight. But such gaieties belong to the biography of one of the other Franklins, not to that of the Statesman with whom we are here concerned.

If the treaty of alliance lifted the weight of anxiety from the envoys, it also increased the burden of work, the main share of which was from the first borne by Franklin. The outbreak of war between France and England rendered possible a resumption of those naval operations into the direction of which he had thrown himself with such zest in the spring and summer of the previous year. The business of the brave had been hampered then by the want of any port to fly to, for safety or supplies, nearer than the other side of the Atlantic. To be sure, nearer ports *had* been sought; but difficulties had been apt to result, which were not to be created too often. The cessation of France's neutrality threw open all French seaports to the so-called privateers, which preyed upon British commerce, and sometimes engaged British warships not unsuccessfully. With the buying, equipping, commissioning of these craft Franklin had everything to do; and when they returned from conquest, he was the prize court that kept them on the right side of the law and also apportioned the spoils. Adjudicating the quarrels or disarming the jealousies of rival captains was a harder and more perilous task, but he faced it with skill and courage. As an example of his courage one would like to quote a letter which he wrote to a certain Captain Landais, undeterred by the fact that this captain was a Frenchman and half a maniac. But the most important business growing out of the new conditions on which the war was waged, was that with reference to the American prisoners in England. A few days after receiving the great news of December 4, the envoys had written to Lord North requesting that agents appointed by them might be permitted to have access to these prisoners and do something, by periodical small doles of money and the distribution of comforts, to render their condition less wretched. His lordship returned a courteous and even conciliatory reply, and practically granted the request. He even said something now about an *exchange* of prisoners: which was equal to recognising the rebels as belligerents. But a little later Government showed more reluctance to commit itself definitely to that position; and although an engagement to make an exchange was given in the spring or early summer of 1778, it was not until the end of March in the following year that the first cartel ship sailed for France. Into no business did Franklin ever put his heart so greatly and simply and transparently as into this. He stuck to his task and maintained his plea indefatigably through months of discouragement and disappointment, and some of the letters which he wrote in this cause are among the finest monuments to his character.

At the same time he was rearing another such monument, not immediately visible to all, and least pleasing to those who were privileged to watch it rise, in the steady mind with which he met a long series of secret overtures made to him by the English Government. From the moment when the news of

Burgoyne's capitulation reached Europe, that Government had recognised the danger if not the certainty of a Franco-American alliance being ratified forthwith. The prospect caused a singular sweetening of temper towards the rebels, a desire to end the quarrel with them, even upon terms which a little earlier it would have been considered an insult for the rebels themselves to have proposed. Hence the procession of secret emissaries who began to appear at the Hôtel Valentinois about the middle of December 1777. The object of these first comers was to avert, while yet there was time, any "fatal treaty with the House of Bourbon." Their arrival did not interrupt the work, then going on, of drafting the three treaties. When the Treaty of Amity and Commerce was formally announced, war against France was the only reply which the feeling of the country, to say nothing of the pride of Kings, made possible. But the procession of secret emissaries kept on its way, all the same, right up to high summer of 1779. The object now was to sunder the allies, that France might be left to fight alone; and to secure this, England was now willing to grant any concessions, short of absolute and formal independence, which the colonists could dream of enjoying. Though the earlier of these appeals implied an assumption that the colonists were fools, and the later ones that they were caitiffs, yet they were mostly good if misguided men who came on that errand. Also they were sufficiently numerous, and they were sufficiently varied in their personal attributes and social style, to contribute, by their regular apparition from time to time, a distinct strain of human interest to life at Passy, during a period of twenty months, and even to enrich Benjamin Franklin's acquaintance with the moral types of mankind. Which is all that needs to be said about them here.

One would be glad to dismiss in like summary fashion two or three other persons who, during half the period, at least, of Franklin's service in France, made life interesting in a very different sense. Their claim to be more intimately remembered, however, cannot be passed over; for to ignore the degree in which they increased the difficulties of his position and his task would be to leave the account of his services, and of the merit implied in rendering them at all, vitally imperfect. It was a period in which his endurance, his self-forgetting patience, was as magnanimous and rare as his wisdom in counsel and in management was unmatched. The touchstone of one half of the greater qualities of Benjamin Franklin was the active-minded, small-brained, self-enamoured and evil-thinking Arthur Lee of Virginia. If that great colony gave to the Revolution its *Complete Hero* in George Washington, it gave also, in Arthur Lee, one whom it is only not quite accurate to describe as the *Complete Cretin* or the *Complete Cad* of the Revolution. He was not really a cretin, for he had plenty of intelligence of a trivial kind, and a deplorable abundance of uncontrolled and misdirected reasoning power. Neither was he exactly what you would call a cad; for besides belonging to a very good family, and having had an English Public School and University education, he was a fairly honest patriot of his shallow kind, and even wore a certain pseudo-elevation of style about him so constantly that the theatrical property became the man. But he was fussy, as only a fool is fussy. He was vain, as only a being imperfectly developed, and therefore self-conscious and uneasy, can be vain. He was jealous, as only a man of acute narrow intelligence and restive conceit can be jealous. He had a mania for doing, and for meddling, and for modifying. Above all, he had a mania for SUSPECTING, whenever anything was being done, or was not being done, for reasons of which he was not advised, or in a way of which he did not approve. The fact that the thing was being done by somebody else, or that the way was somebody else's way, was a sufficient reason why Arthur Lee should first disapprove; and then suspect; and then hint his suspicions of that person; and finally reach the stage of boldly slandering him with perfect honesty and conviction, and an abundance of avouched lies. Thanks to this happy disposition and a complete lack of scruple in indulging it—thanks, also, to the fact that he was personally unknown in America, and at the same time was covered by the great respect in which his powerful and patriotic family was held there—he was able for years to run a career of mischief-making and of petty infamy at a high plane of things. "The disturbance he wrought," says Mr Morse, "was great enough to constitute an important element in history. . . . He buzzed about Europe like an angry hornet, thrusting his venomous sting into every respectable and useful servant of his country, and irritating exceedingly the foreigners whom it was of the first importance to conciliate." Another American writer describes him as having caused to his fellow-commissioners, first and last, "about as much trouble as did the backwardness of the French ministry, the zeal of the British cruisers, the laxity of the over-pressed Congress, and the low state of American credit, all put together." The same writer adds that "His was one of those characters which, though probably reasonable enough to their possessors, seem to others to be almost miraculous in their littleness and meanness." The ill-will which a pushing, punctilious, fussy, pragmatic, mandarinic idiot like this must immediately conceive on finding himself in the smallest degree overlooked in any transactions, or consultations, or social attentions which might be going forward, was pretty sure to come speedily into constant play when he found himself placed beside such an overshadowing colleague as Dr Franklin, among such a people as the French. Nevertheless, Franklin was not the chief mark of his malice during 'Seventy-Seven: Silas Deane occupied his thoughts and his pen at that time. But when he had accomplished the destruction of that victim (who was recalled at the beginning of the following year, to be treated by Congress with an injustice which practically unsettled his wits, and caused him to abjure his country), then Arthur Lee permitted his mind to settle upon Franklin. It was very bad for his mind. For the task of subverting such a man was a long task, and the effort was, in effect, futile; so that what with the glooms of disappointment, and an almost hysterical exacerbation of animosity, which the long obsession had created, Arthur Lee makes his exit from Europe in the condition of a quite presentable and well-dressed monomaniac, but a monomaniac all the same. But in the interval he was able to do a vast amount of mischief, and to create an atmosphere of anxiety and uncertainty, an atmosphere of conflict and cabal, in the midst of which Franklin had to keep his patience and serve his country as best he could. His country in the meanwhile, as he was perfectly aware, was well on the way, at any moment, to treat him as unjustly as it had treated the luckless Deane; so consistently and continuously did the wretched Lee send his official packets full of insinuation, and his private letters full of lies, across the Atlantic. For Lee could command a powerful interest there; and for his policy of thwarting and stinging and teasing, he had the support in Paris of his brother, William Lee, and his melodramatic crony, Ralph Izard, both members of legation.

Such men are, in the literal sense of a valuable and misused phrase, not worth a damn, so we need not damn them. But the attention would not be altogether wasted on a much better man, Mr John Adams. That is a name for which Americans have a respect, but which it is permitted to a British person who is, anyhow, more interested in Franklin, to regard with some dislike and contempt. A perception of the good points of Mr Adams lessens the dislike, but rather increases the contempt: for such a man ought to have known better. At any rate, when John Adams—the strong and honest John Adams, second President of the United States—came to Paris in the spring of 1778, taking the place of Deane, he fairly threw himself into the arms of the Lee coterie, and, without directly countenancing the extravagancies of Lee himself, yet took up an attitude of ill-disposition towards Franklin, which was an invaluable support to those weak-minded malcontents. For this unfortunate and dishonouring attitude of Adams towards his great countryman, Lee is largely to blame, since he "initiated" his new colleague to such effect, that it took Adams, working hard at the accounts and the general state of things, the better part of a year to unlearn what he had been taught, upon his arrival, in a few conversations or a short course of hints. But the bulk of the blame must fall directly on Adams himself, for the root of the evil was in his own nature. His vice was the vice of Arthur Lee, with a personal difference. Arthur Lee was suspicious and also jealous; John Adams was jealous, morbidly jealous, and only rarely, and as a consequence, suspicious. He was jealous of the greatness, the importance, of other men. On that account he was jealous of Washington, of Hamilton, and of Franklin; and years after all three were dead he would become almost furious at the mention of their names, or at the citation of an opinion of theirs, though it were in his own praise. Of course he did not arrive at that stage in a day; but even for the John Adams of 1778, France was not the proper place, nor Franklin—"the illustrious Dr Franklin!"—the most fortunate colleague. Not to linger over the matter, let me merely say that this covert ill-will of Adams, as yet not very definite nor very hearty,[1]

[1] That came later; but as I shall not be able to find room in the text for the train of minor events out of which Mr Adams's more confirmed animosity arose, I may refer to the matter here.

Upon the Joint Commission being dissolved, Adams returned to America in the spring of 1779. But by next February he was back in Europe, having been sent thither by Congress, somewhat prematurely, in the capacity of a Peace Commissioner. De Vergennes, who had not much liking for Mr Adams, yet wished to make the best of him, and showed him a great deal of civility upon his return, and invited him to communicate from time to time. Very pleased with himself thereat was Mr Adams; and being pleased, became fatuous, and went headlong. That is, he fell into a way of communicating his views, generally on affairs that were not within his province, in very long letters to de Vergennes, too often, and for insufficient reasons. He argued with this great man of affairs about things that did not matter; and upon things that did matter, but which were no business of his, he presented his views in epistolary treatises which displayed a vast deal of intelligence and an astonishing want of sense. The remorseless correctness of Mr Adams's logic did not inspire so much confidence as the absence of tact and almost of courtesy created disgust in the mind of a French diplomatist. He was not only rude—for the amiable expressions of the king himself, as reported by de Vergennes, could not escape the schoolmasterly corrections and settings right of this superfluous and precise self-constituted colleague of the Foreign Office—but he was tiresome intolerably! At length there came a rupture, and de Vergennes reminded him that, after all, Dr Franklin was the only person with whom This Court need discuss the matters in question. He also appealed to Franklin for a disclaimer, on the part of Congress, of a certain policy (with regard to the redemption of the depreciated American paper currency) which had an appearance of being unjust to French merchants and others, but which Adams had gone out of his way to champion and explain, much in the manner of a schoolmaster driving knowledge into an unwilling head. Finally he (de Vergennes) sent the whole correspondence to Franklin, and required him to transmit it to Congress. Here is an example of the kind of situation that was made for Franklin from time to and the ceaseless, plotting, bitter hostility of the microcephalic Lee, united in contributing additional aspects of hardship, anxiety, and almost of thanklessness to that noble task—of helping his country to come prosperously through her struggle for Independence—to which Franklin had devoted the

time by so-called colleagues. It was serious beyond words. In dealing with this particular instance, as with others, it has been acknowledged (by all the world save Adams and the sons of Adams) that Franklin showed the greatest wisdom, moderation, generosity, tact. Any other man would have taken up a high position, not without cause, about the gratuitousness, the meddlesomeness of all this mischief-making. But not by a syllable did Franklin remind Adams that he had been wandering out of his province; and he gently suggested a way, as though Adams were a colleague who had blundered a little, by which he could easily make matters right. But Adams, for good and evil, was not of the compromising, flexible kind. He did not want that matters should be put right, but that he should be defended, justified, vindicated, at whatever cost to the general system of things, including his country. So his only reply was a short note to Franklin, saying that he also had sent the correspondence to Congress.

From this time dates that animosity against Franklin which was a quenchless, though quiet and smouldering fire in the breast of John Adams as long as he lived, a fire which it has become a duty of piety in his successors to keep alive. They have had a fortunate degree of success. Franklin's family may be said, for historical purposes, to have died with him, his only descendants being by the female line; whereas the "House of Adams" is one of the acknowledged institutions of America, both in politics and literature. It is very conscious of itself, and perhaps dreams of a destiny. No minutest particular regarding it is allowed to perish. It has a fire-proof building for its archives, as though it were the House of Hapsburg. Its influence, travelling underground, reappears in strange places. In the Cambridge "History of the United States," for instance, there is a passage about Franklin—absurd, and to my mind disgraceful in a work of that importance—which says that, "The whole tenor of his life shows him to have been a man of no delicate sense of honour," and that "in what he believed to be a good cause he could be unscrupulous in his choice of means." I am not concerned here to examine or refute this. I only say that the writer (Mr Doyle) is better acquainted with the work of John Adams than with the character or even the career of Benjamin Franklin; and that in writing the above words he was influenced by an unconscious recollection—almost resulting in verbatim quotation—of a particularly malevolent and absurd passage in the Life of John Adams, by his son.

remaining years and energies of a life already so full of works, and service, and praise, and the right to rest. In the story of what he had to endure from these causes during a course of years—years in which he was doing such great things for his country—there would be something pathetic were there not something magnificent and strong. The patience which he had with those people, his self-effacing endurance, his determination not even to recognise the evil intention or the unfriendly act by defending himself, until the Independence of America was achieved—these are a measure of the moral reserves of wisdom and justice and strength within that rich and profound nature. Be it added that the importance, at least, of seeing that his services were not lost to his country, or rendered ineffective, was finally recognised by Congress at the beginning of 1779, when it sent Lafayette to France with a paper annulling the existing Commission, and appointing Franklin sole Minister-Plenipotentiary to the French Court. At the end of that year it took a still stronger step, by commanding Lee and his associates [1] —who had lingered on in Paris, doing more mischief than ever, as being more desperate with rage—to return to the States. Once they arrived there, family interest was strong enough to secure for them not only immunity but reward, and to enable them to exercise their animosity, if not to achieve their vengeance, upon the name of Franklin for many years.

It is time now to say something about what was, from first to last, the chief subject of Franklin's labours in Europe, and the special sphere of his victories: the Financing of the Revolution. That is a

[1] William Lee and Izard. John Adams had returned to the States early in the year, upon the joint-Commission being cancelled. He had even expressed an emphatic approval of that "masterly stroke," as he called it.

subject which would require for its proper setting forth, merely in a historical and descriptive way, an article fully as long as this memoir. Only a page or two are here available in which to indicate briefly some of the causes and the conditions of his task, and the way in which he achieved it.

When the Colonists decided to accept the alternative of a war with England rather than recede from their claims to essential autonomy, they estimated very imperfectly the vast reserves of power at the disposal of a great and organised Kingdom. Still less did they estimate fully the effect which their own want of organisation was likely to have in keeping them weak, in spite of vitality and a stubborn purpose to be free. Of course they entered upon the war with scarce a vestige of that material provision which is a primary requisite, a condition taken for granted, whenever civilised peoples enter upon the long and exhausting labour of murdering each other in masses large enough to cover a field or fill a landscape. But this want of material provision was a small thing compared to the want of means of remedying the defect, the want of means of mobilising the resources of the country to that good end: in other words, the want of a Government. Whatever the improvised body called Congress might be, it was not in those days a Government; and in its varied lack of organic powers, the most vital deficiency was the lack of power to raise a revenue. Of three makeshifts in lieu of that power which were within its function, one served for a time, and served disastrously. The second served all the time, but not well enough to ensure success or to keep disaster at a year's distance. If the third, and the least likely of all, served incomparably well and to victorious effect, that was because this expedient was entrusted to a man in whose hands an oaten straw became as strong as a quarter-staff in those of others, and to whom the utter desperation of things was but a casual difficulty to be removed by thought and patience. The expedient was that of borrowing money upon the sole credit of a young nation fighting for existence against the greatest power in the world.

Naturally the attempt to do anything so difficult did not occupy a prominent place in the plans of Congress at first. Danger and need compelled recourse to it. But the attempt having once or twice succeeded beyond expectation, though not beyond demand, the lesson of experience was sagely remembered and confidently put to use. To borrow money abroad at intervals, and at intervals that grew shorter and shorter, soon became a main part of the budget of such substitute for a Chancellor of the Exchequer as the inchoate Government of the United States then possessed. Which means that that Government depended more and more upon Franklin to keep it, and the whole system of things to which it belonged, in existence. It was his business to maintain the struggle for Independence by his great labours at this side of the world as truly as it was Washington's at that. And for the upholding of the cause in Europe his services were as great, his qualities as perfect, his trials as constant and more severe, his personality as indispensable to the saving of the situation from day to day, and the achievement of a crowning success in the end, as those of Washington in America. The story of the financing of the Revolution by the one is indeed the necessary counterpart of the story, more obviously epic, of the captaining of its armies by the other; and of the two, this is not the less heroic. The greater difficulty of making *this* story interesting to readers does not affect us here, where obvious lack of space, and the scheme of this article, preclude the effort to try. A word or two only must be said of the two main forms which those ceaseless demands for money and aid, the burden of his days and nights during seven years, were wont to take.

The first was, a demand for loans, usually in impossible amounts. An effective borrowing power was one of the advantages immediately accruing to Congress from Franklin's presence in Europe; and as soon as the fact was perceived, it was taken into account for all, and if possible for more than all, it was worth. First and last, it was worth an additional annual revenue, without which, under the existing condition of semi-organisation and the essential separatism of the States, the flag could not have been kept flying at all. And it was Franklin, and Franklin alone, who could find that revenue; for no other American had a grain of personal weight or influence with those whom it was necessary to deal with for these occasions, and who had to be induced to make efforts that were often extremely difficult, with the best will in the world to oblige. A stage was soon reached, and it was reached again too often, when he found it even difficult to set out upon the errand enjoined him: the demand would be so impracticably large, or (more often) would come so unconscionably quick upon the heels of the granting of one which had been a difficult business, but which (he had told himself and others) would be the last for many months. This was what he called "an after-clap"; and indeed his life was passed in a kind of sporadic thunderstorm of such claps and after-claps in those years. The other guise in which the demands upon his influence came may rather be compared to a snowstorm. Congress soon got into a way of taking his success for granted, and would draw upon him freely on the strength of a loan which had yet to be negotiated. Perhaps the first mention of the said loan, and a shower of bills for the absorption thereof, would reach him by the same post or the same packet. Still worse, it got into a way of drawing upon him for great total amounts, in a bewildering multitude of bills of all denominations, without any reference to a given loan, and with but a bare general intimation that it was doing so, or had done so; and sometimes without even that. Whatever transaction Congress engaged in that had its reference and effect in Europe, that effect was a burden thrown upon Franklin. If it sent other patriots thither on "financial missions," the result was only that Franklin had to keep those missionaries alive, besides taking up, "for the honour of Congress," the bills which Congress had drawn upon *them*. Not one of them could ever raise a shilling. And he himself had practically but one resource: his influence, essentially a personal and individual influence, with the French ministry. Congress seems to have imagined it was impossible to exhaust that resource, or had no reluctance to abuse that influence.[1] Franklin both feared the one—a fear entirely for his country's sake—and had, in regard to the other, scruples that are nobly to his credit. But his patriotism, his one duty of leaving no effort unmade when his country required him, had always the last word, and bade him go forth once more. And if he went often when the circumstances were such that he felt, and felt with unselfish resentment, that the dignity of America was being made questionable in the eyes of strangers, and his own opinion of Congress was for the moment, at least, anything but high—yet he went: and he never went in vain. The fact that he had, in many cases, to ask for what he himself felt to be unreasonable and knew to be difficult—this was one of the circumstances which made his service so hard. But there were more such

[1] More accurately, the devil drove, and it could not help itself; though folk in Europe did not quite see that, not even Franklin.

circumstances—moral circumstances, material circumstances—than it is even possible to glance at here. He had no help, not even sufficient clerical help, and he had powerful plotting enemies, this one man whose call and mission it was to keep the credit of his country among the nations of the world, to provide for all her manifold purposes and outlays in Europe, and even, in large part, for the effective maintenance of the war of liberation within her borders. What it cost him, in mental and moral wear and tear, to have rendered these services, we cannot estimate, but we may say with confidence that it was more than any other man then living in the world had it in him to have paid.

At least it was not paid in vain: and the greatest effort, perhaps, which he ever put forth is memorably associated with Washington's final campaign of triumph. The gravity with which all men in America, and chiefly Washington, looked forward to the campaign of 1781 is matter of history; so is the resolution of England to end the rebellion that year. It was then that Congress wrote to Franklin with such urgency as it had seldom used. It was then that Washington himself wrote to Franklin, virtually saying that it now lay with him, away there in Passy, to save his country, if she was to be saved at all. And it was then that Franklin, who was at that hour at the utter end of all effort, not sheerly miraculous, made one effort more: and pleading in this direction, and pressing in that, and making advantage for his country in all, accumulated a more generous subsidy of money and aids for the imperilled cause than ever before. With this vital reinforcement the campaign of 1781—marked beyond all others by energy, dash and brilliance, not less than by victory—began. It closed, for all the purposes of history, when

Lord Cornwallis capitulated at Yorktown on the 19th of October. And then, though Franklin's labours were not at an end, at least his work was achieved: for the Independence of America was won beyond recall.

If his financial troubles were not yet over, that was because it was still to be proved that Yorktown was really the *End*. The war against the European allies was prosecuted for some months longer, and operations would even have been resumed in America, could King George have had his way. But the country was determined to support him no further in a folly that had brought so many losses and so much disgrace, and this feeling was voiced by Parliament in such terms as even he could not disregard. On the 20th of March 1782, Lord North's Administration (so-called) fell; which means that the king was compelled to dismiss his sorely-tried favourites and to resign the government of the country into the hands of statesmen. The men who were now called to power, and who really had a commission from the country to end the war, were all old-time friends to Franklin and to the American cause: Rockingham, Shelburne, Conway, Burke, Dunning, Howe, to say nothing of Charles James Fox, who had visited Franklin at Passy. A friendly letter from Franklin to Shelburne on March 22, deftly set a-going what two hemispheres were anxiously expecting — the Negotiations for Peace. And vastly interesting Negotiations they presently proved. All the circumstances which go to make the secret history of great treaties and great diplomatic congresses so ravishing were here present in a very high degree, but I can only call attention to one fact that made for complexity and had its moral consequences. America belonged to that "Northern department," of the foreign world over which Lord Shelburne, as it happened, exercised official cognisance: whereas France belonged to the "Southern department," and here Mr Fox was the presiding genius. Consequently, the envoy who should treat with Franklin was appointed by Shelburne, and was answerable to him alone; while he who should treat with de Vergennes was one who came and went at the bidding of Mr Fox. The envoy of Shelburne was Mr Richard Oswald, a retired merchant, whose talent as a negotiator consisted in an absolute honesty and guilelessness which is only to be found in his (and my) dear country.[1] In their earlier, tentative conferences, Franklin managed to negotiate in such a way as to make the question at issue concern, not the independence of America, which he took for granted, but how much England was prepared to surrender along with the Colonies. He was playing for Canada, Nova Scotia, and, in fine, for the residue of this poor country's possessions in North America: though he was willing that she should keep the Islands.[2] And, by all appearance, he was playing a winning game, when the introcession of his partner spoilt his hand. The Peace Commission consisted of four members, of whom he alone was virtually "in office" at this time. John Jay was in Madrid, John Adams in Holland, and Henry Laurens a prisoner (or very lately a prisoner) in England. Sudden ill-health caused Franklin to summon Jay to his assistance, who arrived at the end of June. Now Jay was the most estimable American of his generation and almost the most likeable, but he was not a cosmopolite. He was apt to feel that foreigners

[1] Though a London merchant, Oswald was a pure Scot. He was quite a stranger to Franklin, *pace* an important History of the United States, which apparently confuses him with David Hartley.

[2] Meaning, of course, not Great Britain and Ireland, but the West India Islands. They were commonly referred to in the Colonies, and even in England, as the Islands in those days. The bad habit of ignoring their geographical relation to America is a product of later ignorance.

were strange folk, anyhow; and now, with or without good reason, he became possessed by a spirit of suspicion so sincere that it would be easy to make fun of it. With or without information on the point, he was convinced that when the diplomatists of Europe met round a table, no Americans being present, they would certainly arrange matters, on terms of mutual accommodation, to the disadvantage of America. Seeing ulterior motives and sinister designs where Franklin saw nothing but an ordinary effect of official conservatism, he took alarm at the term "Plantations or Colonies" in the formal commission to treat which was given to Oswald early in July. Until these fears were removed by the substitution of "The United States," business had to stand still. Then, at the end of September, the time was gone by for asking Canada, Nova Scotia, etc. And now enters John Adams, full of satisfaction with himself on the score of some successes among the Dutch money-lenders, but still fuller of a certain secret resentment, the origin of which has been referred to on the margin of a former page. Therefore he now expressed his approval of Mr Jay's noble conduct with aggressive emphasis: an emphasis in which there speaks the *humourless* patriot, but still more the provincial; and, more than either patriot or provincial, the bitter, wounded, vain man with a rankling grudge, happy to take or support any course which he knew to be contrary to the feeling and sense of his illustrious colleague. John Jay next renewed his proposal that they should not communicate with the French ministry regarding the progress of their negotiations with England: and John Adams impressively approved. The commission was instructed by Congress to do nothing without the knowledge and concurrence of their generous ally; but these two now said they would break that instruction without a scruple. This placed Franklin in a difficult position, and whatever course he took he could hardly be in the right. But he saw that the greater evil would be to place himself in conflict with his colleagues just then. The juncture was critical. Ministerial changes in England were anticipated which might quash the peace negotiations even yet and reopen the war. In the interests of all it was desirable that not an hour should be wasted in conflict or friction of any sort. He therefore gave in, without further protest, to the will of the majority.

This was in October, and matters now went on apace. Waiving details, there were three questions of outstanding difficulty; questions upon which each party was either very sure of its right, or greatly interested in asserting one. The first, second, and third of these were disputed on behalf of the States with good effect by Jay, Adams, and Franklin respectively. Jay upheld manfully the right of the States to expand westward, in defiance of some restrictive Spanish claims which England was inclined to favour. Adams vindicated the claim of the States to share in the Newfoundland fisheries —not as a liberty granted by men or treaties, but as a right belonging to them from the creation of things—in a fine burst of angry eloquence in which we have, for the only time in Europe, I think, a glimpse of the better John Adams. But the third question was the one that, from the very beginning of the negotiations, had been found most intractable. It had often been taken up, and been often put aside again. Up to the last moment it appeared that upon this question the treaty would be wrecked, even within sight of signature. It was the question of compensation to the Loyalists, or those Americans who had decided to stand by their king rather than their country when the sundering hour had come in

'76. If anything could exceed the opposition to such a claim by American feeling and American opinion, it was the stress laid upon maintaining it by the English government and people. When they had lost so much, and saved so little honour, they were not going to forsake their friends in the act of settlement. It was an honest feeling, though the thought involved in it had certainly been submitted to insufficient analysis. The reasons for a very different feeling towards those unfortunates on the part of their countrymen will readily occur to the reader. No man in America was more convinced than Franklin that the Loyalists (or Royalists, as he called them) ought to accept the consequences of having warred unprosperously against their own land and its liberties. He was none the less inflexible in that opinion because his own son, William Franklin, the late governor of New Jersey, was among those Royalists and now living as a refugee in England. When the question was brought up again at the end of November, the English commissioners (there were now three) made a heroic attempt to carry their point: and it appeared that if they should not succeed, there must be a deadlock to the whole process of peace-making. It was then that Franklin quietly drew from his pocket a piece of paper stating an unexpected counter-claim, so cogent, and of such a kind, that, rather than face it or dispute it, the English commissioners gave up their point at once, and also conceded, without further debate, the other American claims that were still under consideration. All the many difficulties were gone like a dream. On the day (November 30, 1782) following this "masterly stroke," the preliminary treaty was sealed, signed, and delivered.

So far good. But to Franklin now fell the not very agreeable duty of announcing this happy consummation to de Vergennes: of telling him, namely, that his American allies had carried their negotiations to a conclusion without once communicating with him, and had settled all questions between themselves and England without even the semblance of a respect for the interests of France. The fact that this was but a preliminary treaty, and that it definitely concluded nothing, did not lessen the extreme peculiarity, to employ a mild phrase, of the course taken by the American commissioners. But it enabled Franklin to offer, for what he acknowledged to have been "a lack of *bienséance*," an ostensible excuse or extenuation, which de Vergennes made a virtue of accepting. He divined, however, that his old friend had a better excuse which he was bound in honour not to plead, and that his own disposition had been overborne by his colleagues. Regarding them, he said a little later, "*They* do not pretend to recognise the rules of courtesy towards us:" which was a little hard on Jay, though no injustice to Adams. At any rate peace was secured, and by this secrecy and celerity was snatched, apparently, from complications and perils that would soon have subverted the labours of all the peacemakers.[1] The definitive

[1] For it must be added that in so profoundly distrusting the intentions of the other Allies towards America at the last stage of their adventure in common, Jay was either acting more wisely than he knew, or else was possessed of definite knowledge which he did not impart to either of his colleagues, certainly not to both of them. I am not aware that the latter supposition has ever been proved, and I think it is unlikely. He seems to have been influenced by a certain intercepted document, which was also known to Franklin, but which was not sufficient to shake Franklin's confidence in the good faith of his friends. Nevertheless, the more recent opening of the archives has shown that when Spain became a party to the Alliance in 1779, the price of that accession of strength was a *Secret Treaty* between France and Spain, containing articles which were likely to have greatly prejudiced the interests of America when it came to settling the terms of peace.

It ought also to be added, to avert misconception on the part of English readers who do not know their men, that though

Treaty of Peace which was signed about a year later (September 3, 1783) was virtually identical, as far as concerned America, with this preliminary treaty, negotiated so ably by Jay, Adams, and Franklin; in which, to the astonishment of all the world and the disgust of a large part of it, the Americans got everything and gave nothing.

Franklin was kept long enough in France to be a signatory to the definitive treaty, though he had asked leave to return to America shortly after the preliminary treaty was achieved. Congress ignored his request, which was too reasonable a one for it to acknowledge and yet refuse. After the signing of the definitive treaty, he again urged his desire to be released. Still no notice was taken, save that in August 1784 Jefferson was sent over to assist him in transacting the "commercial business" of the Republic: which business consisted in arranging commercial treaties with various ancient European kingdoms. Finally, in March 1785, Congress passed a resolution permitting "the Honourable Benjamin Franklin to return to America as soon as convenient." Regarding the interval covered by those dates, I can only say that it was filled with public services, not more dignified, but less uneasy, than those of previous years; and with the enjoyment of an official status and esteem, and an enthusiastic social respect and liking, that are unparalleled in the history of legations, if not of men. So when leave to return was at last granted, and the venerable old man set out from Passy upon his homeward journey one day in July,

Franklin could not share Jay's suspicions against those whom *he* had every reason to trust and feel grateful to, this difference did not indicate, nor create, any the smallest personal antagonism between the two men. Jay was not an Arthur Lee nor a John Adams—the only personal enemies Franklin ever had, and both of them monomaniacs of vanity—but cherished for Franklin, then and to the end of his life, an affection and a noble reverence which were equally an honour to both good men.

it was, says Jefferson, "as if the village had lost its patriarch:" and the slow progress of his party towards the coast was marked by a series of ovations. It was indeed a sort of royal progress in other senses; for upon it becoming known that the state of his health would ill stand the joltings of a long carriage journey, one of the Queen's litters was placed at his service. He carried with him also, besides written memorials of the approval and respect with which the court regarded his whole conduct while in France, a portrait of the King framed in four hundred and eight diamonds. From Havre he crossed to Southampton, to meet the ship that was appointed by Congress to bring him home. Everything, including the courtesies extended to him by the British government, went to make those few days on English soil a kind of moral Easter, a resurrection time of kinder feelings, if not of the old endearment. Here the old associates within possible reach rallied to him. Here he had a reunion and a sufficient reconciliation with his royalist son. And here, especially, he had three days of happy communion with his dearest English friends, the good Bishop of St Asaph and his family: who, not to lose an hour of his company till he sailed, came and took up their quarters at his inn. When the time came, they saw him aboard; and on the night of July 27 the good ship put to sea—homeward bound.

On September 13 she arrived in the Delaware, opposite Philadelphia. And behold, upon the shore, a vast multitude of people, filling the air with their huzzas and thrice-welcomes!

AGAIN HE had appeared just where and when he was needed. That was a fateful period in American history, and we cannot doubt that a perception of the new dangers and the new needs of his country was among the things that had made him most eager to be home. The first effect of the cessation of war had been to reveal the imminence of anarchy, and all the evils due to an economic derangement, a social unsettlement, and a political inchoateness or invalidity, such as no country ever displayed on the morrow of its entry among the great nations of the earth. In the language of physiology, one may say that the United States was born non-viable according to all the accepted signs or criteria: and some who had viewed its birth as a hateful portent, now expected its timely decease as the rectification of an error of nature. There were many in America whose eyes strained seaward toward the home-coming Franklin as toward the one man whose coming would yet save the country: Americans, just like the English Government in 1782, "expected everything from the comprehensive mind of Dr Franklin." So, whatever he was coming home to do, it was apparently not to rest; for it seemed that his countrymen would never recognise that he was an old man so long as he was a living one. His own Pennsylvania made the first demand upon him, as having the first claim; as having, also, her own crisis as a commonwealth to weather, a crisis which was viewed with concern by all the other States. In the month following his arrival he was elected to the Legislative Council of Pennsylvania, and then made President of the State by an all but unanimous vote: his own vote being the only one cast against him. So it was in the following year, and so also in the third year; at the end of which term, the law forbidding a fourth election of the same president permitted him to make his escape from office. During that time he did much to consolidate the political situation, and to improve the social feeling and outlook in Pennsylvania. A peculiar care for public instruction still possessed him, and he was now able to carry out a long-cherished scheme of his, in the founding and inaugurating of a college for the education of young Germans; an enormous part of the whole population of Pennsylvania—at one time about a third—being of that nationality.

During one of these years, however, he rendered more important services upon a greater plane of things. A Convention of Delegates from all the States was appointed in 1787, and began its sittings on the 25th of May. Its mandate was to frame a Constitution, in which the country might know itself, and by which the Union might live. Despite his age and physical infirmities—for he was now in his eighty-second year, and racked by those two most agonising of ailments, stone and acute gout—it was felt to be needful that Franklin, not less than Washington, should be of that body. And it is doing no injustice, even to Washington, to say that the man in all that assembly whose presence could least have been spared was Franklin. Of the character of the Convention and the history of its momentous labours I can have few words to say here. As to the first, however, it is to be noted that, apart from the strife of interests as between State and State, the Convention was marked by a line of cleavage, then appearing for the first time and never afterwards obliterated or closed, but running through all American history. On the one side was the Strong-government or Federal party, headed by Hamilton, and sympathised with by Washington. On the other side was that party, associated with the name of Jefferson, but of which Franklin was really the moral father and founder: the party of those whose more anxious care was to give all possible scope to the principle of local autonomy, and to safeguard the fact of popular freedom.[1] Franklin's voice was always in favour of the more generous provision, the ampler liberty; was always earnestly opposed to whatever might tend to make governmental oppression at some future time possible, and still more to whatever could have a tendency to depress the self-respect or inhibit the honest ambition of the poorest man. Some of his finest utterances were in maintenance of that plea; and it is a symptom of the noble feeling with which Franklin was regarded by the noblest men, that Hamilton would give his support to Franklin's recommendations, though they were essentially moral criticisms of the policy which he himself thought best for the country. Many times in the course of the four months' labour of the Convention did Franklin's wisdom and his humour, and still more that spirit of cheerfulness and good-will, and that suggestion, which his every word somehow conveyed, of a common purpose animating them all alike, and making them all friends and assistants of each other in the same quest—many a time did this rare and complex talent of Franklin's remove a difficulty, or inspire the right temper in which to approach it. Yet there was one question upon which, it seemed, for all that could be argued by the ablest or urged by the best, the Union must go to pieces. This was the question of the proportion in which the different States, varying so vastly as they did in size and population and wealth and historical importance, should be represented in the Legislature. The small States, like New Jersey, claimed to count equally

[1] Called at first Republican, and at a later time Democratic. The two terms are now opposed, the latter designating the school of Franklin and Jefferson, and the former—a more Ancient Influence in human affairs, I suspect.

with great ones, like Pennsylvania and Virginia. Round this question it was war utter and uncompromising: war to the death, or to the disruption of the Union. For those who were in the right could not give way, and those who were in the wrong would not. A way out was found in the end by Franklin, who, not in one act, but by two approximations, developed his plan for allaying the fears of the little States, lest they be overborne, and yet saving the larger ones from what would have become, had it been practicable at all, a tyranny as impudent as it was unjust. The plan was to have two Houses, and give a proportional representation in the one and an equal representation in the other, and to divide or balance their functions so as to secure just government for the whole. This, the central or the basic article in the Constitution of the United States, was a gift of Franklin to his country not unworthy to rank with his earlier services. And when at last the draft Constitution was framed, and it was time to put it to the House for acceptance in its entirety, that it might then be submitted to the nation for approval, it was Franklin who carried it over its final perils by a speech of matchless wisdom, tolerance, and humour. His labours had the only reward which a heart like his could desire. For though but two and a half years of life remained to him when the Convention finished its work in September 1787, he yet lived long enough to see justified that confidence in the good-citizen qualities of his countrymen, and that faith in the great future of the nation, which he had held unwaveringly, and without an effort, in the midst of conditions and in spite of signs that had seemed to other men desperate.

Yet even the termination of his third Presidentship of Pennsylvania in the autumn of 1788, if it ended his official career, did not end his public services.

He still plied, from time to time, a pen that influenced opinion, in spite of anonymity, as no other could. Some of the wisest and wittiest of his writings belong to the last two years of his life, so full of suffering as those years were. Most of that period was passed in bed, and the intermissions of agonising pain were few and brief; yet through all he kept at bay alike the dullness of old age and the peevishness of physical distress. His last public act was to forward, as President of an Abolition Society, a memorial to Congress asking it "to devise a means of removing this inconsistency [the maintenance of negro slavery] from the character of the American people." His last contribution to literature was a brilliant letter, signed "Historicus," in refutation of a pro-slavery speech in Congress. That was on March 23, 1790. He was now bearing up, with patience though not with success, against a crushing combination of maladies. One day his breathing ceased altogether, and he was thought to be dead. But he rallied, and at once resumed his cheerful and benevolent interest in all good causes and efforts. On April 17 he passed into a state of coma, and died in the evening about ten o'clock.

His own State honoured him with great obsequies; and Congress voted that "the usual badge of mourning be worn for a month." It was not much. But it was all the recognition of Franklin's unequalled services which Congress had ever vouchsafed to make. The true scene of national mourning for the death of Franklin was in France; and there the most striking tributes, both of affection and of intellectual commemoration by the greatest men, were paid to his worth. Later generations of Americans have recognised with pain that the glories of their Revolution are a little imperfect because of an act of justice forgone, are a little dimmed to all honest eyes by an appearance of insufficient gratitude—even the costless gratitude of a " thank you " was begrudged—to such a servant, citizen, and patriot as no other country ever had in the history of man.

CPSIA information can be obtained
at www.ICGtesting.com
Printed in the USA
LVHW040247181222
735388LV00009B/211